INVASION

INVASION

THE FORGOTTEN FRENCH BID TO CONQUER ENGLAND

DUNCAN CAMERON

AMBERLEY

To Jenny

Jacket illustrations: Front: Bataille de la Rochelle, 1372. From Froissart's Chronicle. (Courtesy of the Bibliothèque Nationale de France); *Back:* Rye Landgate. (Courtesy of DeFacto under Creative Commons 4.0)

First published 2019

Amberley Publishing
The Hill, Stroud
Gloucestershire, GL5 4EP

www.amberley-books.com

Copyright © Duncan Cameron, 2019

The right of Duncan Cameron to be identified as the Author of this work has been asserted in accordance with the Copyrights, Designs and Patents Act 1988.

ISBN 978 1 4456 9024 7 (hardback)
ISBN 978 1 4456 9025 4 (ebook)

British Library Cataloguing in Publication Data. A catalogue record for this book is available from the British Library.

Typesetting by Aura Technology and Software Services, India.
Printed in the UK.

CONTENTS

PREFACE

It is May 1338, and Plymouth Sound is filling up with English ships coming in from the dangerous waters of the English Channel. Small fishing boats, merchant vessels trading with South West France, cargo vessels, coastal traders – every boat that can make it is heading for safety. It is an excellent refuge. The outer harbour is wide and spacious, indented with many useful hiding places, and further into the harbour is Plymouth itself. The small walled town defended by one small fortress to the west of what is now known as Sutton Pool is well hidden away from marauders.

A French-led fleet of Genoese and Monegasque warships appeared along the coasts of Devon and Cornwall a few days earlier and the entire South Western Peninsula is now lying open to the French-led invaders.

Devon and Cornwall had many small harbours full of ships, and the busy coastal trade made it good raiding territory. The galleys, long slender and low, mostly from Genoa or Monaco, made up the attack front, and the cogs, big fat converted merchant vessels used for the storage of loot and transportation, were engaged in low-risk freebooting all along this coastline. Plunder was an important part of any campaign that involved the Genoese or the Monegasques, paid allies of the King of France. Plunder rewarded the mercenary crews for the risks they were taking in making their skills available to their employer.

Again and again the same routine – approach a likely ship on the high seas, grapple with hooks, board, throw the crew overboard to their deaths, take everything of value, set the ship alight and move on to the next one. If the ship was large or valuable enough, it might itself be captured and sailed back to a friendly port on the other side of the English Channel.

In the summer of 1338 King Edward III had spies in France who had passed the word that the French were planning an invasion of England. Kent, Sussex and Hampshire were ready, with keen-eyed sea watchers ranged all the way from Sandwich to the Isle of Wight and beyond, to pass on warnings and light beacons and if necessary, descend on the French landing places. But beyond Dorset the local people were still unprepared and the galleys started to do what they were best at doing.

By now someone surely would have spotted the fleet making for Plymouth once it appeared over the horizon. As the maximum speed for the Genoese and Monegasque galleys over a distance was not more than a fast walking pace, the citizens should have had plenty of time to mount a defence. But none of the chroniclers mention any attempt to stop the incursion when it started.

Perhaps the sight of the warships approaching Plymouth Sound slowly yet relentlessly was so terrifying that the people who had been appointed to mount a defence ran away. The fleet was supposed to be frightening and various forms of display were used to heighten the effect. Unlike twenty-first-century warfare, the fourteenth-century military believed in dressing up for battle. The French fleet and crew would have been arrayed in their finest gear, and the ships brightly painted. The blue royal standard of France with gold fleurs-de-lis was sewn into the sails of the

French ships. The red-and-white lozenges of Monaco identified the Monegasque ships and, a little confusingly, the Saint George's cross of Genoa, so similar to the English cross, was also visible. The masts were flying pennants, identifying each high-status aristocratic leader on each ship. The message was underlined by the shields lining the gunwales, each emblazoned with its owner's coat of arms. The rear of each galley was covered in a tent in matching colours and designs to the flags and shields, in order to shield each commander and his inner circle from view.

The decks were crammed with fighting men, tightly packed together. The high status warriors, those with iron helmets or breastplates, burnished their armour so that it gleamed in the sun. The new style high-status armour encased the whole body in steel, and exaggerated the breadth of the shoulders and the thickness of the legs. When the visor of the bascinet was closed for battle, covering the face completely, the pointed, pig-like shape of the face with two small slitty eyes gave an animalistic appearance to the leaders. Some of the galleys were plated in copper, polished until it shone and reflected light onto the waves. As they got nearer to the entrance of the harbour, the noise added to the effect. Brass trumpets blown on the approach were designed to terrify, while also carrying commands to the fleet. All aspects of design were coordinated with the well-timed set of manoeuvres that added to the sense of menace felt by the people on the shore.

The attackers shouted battle cries such as '*Montjoie Saint Denis!*' This was an ancient slogan going back to the early days of the French people, redolent of past feats of daring in the Holy Land, instilling fear into the hearts of the foe, and strength and courage in the hearts of the invaders.

The Genoese and the Monaco warriors were marines, able to handle their galleys at sea whether rowing or sailing. And as soon as the galley landed the same men leaped out onto land, sword in hand, ready for action and eager to switch into fighting mode.

The French-crewed cogs acted as support vessels and were safely waiting outside harbour, ready to store loot. Sailing vessels of the period were unhandy and had difficulty making way unless there was a wind in the right direction, so they were always liable to be trapped in port if the wind changed. The advantage of the galley was that the banks of rowers made them independent of the vagaries of the weather. They can be described as precision attack vessels.

The real prize in Plymouth harbour was the seven merchant vessels from Bristol with high-value cargoes. The Genoese descended on them, disposed of the crew overboard, then transferred the cargoes into the merchant cogs, and burnt the ships. Plymouth harbour was starting to fill up with bodies and burnt timbers.

* * *

Hugh Courtenay was the highest ranking local dignitary and was responsible for maintaining the defence force. Yet he had not carried out his obligation of summoning the militias that he himself led. Maybe the keepers of the coastal lands in Devon and Cornwall thought that the isolation and relative poverty of their part of England, compared to the territory further east, meant that they would not be bothered by the French raiders. If the coastal defenders further east in Kent and Sussex had not been so well prepared, the population of Devon and Cornwall could well have been left in peace.

When the invasion fleet entered the harbour some local people must have ridden off to find the Earl. After the Franco-Genoese crew finished with the ships in harbour, they moved on to dry land and began burning and looting. It was about this time that Hugh appeared with his band of militiamen.

His background was very much within the high chivalric tradition. A battle-hardened and ferocious veteran of the Scottish wars, he was said by Adam Murimuth the Chronicler to be eighty years old at the time. If true, this was a very remarkable achievement in a world where life expectancy was little over forty years, but equally the chronicler might well have used unreliable sources of information. Hugh had been close to King Edward III during the great English victory over the Scots at Halidon Hill near Berwick. On that day tens of thousands of Scots had been hacked to death by the ranks of dismounted English knights and Hugh Courtenay was among them. So he was very much at home with bloody warfare. Doubtless the invasion gave the elderly Earl a chance to relive his early days, once the messengers from Plymouth located him.

Courtenay and his followers arrived too late to save the shipping in the harbour – but they were in time to stop the force before they had burnt the entire town. As was so often to happen in following years, they showed the invaders how fiercely the English could fight back when they were under attack. After a bloody battle in which there were many deaths on both sides, the interlopers retreated under pressure to the ships. In the confusion that can develop during an unplanned retreat, local people joined in and did their bit by attacking the invaders. At this stage the invaders became vulnerable and many were pushed or fell into the sea where those in heavy armour were almost certain to drown.

Adam Murimuth the Chronicler claims that 'five hundred' of the invaders died in the operation. This could be an exaggeration – like the Earl's age.[1]

The flotilla sailed away, back to harbour in Normandy, after an expedition that had not been wholly successful. They had started by approaching the prime targets – leading ports such as Southampton, Sandwich, Portsmouth – which should have been full of high-quality ships and well-stocked warehouses. Having failed to effect a landing on any of these they descended on a target of secondary importance.

Why was Plymouth not defended? We can assume that the warnings of imminent attack would have been acted upon as fast as possible – but as it was impossible to predict exactly when and where a raid would take place there was bound to be a time lag. The party included foot soldiers who could only move at walking pace and just a little delay to Earl Hugh's muster would have allowed the invaders to succeed.[2]

This episode is typical of many invasion events during this period. Plans are made and do not get carried out. Campaigns are launched with little planning on just where the fleet will go. Rather, fleets cruise the coastal waters looking for action, and respond to circumstances. Surprisingly, rarely is an enemy fleet in English waters driven off by English ships.

Typically, when an opportunity presents itself the response is quick and ruthless. Ultra-violence is a basic tool of fourteenth-century warfare, and there are few limits. Post twentieth-century notions of war crimes, the rights of non-combatants and of individual culpability have no relevance in this theatre of war. Once the king has declared war, the mass slaughter of innocent civilians and of ordinary townspeople was the norm, not to mention wholesale destruction of property. The fourteenth century had no need for weapons of mass destruction – a dedicated team of experienced warriors with hand-held weapons and firebrands acting on behalf of their leader could carry out a lot of carnage in a short time.

Looting was an important weapon. In an age when states lacked access to the vast flows of cash that the modern world uses to finance warfare, the ideal was for each expedition to be self-financing. Everything of value that the raiders came upon was to be taken and distributed. For inflammable non-moveable items, fire was the key weapon of mass destruction so after the looting and the killing came the torch.

To return to the question of plunder, this was of crucial importance in any raid. Fleets should return home with their holds full of valuable goods, and there were agreed systems for the distribution of plunder. In the Portsmouth incursion, for example, the King of France, Phillip VI, would receive 50 per cent of the value of goods brought back to France, with diminishing portions for the people further down the scale. Plunder might include people held hostage against a fat ransom – on occasion the most profitable form of plunder that there was.

As the Plymouth raid illustrates, the French incursions were not unchallenged. The English often fought back, given the right circumstances. Indeed, the English Crown throughout the period repeatedly sent out long-winded, rambling proclamations such as the following, which was sent out only a year before the Plymouth raid.[3]

Since we have learnt from several sources that people from abroad, our enemies, with galleys and ships of war, are coming in great numbers to parts of Dorset planning to turn aside and to invade those parts with hostile intent...

Wishing, with the help of God, to protect against these dangers, we ask in the faith that we have in you, we strictly ask you as soon as possible, with all your strength in person, you and your people, with as much force as possible, take yourselves to that region, you with other loyal people, defend yourselves against these hostile invaders, and attack these enemies bravely, if they presume in those parts to ... etc.

These were public proclamations meant to be listened to and read aloud – so the repetitions and parallels in the text probably served to emphasise the message, the words were designed to have a powerful impact. This edict was issued from Edward III's Westminster-based Chancery, and it came out in 1338, a year before the invasion of Plymouth. The people of Devon had definitely been instructed to be ready against attackers. Nevertheless, once the immediate crisis that provoked the edict had passed, arrangements were often let slip.

During this period the traditional English belief that their king was sovereign of all the seas around the island of Britain came into conflict with the French response to English aggression, taking the war to the seas and the English coastal regions.

Edward III responded to the French threat by reviving ancient laws going back to Anglo-Saxon times. All able-bodied males between the ages of sixteen and sixty living near the English coast were called upon to fight off any hostile landings on English soil and in at least some locations, they were ready for action. By the time of the Plymouth raid, in theory at least, the able-bodied male inhabitants of the coastal regions of England should have belonged to militias, possessed equipment according to their status, and undergone some sort of training. The previous sailing season of 1338 had had its share of Franco-Genoese successes in the form of towns razed, male inhabitants killed and females raped and killed. Some but by no means all landings had been fought off. In following years the defenders were better prepared.

To return to the narrative – in May 1339, at the start of the campaigning season, the French southern fleet accompanied by its paid allies from Genoa and Monaco had sailed out from the French king's naval dockyard in Rouen, up the Seine Estuary, and into action in the English Channel. They started by making for Southampton Water looking for a suitable landing – an obvious choice since they had carried out a successful attack on the same important port a year earlier.

Southampton itself, despite still not having acquired the stone fortifications that had been promised by a rattled English government after the previous French attack, had at least got some temporary wooden defences. Much more importantly, the newly formed coastal levies were ranged all along the southern coastline – as they should have been further west – ready for action and no doubt eager to revenge their humiliations of the previous years. So it was impossible to land in Southampton itself, and it would have taken just a few English ships in the entrance to the Solent for the Franco-Genoese fleet to be trapped.

The Mediterraneans took off to the more open waters around the Isle of Wight, but armed levies were similarly arrayed all along the low cliffs on the north of the island. The galleys moved west away from danger and cruised along until they crossed the invisible line that separated Southern England from the west, saw the undefended coastlines of Devon and Cornwall, and started to attack ships on the high seas before mounting the May 1339 raid upon Plymouth.

I

BACKGROUND TO THE ATTACK

The Plymouth raid is just one episode in our book – there will be many others. There were at least seventy known incursions during the fourteenth century and there were certainly many more that did not attract the attention of the chroniclers of the time. These episodes are little known today, compared with the three failed attempts that have entered the British national story. Certainly there are many good histories of the Spanish Armada, and the Napoleonic and Nazi plans but few about the fourteenth-century invasion crisis. Yet it can be argued that the fourteenth-century French invasions had more impact than the Spanish attempt against England in the sixteenth century, or the Napoleonic invasion attempt at the start of the nineteenth – even the invasion of 1216 that at one stage took half the kingdom. The repeated French incursions in the fourteenth century had perhaps more in common with a combination of the threat of Hitler's invasion in 1940 with the effect of the bombing of cities in later years of the war.

The incursions caused death and destruction on the English mainland, in the form of trading towns razed and inhabitants massacred. The economic damage caused by the destruction of entire trading centres such as Portsmouth and Southampton had important effects. The incursions caused major economic damage to the beginnings of England's trading economy. The French navy and its allies were able to take command of English seas and the sea routes that linked England with their economic partners in South West France for example, thus compounding the damage. The economic, social and political damage deliberately inflicted upon the English by the French had consequences, which, it can be suggested, resulted in long-term changes to society.

There was no large-scale invasion of England during the fourteenth century on a par with the Norman Conquest. But that was not for want of trying. On perhaps four occasions France put together a fully fledged campaign involving French boots on the soil of England and an attempt to remove the troublesome English royal family entirely and replace them with more compliant Francophile rulers.

For England, the fourteenth century was its most invaded century after the end of the Dark Ages in 1066. Most of the action is connected to the disastrous and long-lasting series of conflicts known as the Hundred Years' War, which continued well into the following century. It is not the intention to write a history of this war but it will be, for much of the narrative, a background to events. And behind the war stands the giant figure of Edward III, the winner of many battles. Winning battles was perhaps what Edward was best at doing – but he never achieved his overall war aim. Edward's England did not rule the waves.

During the Middle Ages the seas were dangerous territory. Many people would do their utmost to avoid going about on the high seas on a ship, as shipwreck was an ever-present danger. In England and France especially, the knightly classes tended to avoid ships as much as they could. The Scottish Ballad 'Sir Patrick Spens', describing a shipwreck when many of the royal party were drowned during a great storm on a journey from Norway to Scotland, sums up the terror of the sea for the high-born:[1]

> O loth, loth, were our good Scots lords
> To wet their cork-heel'd shoon [shoes],
> But long ere all the play was play'd
> They wet their hats aboon [on the top].
>
> And many was the feather-bed
> That fluttered on the foam;
> And many was the good lord's son
> That never more came home.

In addition to the danger of death by drowning, the seas were lawless. Piracy was a parallel lifestyle to trading and fishing. Life in coastal communities was risky and pirates were liable to turn up at any time in order to rob and kill. Pirates could be of a different nationality, but equally they could be from neighbouring settlements. In England a rivalry between Yarmouth in East Anglia and Winchelsea in Sussex led to a bloody piratical raid upon the Sussex settlement in the 1340s.

Before the start of the period there had been attacks upon the English coastline by French naval forces and they would continue into the fifteenth century. Our period is exceptional because of the severity of the attacks, their year-on-year relentlessness, and the fact that they were planned and carefully carried out with the intention of causing the greatest possible damage. However, incursions were not evenly distributed throughout the century. There are certain decades with hardly any action, and other short periods of very intense activity. It is the intention to describe and analyse each significant incursion, and in addition other acts of aggression in the English Channel and on occasion in the sea routes round Brittany to Western France.

The chain of events that led to the century of invasions commences with two exceptional people who stand out from the background characters in strikingly contrasting colours. Their actions prematurely catapulted Edward III onto the English throne, ready to reorganise his kingdom, eager to go into battle, (with little awareness of the long-term consequences of his actions), and to turn England into a fierce fighting force.

The first was the father of King Edward III. An eccentric, whose physically passionate and open devotion to his non-regal male favourites, wholly unacceptable in his era, led him to assign power to people seen by his contemporaries as being unworthy, and whose violence and brutality caused many of the English aristocracy to turn against him. The actions of Edward II are part of the reason for ensuing events.

Secondly, there is Isabella, Edward II's wife, young Edward's mother, sister to the King of France. She would have been outstanding in any period but in the fourteenth century with its many shadowy royal queens and princesses about whose character little is known, she shines forth. In a series of actions totally outside the norm for fourteenth-century royal female behaviour she turned from being a traditional royal queen and princess to working as a skilled diplomat, plotting to bring down her husband via an invasion, and taking part in the invasion itself. Not only that, she carried her plot through with total success.

Our story falls into five sections:

One – Isabella's invasion of England:

Edward III is still a young prince and he and his mother Isabella becomes embroiled in the complex series of political conflicts, stemming from the strangely inappropriate behaviour of Isabella's husband, the King of England. Young Edward (son of Edward II) became king only after his mother Isabella, assisted by her lover Roger Mortimer, put together an invasion of England on behalf of her son when he was only fifteen years old, and deposed Edward's father, Isabella's husband.

The campaign was launched from the small Flemish state of Hainault on Edward's behalf. It was manned by a motley array of German and Flemish mercenaries, beefed up and validated by a number of exiled English knights – and was a success. If this invasion had failed, Edward III's reign might well have been one of history's 'might-have-beens' and none of the incursions that we describe would have taken place.

Two – Scottish attacks on English coastal targets:

The second part of the narrative starts in the early years of Edward III's reign, when his lifetime of fighting starts with his attempts to snuff out Scottish independence – and a short time later when Edward outrages the entire French political establishment by making his claim to the French throne.

As a result of annoying two neighbours, one to the north and one to the south, England becomes embroiled in a proxy war with Scotland, with a potential for war on two fronts. The powerful French state supports the weak Scottish one from attack by a third, also powerful state – England. As a result, between 1334 and 1337 Scottish ships appear in English coastal waters, attacking coastal locations as far south as the Channel Islands and in various places on the English coast, with the assistance and connivance of their French friends.

Three – Intense raiding and invasion plans by France:

While the Scottish conflict rumbles on, France gradually becomes committed to all-out war until, in 1338, full-scale hostilities break out between France and England. For a number of years Edward struggles as he tries to fight back against the French on multiple fronts. One result of his diplomatic failure is that for six years, from 1338 until the late 1340s, settlements on the

English coast are repeatedly attacked. At first the French navy acts on its own. But soon France enters into a treaty relationship with Genoa and Monaco, and later with Castile, in order to access their superior Mediterranean-based naval technology. During this period the Mediterranean oared galley makes its appearance on the English coast.

By now the French are planning a full-scale invasion of England, hoping to bring about regime change. What has often been called the 'Auld Alliance' between Scotland and France – dating back to the previous century – was strengthened. As a result, a joint Franco-Scottish invasion of England became a possibility for the following decades.

Four – New invasion plans and more raiding:

The next episode starts more than ten years later in a desolate and war-damaged post-Poitiers France, when Edward III is well past his peak as a leader.

The young French King Charles, known perhaps appropriately as 'The Wise', leads a fightback against the English. The plan of engaging the English on two fronts re-emerges and a number of invasion plans are launched, some in alliance with other anti-English allies.

Charles also makes a long-term strategic decision to build up a professional navy from the Royal Arsenal in Rouen – the Clos des Galées. He appoints Jean de Vienne, a distinguished aristocratic fighting man, as Admiral de France to plan and lead the forthcoming invasion of England. This campaign is well organised. It reaches its climax in 1377 – England's year of invasions – when fifteen locations on the English coast are attacked by French naval forces. By chance Edward III dies at about the same time that the invasion is launched. Jean de Vienne is little known in England but he was responsible for many wrecked towns, burnt ships, and dead citizens floating in the sea.

Five – The Franco-Scottish invasion of England:

After the death of Edward III, England is no longer a fierce warrior kingdom punching above its weight on the European scene. After 1380, at the start of the reign of Richard II, the French return to planning a war on two fronts, with the intention of catching the English in a pincer movement between a Scottish land invasion and a Southern England naval landing turning into a second land invasion. Attempts are made to reform an alliance with the Scottish King Robert II. The French invading army lands in Scotland and a joint invasion is carried out.

* * *

Although they have never become part of the English national story these episodes have not disappeared from the history books. All over Southern England, which bore the brunt of the French onslaughts, local histories record these events. But they are often described as mere 'piracy', which diminishes their importance. As an example, a battlefield guide written in the 1970s says of a 1377 French landing that it was carried out by 'pirates' who were driven by 'a subconscious hatred of the English because of their victories at Crecy and Poitiers only 31 and 21 years earlier.'[2]

This is a common misunderstanding. In reality the Rottingdean landing, as were the nearly seventy other actions in the long-drawn out campaign, was part of the large-scale, carefully thought-out, and very 'conscious' strategy, which is the subject of this book. The forces that landed were well-trained soldiers and seamen led by aristocratic warriors from France's knightly class. They were supported by the inner circle of the French monarchy, and answered to the French monarch of the time, who had been planning the campaign for years.

As another example of English misunderstanding, the Wikipedia history of Seaford, in East Sussex, says that the town, which was a member of the Cinque Ports and of real maritime importance before the fourteenth century, declined 'due to repeated raids by pirates'.[3]

The eclipse of Seaford from the economic map of England between the late medieval period when it was a Cinque Port and the coming of the railways when it became a holiday resort also happened because the medieval port was all too often in the sights of French warships, answerable to the French Crown. Seaford was an economic casualty of the fourteenth-century French campaigns, as were many other ports. The economic disruption caused by the war meant that when changes took place in the set of the coast to the sea, the town was abandoned rather than rebuilt.

At the start of the century shipping tended to be associated with the merchant class, and the ships themselves were manned by people of low socio-economic status. In England merchant ships were routinely pressed into service by the state and converted to temporary military use. They transported fighting men – and on occasion battles were fought on the decks of privately owned ships by armed knights and archers, as though they were fighting on a small land battlefield. But the skills that were needed to man the ships were not provided by the warriors.

In the Mediterranean, trading had a higher status and shipping was of a higher standard, possibly as a result of influence from Byzantium and the Muslim cultures of North Africa and the Middle East. A key storyline is how the French fighting machine learnt the importance of ships as a weapon against English aggression, and formed alliances with the leading naval powers of southern Europe, with Genoa and Castile in the vanguard, when it was normal for princes and dukes to be professional sailors, in contrast to the northern European view. By an extraordinary twist of historical fate, Monaco plays a part in the story as a small but fierce fourteenth-century naval power operating from a fortress on the rock of Monte Carlo. For much of the period the leaders of the Monegasque navy were Carlo and Rainier II Grimaldi, father and son, who between them spent many years in the English Channel and both of whom in person led a significant number of hostile landings on English soil. The Grimaldis were probably responsible for more death and destruction than almost any other leaders of the era. Significantly, the marines who manned the Mediterranean galleys, so important to the French war effort, were, unlike their northern counterparts, both able to man a ship and fight a battle.

When reflecting on the relentless continuity of warfare during this period it is important to bear in mind that the male members of the ruling classes in both England and France subscribed to the chivalric view of the world, in which warfare was a duty and an obligation. The highest class in the tripartite division of society was the knight, the aristocrat. The aristocracy held lands and took income from their lands tax free, and were able to enjoy the fruits of their ancestral possessions as they wished. But it was an essential obligation for a knight to spend his early years preparing for war by mock fights and tournaments, and later by attaching himself to a military expedition. And when the time came, he was obliged to fight for his king, even unto death, in order to protect the other two layers of society against their enemies.

The second order was the clergy, whose contribution was to ensure that society maintained its relationship with the Almighty. Modern clerics tend to have a bent towards pacifism, a tendency to stress the values of peace and love but not so the fourteenth-century clergy who might have taken as their motto Christ's words – 'Think not that I am come to send peace in earth: I came not to send peace, but a sword'[4] and in the words of the much fiercer Old Testament, 'My lord fighteth the battles of the Lord'[5] where the 'lord' is the earthly leader and the 'Lord' is God Almighty himself. This was the prevailing attitude rather than the philosophy behind the phrase 'Turn the other cheek'.

The knightly classes and the clergy did not see war as an aberration, to be avoided at all costs, but rather as an integral part of the functioning of society. And to take part in a just war would bring a warrior credit in the afterlife and benefit society as a whole, as well as enriching him himself via loot and the extortion of ransoms from prisoners of war. The fact that Medieval ultra-violence co-existed with a powerful and influential Church meant that on occasion the princes of the Church in England themselves, in their role as chief executives of large and prosperous estates, could be summoned to don a suit of armour, mount a suitable warhorse, and ride into battle at the head of a motley but determined array of local militias, carrying out the Lord's work.

For a young man of knightly stock wishing to follow in his father's footsteps, the search for suitable work experience was a serious business, so in periods of relative peace, in France for example, peripheral wars in Scotland, fighting against the English, would be a draw to young Frenchman from aristocratic families. Another alternative was to fight against Europe's pagan neighbours, for example the Lithuanians, thus gaining variable hands-on experience at the same time as gaining kudos for fighting for both God and Christendom as well as encouraging the recipients of the violence to convert.

However, the vast majority of people did not belong to either the knightly classes or the clerics. They constituted the labourers, the workers. Their job was to work and to produce, not just to support themselves by their work but also to support the two other orders in their martial and spiritual labours on behalf of the workers. The Third Estate constituted the vast majority of society and included everyone from poor independent peasants up to rich commercial magnates in possession of huge fortunes.

While it is quite a valid exercise to narrate the decades of raids, incursions and maritime fighting in the English Channel and the

North Sea as an aspect of the complex set of political and military manoeuvres that goes under the name of the Hundred Years' War, the ordinary inhabitants of Southern England had little sense of being engaged in such a protracted and definable martial endeavour. For an ordinary mariner from the Cinque Ports, for example, the French on the other side of the English Channel had always been an enemy; private raids in which the marines of a Cinque Port would descend on Le Crotoy or Boulogne from time to time were the norm. And vice versa. Like rival football teams, an opportunity to avenge some past humiliation was rarely passed up. For the sailors of the south coast the incursions of the Hundred Years' War followed a familiar pattern.

Quite apart from the tragedies of war, the fourteenth century was a time of huge unforeseen catastrophes. Within the space of twenty years two great crises hit Europe – climate change plus mass deaths from epidemics – so by the end of the century, the population of Europe was less than half what it had been at the start.

In this one universal fear the fourteenth century has links to the twenty-first, haunted by the idea that civilization is threatened by climate change. The fourteenth century opened with freezing weather and icy summer rains. Cold, storms, and continuous rain and hail mean that harvests failed year after year and animals sickened and died, causing mass starvation. Again and again military campaigns had to be launched during periods of terrible weather, when knights on horseback sunk deep into treacherous mud and supply carriages became bogged down in the morasses caused by thousands of human and animal feet passing over waterlogged soil. Marginal settlements were abandoned to snow and ice, glaciers in the far north grew and swallowed up villages and farmland. Fields were abandoned and forests spread.

On the other hand, while the twenty-first century struggles with the impact of population growth, with human activity spreading to more and more parts of the environment, in the fourteenth century the human ecosystem was in retreat. With its famines and the great epidemiological disaster known as the Black Death, the fourteenth century was a period when all over the world the number of human beings was in sharp decline. As the human biosphere retreated, the animals of the wild came out of the woods and wild places and into the deserted farmland and abandoned settlements.

* * *

The threat of French invasion led to a wide-ranging reorganisation of English society by the Crown, with much of the adult male population being liable to serve as defenders of the English shores against enemy invasion. The invasion crisis increased the reach of the English state, which of course had an impact English society.

By the early fourteenth century, England and France had shared a long history of uneasy and distrustful relations, made all the more complicated by the fact that their ruling classes were so closely entwined that sometimes it was difficult to separate them. It is ironic that almost 300 years after William the Conqueror had almost completely replaced the Anglo-Saxon aristocracy with his Norman-French-speaking supporters, Edward III was a Norman-French speaker with a French wife who spoke Parisian French, so both of them may have had trouble in understanding what Edward's English subjects said.

An important factor behind the Gallicisation of England was the 'immigration policy' followed in the century after the Norman takeover of England. During that time many Normans settled in England, attracted by the many excellent opportunities that a new life in England offered them. In the early years of the conflict, there may well have been little to distinguish high status representatives of the two sides. The language spoken and the choice of clothing, fashions, food and drink customs, etiquette, and respect for the tradition of chivalry would have been very similar. But as the years passed and the French remained a threat to the English homeland, English identity began to draw away from the French. Frenchmen acquired negative stereotypes; individual Frenchmen in England were targeted as potential 'fifth columnists'. The links that religious institutions in England possessed with the Continent were seen as questionable. Travel overseas became suspect. Speaking French became rather less essential to success. The threat of invasion from France helped this process along.

Edicts flowed out from the Westminster government offices warning against the dangers posed by foreigners – especially French ones. In the real world, high officials were required to keep an eye on dubious activity. English ports facing the French coast just a short distance across the water were aware of the source of danger. Citizens were encouraged to watch out for spies and to inform the authorities of suspicious characters passing through. Here is just one example – in one proclamation the Archbishop of Canterbury himself acts as a sort of intelligence agent on behalf of the Crown. This is an edict of 1337 issued by the Crown, under Edward's name:[6]

To the Mayor and Bailiffs of his Port of Dover – Greetings!

In relation to some news that has come to our ears, we inform you, that certain men, of various conditions, status, or religion, in the above-mentioned port, are wishing to travel to overseas regions ... search them very carefully, and see whether they are secretly carrying letters or other things ... And any letters whatsoever with them or on their persons ... send to our venerable father, John, Archbishop of Canterbury, as soon as possible...

In English popular culture we can see the emergence of literature portraying the French and their monarch in satirically negative terms. The French are seen as being

> Shrewd, siren-like, cruel, sour of mind,
> Under their Duke Philip, nicknamed the blind![7]

In this period, the English Channel had truly become an invasion front.

2

HOW THE QUEEN ORGANISED AN INVASION OF ENGLAND

The events that catapulted Edward onto the throne of England while he was still a teenager with few restrictions on his warlike plans were driven by the actions of his mother Queen Isabella. After a period of behaving as a conventional wife, Isabella abandoned the constraints of her royal upbringing and became a vibrant, politically skilful and dominant figure in English politics – almost unheard of for a queen, even one like Isabella who by virtue of being the sister of Charles IV the King of France was as well connected as it was possible to be. Isabella's invasion of England from Flemish territory, on behalf of her son, started the chain of events that led to decades of warfare between England and France and the many French incursions onto English territory. This Isabella-organised invasion opened the way for her son to seize power very early in life.

If Prince Edward had assumed the throne in the usual way, upon the death of his father, the multiple invasions of England in the following decades would never have occurred. This is the event from which the rest of this narrative flows.

Not surprisingly, the highly effective Isabella did not get a good press during the Middle Ages, which is when she acquired the title 'The She-Wolf of France'. Her reputation has, however, greatly improved in recent years through writers who see her as a proto-feminist disavowing her unworthy husband and out-plotting a whole raft of less clever males.

The events that led up to the Isabelline invasion were the result of the eccentric and chaotic reign of Isabella's husband Edward II. The peculiarities of his style of kingship are well known. As a war leader he demonstrated poor judgement and had an unfortunate tendency to lose battles – never a plus in medieval Europe. Though historians such as Stephen Spinks have pointed out that Edward II inherited a poisoned chalice of huge debt and baronial disaffection from his father. The events that led to the invasion stem mainly, however, from the fact that during his reign Edward had close and apparently intense relationships with two male favourites – firstly Piers Gaveston, and secondly, Hugh Despenser. The proximate event was the overwhelming Despenser influence on the English government, and the use of extreme and often arbitrary violence against enemies, many from the knightly class. As a result, the number of opponents to his regime grew as Edward II's reign progressed. The growing political turmoil in the English court posed a danger to Isabella, the rejected wife of the ruler at the eye of the storm, and to her oldest son Prince Edward. When Isabella was in danger of falling into serious disfavour with her estranged husband, she extricated herself from this danger with great skill.[1]

In a modern twist to the plot, after Isabella disavowed her relationship with her bisexual husband she formed a close but informal liaison with Sir Roger Mortimer, a non-royal from a provincial knightly family. Isabella had brains, political skills and regal family contacts; Roger Mortimer was a charismatic fighting man who could deal with the male supporters of the audacious invasion. Together they formed a fourteenth-century power couple.

Circumstantial evidence points to the narrative starting in 1323 when Sir Roger Mortimer, a member of a family from the Welsh Marches that had aroused the ire of Edward II by rebelling against his regime, was in a dungeon in the Tower of London. It is highly probable that Isabella had formed some kind of liaison with Mortimer before he was sent to the Tower, and a Flemish chronicler of the time suggests that one reason for Roger being singled out for this treatment is that Edward had received intelligence that his wife had already some form of illicit relationship with Mortimer.[2]

Roger Mortimer was in the Tower in the aftermath of the rebellion, which resulted in the deaths of many aristocratic leaders including the Duke of Lancaster. The Duke was tried by a tribunal made up of Edward's supporters, convicted of treason and beheaded on 22 March near Pontefract Castle. These ruthless actions set many of the English court against their monarch, but it was Isabella who tapped their discontent with Edward's rule and succeeded in having her husband removed from his throne.

It was surely not a coincidence that Isabella was in residence in the Royal Quarters of the Tower on the day that Roger Mortimer escaped from his dungeon in the same building in August. There had not been an escape from the Tower for nearly 250 years. Although it took determination and physical courage to break out of the dungeon, the intricate arrangements have all the signs of an inside job and Isabella was on the spot.

The getaway took place on Mortimer's birthday, in celebration of which he had delivered to his cell an elaborate feast with all the trimmings, including wine. This he shared with his guards and even the Constable of the Tower. The wine was drugged and most of the party fell asleep. An associate of Mortimer's happened to have a pickaxe and crowbar, which were used to make a hole in the wall of the dungeon through which Mortimer escaped. With one companion, he climbed out of the tower via a chimney.

Once on the roof, he descended to the riverside using rope ladders to reach a waiting boat. After crossing to the south side of the river, horses were waiting and Sir Roger then galloped all night, covering the 70 miles or so to the banks of the Solent. In Netley, 2 miles to the south of the port of Southampton, a ship was waiting to take him to France. After arriving in French territory, he galloped as fast as possible to Paris and a meeting with none other than Isabella's brother, Charles IV.[3]

The escape was complex, well planned, faultlessly coordinated and carried out by someone who was very well connected and at ease with secret plots. The final stage, especially, shows the hand of Isabella. It is unthinkable that the King of France would have met with an escapee from England, with no royal connections, unless an introduction had been arranged. Isabella was undoubtedly the catalyst.[4] Now Roger Mortimer was in Europe, setting up networks of exiles, while Isabella bided her time, waiting for her opportunity – for nearly two years.

Edward II's lack of diplomatic skills had led to strained relations with the King of France, placing the English landholdings in Gascony in South West France in jeopardy. This was a major diplomatic crisis. With great skill, Isabella persuaded the royal favourite Hugh Despenser to advise Edward, his lover and Isabella's husband, to send her to France to the court of her brother King Charles as an ambassador to negotiate a solution to the Gascony crisis.

In February 1325 Isabella left for Paris. There she negotiated a treaty with her brother King Charles. Her son Prince Edward would travel to France to pay homage to his uncle King Charles, guaranteeing possession of the province by the English royal family in his name. The terms were fulfilled when in December that year Edward kissed his Uncle Charles's hand in formal recognition of the feudal relationship between them. Through brilliant diplomacy Isabella had removed herself and her son from the growing anti-Despenser storm in England while solving, for the time being, a tricky diplomatic problem.

A woman with Isabella's diplomatic skills did not stop once she had ensured her son's possession of Gascony. Her main aim in going to France was to form connections with English anti-Despenser aristocratic exiles. With an adroitness that put her ill-advised husband in the shade, she began to pull together her plan for invading England and arranging for her son to replace her husband as king.

The French king was not prepared to intervene in a court struggle in England where the stakes were so high. If the plan had failed the very best outcome would be for Isabella and her son to spend the rest of their lives as hangers-on in European courts. The worst was humiliation and execution. But Isabella knew her eleven-year-old son was her best asset, and as was to happen on many occasions during Edward's life, a chance event came to his aid.

By an amazing stroke of good fortune in January 1326, Count Charles of Valois died and as a result Paris was filled with Europe's Francophile aristocracy who were there to attend his funeral. Isabella managed to turn the death of her brother into the perfect networking event to further her plans. Joan of Valois was there too with her children, including her nine-year-old daughter Philippa. Joan and Isabella were cousins and both had marriageable children. Joan was consort to the Count of Hainault, a small but wealthy state in Flanders, with a handy port in its territory – Dortrecht. The ruling family of Hainault were French speakers, but their power base was outside the area of France, giving them access to the sort of practical support that was needed.

As it happens the Hainault royal family were the perfect partners. Like the English monarch, the Duke of Hainault owed feudal allegiance to the King of France and – like the English – the Hainaulters would have been happy to escape this historic obligation. What is more, Hainault was closely linked to England, via the wool trade. The Hainault port of Dortrecht's location on a branch of the Rhine estuary gave the town excellent links into the interior of the European continent. Most importantly, the small but wealthy state had already become the residence of a group of exiled English anti-Despenser aristocrats – including Roger Mortimer, who had turned up at the royal funeral after his meeting with King Philippe in Paris. Mortimer had lost no time in establishing that connection, probably unaware that the future English king, Edward III, would later claim that the French throne should have been his, not Philippe's – but the argument over the niceties of Salic Law lay far in the future.

* * *

Isabella managed to get invited to Hainault after the funeral and a brilliantly advantageous deal was struck. The Duke of Hainault agreed to provide Isabella with an invasion fleet staffed by mercenaries and, in return, the fourteen-year-old Edward was to marry one of the Duke's three daughters. If the deal could be struck then Prince Edward would become Edward III in the near future, and the Duke of Hainault's daughter would be his queen.[5]

Isabella contributed funds by tapping into her dowry as a royal princess. The invasion force added up to about 1,000 warriors, which included 100 English knights led by two royal Earls, of Richmond and of Kent. Seven hundred mercenaries were recruited, for the most part in the small German states. They would have been made up of a number of different categories, including impoverished or ambitious young aristocrats in search of real battlefield experience. A large number of 'other ranks' such as pikemen, crossbowmen, and foot soldiers made up the numbers of the multi-national force of Flemings, Germans, and Frenchmen in addition to the English core. It is said that Mortimer maintained secret communications with clandestine supporters in England by means of letters hidden in barrels – which presupposes the existence of a network of spies on the ground in England.

Roger and Isabella were embarking on a highly risky venture. In medieval terms the behaviour of Isabella as Queen of England was deeply scandalous. Queens of England did not set themselves up in the courts of Europe to undermine their own husbands! If the expedition had not been a success, the She-Wolf of France would have met a dreadful end. But although both her spouse Edward II, his favourite Despenser and her lover Roger Mortimer all came to grief later, fortune smiled on young Edward and Isabella. It could be argued that fortune smiled on Edward III for most of his life.

Edward II's tendency to make big strategic errors when under pressure helped Isabella and Mortimer. Having heard about the planned expedition, King Edward foolishly organised a landing in Normandy, using more than 100 ships. The purpose of the venture may have been to capture Prince Edward and take him back to England. But the prince was in Valenciennes, in Hainault, and Edward's fleet landed in Normandy! The English fleet was decimated by the French defenders – which left Edward badly short of suitable ships when Isabella's invasion took place.

On 27 August 1326 Prince Edward and Philippa of Hainault were betrothed. He was fourteen, his future wife was twelve years old. It is said that he was offered the choice of any of William's three daughters and chose Philippa himself. He appears to have had a warm and loving relationship with her and although he was a womaniser (hardly unusual for a Medieval king) he stayed with his wife, who bore him many children.

On 21 September 1326, 95 ships carrying 700 mercenaries and over 1,000 seamen and warriors left the port of Dordrecht and sailed down the Rhine into the North Sea. As so often happened when invasions were planned to sail from the European mainland to England, the weather turned against them. For two weeks the flotilla of unhandy single-sailed ships battled the winds and storms before landing on the seashore near Orwell, 150 miles across the North Sea. The French chronicler Froissart wrote:

> God's tempest ... took them so far out of their course that they did not know for two days where they were, as a result of which God did them a great favour ... for if they had fallen into the hands of their enemies who knew well that they were coming ... they would have all been killed upon arrival.

The arrival place was almost certainly on the Essex bank of the mouth of the River Orwell – and Frossart's tempest was probably fiction.[6]

It is said that the invading army spent three hours disembarking. A tent constructed of carpets was built for Isabella. Her first action was not to relax and recover from the rigours of the journey but rather to write to the burgers of London, instructing them to support her and Mortimer in the forthcoming struggle.

This may not have been the planned destination. Froissart:[7]

> And there [they] took land on the sands three days without any right haven or port ... and so abode on the sands three days with few supplies or victuals and unshipped their horses and harness and they did not know which part of England they were in.

This may not be true. There are many examples of naval expeditions where the leaders had only an approximate idea of their location and in the absence of compasses and chronometers, navigation could be a hit-and-miss affair. As in the Devon raid more than twenty years later, fleets often sailed with little exact information – and it was quite normal for military fleets to cruise around in enemy waters in search of a landing site according to chance and luck, and with only a generalised awareness of the lie of the land. But the circumstances of this landing were so fortuitous that we can be fairly confident that it had been carefully planned. The fleet was manned by crews from Flanders which, as a major importer of English wool, had a close trading relationship with England. Medieval navigation followed coastlines, meaning that mariners from Flanders would be very familiar with the coastline just 60 miles north of their home port. Ships constantly travelled from Flanders to East Anglia, for example, and it is hard to believe that no one in the fleet was able to read the coastal signals and guide the fleet in the right direction. The fact that Isabella and her entourage soon moved off to Walton Castle, owned by a sympathiser, suggests she knew where she was.

One can picture the young Prince Edward standing on the forecastle of the royal cog as the storm abated, watching events on the water, and seeing the flat Suffolk coast approaching, aware of English ships in the area. It is quite likely that their royal ship would have been painted in bright heraldic colours, the red and gold of the English royal arms and the blue and gold of the Hainaulters. The English flag would have been flying from the cog's masts, and the royal coat of arms of both Hainault and England would have been displayed on the sails of the ships. There were mercenaries from a number of German states, and from the territories of the Count of Bohemia, so their heraldic bearings would have identified each group.

Isabella must have been aware of the tactic followed by Duke William of Normandy in 1066 when after landing his invading forces on English soil he sent his ships back to Normandy. She did the same. There was to be no retreat, no surrender.

Information we possess about King Edward's instructions to the Duke of Norfolk indicates that he knew through spies and informants what was being planned, and that he vainly tried to get his subjects to fight the invading forces. At the start of September Edward II had asked one of his lieutenants, Admiral

John de Sturmy, to take a force of 2,000 fighters to Orwell. But no one showed up. This tells us that there were spies in Isabella's camp, and also that King Edward's authority was already collapsing before the invasion took place.[8] In another telling piece of information, when the Hainaulter ships were returning to Dordrecht after delivering the invasion force, the very ship that Prince Edward and Isabella had been on was apprehended, captured and taken to London.[9]

From his palace in London, King Edward, assisted by his favourite Despenser, responded quickly. Orders were issued to sheriffs to assemble men-at-arms and foot soldiers 'to pursue the rebels and see what harm they can do them'. What chance did the army of rebels have against the nearly 49,000 men-at-arms, foot soldiers and archers who were summoned? Criminals in prisons were offered their freedom on condition that they serve their country in its hour of need. A huge bounty was placed on Mortimer's head. The words of the king's proclamation were read out repeatedly in public places all over the kingdom:

> If any person or persons bring and render to him the body of the said Roger or bring his head, the king … grants that he will pay them £1,000 sterling.[10]

There was one fatal flaw in Edward II's desperate plan. It had little support on the ground. The forces that did appear were small and scattered. Many of the knightly class were unwilling to support their lawful king, and the lower classes were not prepared to act against them.

***

Thomas de Brotherton, Earl of Arundel, was one of England's leading aristocrats. He was a child of Edward I by his second wife, so he was a younger half-brother of Edward II, which made him Prince Edward's uncle and Isabella's brother-in-law. As a leading member of the aristocracy, he had been appointed by Edward II to be protector of East Anglia, charged, ironically, with watching out for invasions from France led by Isabella and Mortimer – which he was doing, but not in the way that King Edward had in mind. Brotherton must have been contacted by the Isabelline party while they were still in Europe and he was already primed to switch allegiance. When the fleet showed up Thomas de Brotherton was there in no time and spoke to Isabella and Mortimer, and doubtless to Prince Edward, his nephew. He publicly abandoned his loyalty to Edward and Hugh Despenser and put his weight and reputation behind the invasion.

So according to this version of events Isabella did not spend her first night on English soil after an absence of eighteen months in a tent or a ship's berth, but rather in the nearby Brotherton residence, at Walton, just a few miles away. There they were introduced to Thomas' companions, who were ready to meet Roger and Isabella.[11]

The following day Isabella started her progress around the country, always dressed in widow's weeds as though in mourning for her unworthy husband, with Prince Edward by her side. The first part of her campaign was to process to Bury St Edmunds, about 40 miles away, so possibly two days of dignified riding, as was suitable for a queen in widow's weeds, accompanied by her son and a small army of well-armed men. Bury St Edmunds was a leading town, rich from the wool trade, and a major centre for pilgrimage, with its shrine to the Saxon Saint Edmund. Isabella and Prince Edward travelled, in the words of the chronicler, 'as if on pilgrimage' to the Abbey of Bury St Edmunds. The effect of this act of piety gave the invading force the appearance of a crusade, an act of devotion being carried out by a mother on behalf of her young son, who had been betrayed by his unworthy father.

While this was going on and the invasion force was moving through England on its way to London, the crew of Isabella and Prince Edward's ship passed on the information to Edward II and the Despensers, also in London, that they had been boarded and removed from their ship by their own forces. The coastal defences had been aware that the invasion force was coming to Suffolk, but had not responded to their presence until after the invasion was a success, thus betraying the king.

Queen Isabella and Prince Edward were welcomed at every town they travelled through. From now onwards the invasion began to take on the appearance of a royal progress. A typical invasion force of the time would do whatever was necessary to recoup the costs of the operation – which meant looting and taking ransoms. At the very start of the campaign, while the royal party were guests of Thomas de Brotherton in Walton-on-the-Naze, the Hainaulter and German mercenaries attacked neighbouring houses, following the usual custom. But the looters were disciplined – and Queen Isabella personally paid compensation to the citizens, much to everyone's astonishment. This style of leadership was in stark contrast to the Edwardian/Despenser brutal, authoritarian government. In twenty-first century terms we could say that Isabella was a master of the significant public relations gesture and the only properties that were taken by the invaders belonged to supporters of Edward II and the Despensers. They were seen as fair game, with the proceeds being split – 25 per cent to Isabella and Mortimer, and 75 per cent going elsewhere.

When Edward II and Hugh Despenser realised that no amount of ferocity against their perceived enemies could save them, they took off west towards Despenser's family base in South Wales in search of loyalists, with a treasury of £30,000 in gold currency. Order collapsed in London. After mobs broke into the Tower and released all the prisoners, an edict was issued freeing all prisoners all over England who had been imprisoned in the King's name.

Fugitives from justice, and people who had been banished by the past regime, were asked to return. The Chronicle of Geoffrey le Baker observes:

> In such confusion good and bad collided and rapacity and murder and in a state of indifference evil deeds were unpunished...[12]

Mortimer and Isabella's army were in pursuit, and it was not impossible either that Edward II might yet raise an army of Welshmen and lead it into battle against his wife and son with England in general relapsing into a state of anarchy. On 2 October Isabella wrote to cities and commonalities asking for their support, and on the same day Edward II wrote to the same cities and commonalities telling them that even to open Isabella's letters would be considered an act of treason. But Isabella was winning the information war.

The Bishop of Hereford publicly accused Hugh Despenser of the sin of sodomy, and preached a sermon on that theme using the quote from Genesis 'I will put enmity between thee and the woman, and between thy seed and her seed.' Although the Bishop did not dare to accuse the king himself, the message was unmistakable when the Bishop likened Hugh Despenser to the snake in the Garden of Eden. The invasion continued to look like a crusade.[13]

Edward and Despenser tried to raise a Welsh army but failed, so with a few followers he took ship for Ireland. The weather changed and they spent days at sea battling the elements. They were blown back to shore and tried again to raise an army in Wales, and eventually almost all their followers deserted them.

From now on, nothing more is heard about the 700 European warriors who had become redundant. They were sent home to Dordrecht, with their wages paid and no doubt a bonus for their having successfully completed their contracts.

By 18 November Edward and Hugh were in captivity, and by the end of the month Hugh Despenser was publicly executed. It is worth noting how Froissart describes his execution,[14]

First to be drawn on a hurdle through all the streets of Hereford and after to be brought to the market place, where all the people were assembled, and there to be tied on high upon a ladder where every man might see him; and in the same place there to be made a great fire, and there his privy members to be cut from him, because they reputed him as a heretic and so deemed and so burnt in the fire before his face. And then his heart to be drawn out of his body and cast into the fire because he was a false traitor of heart ... And then his head was stricken off and sent to London.

The sexual symbolism of this horrible execution needs no further comment.

Edward II was forced to renounce the throne in public. His end is uncertain. Was he killed in a terrible way, or did he live out a quiet life in exile? The chronicler Le Baker says that he was killed in a horrible manner.[15] Many do not believe the tale.

On 7 January 1326 Parliament was called to meet in London and Isabella's wish was granted: Edward II's son became king, but as he was still only fifteen years old, his mother assumed the title of Regent. Unofficially her lover Richard Mortimer wielded day-to-day power, leaving none to Prince Edward.

Edward was crowned in Westminster Abbey on 1 February 1327. It was said that when the Crown of Edward the Confessor – 'of great size and weight' – was placed on his head 'he bore it like a man'. During her son's coronation Isabella reportedly wept continuously, although the chronicler suggests that the tears were not genuine.

3

EDWARD III ARRIVES AND SCOTTISH RAIDS START

Despite being crowned King of England, Edward did not exercise any authority in the next few years. Although Roger Mortimer was not of royal stock, Isabella and Mortimer acted as leaders. In 1337 while Edward was with Mortimer campaigning in Scotland, Edward had tried to assert his authority and came near to trouncing the Scots. He had been overruled by Roger Mortimer – and the English had lost the day. Edward is said to have wept tears of frustration at his stepfather's ineptness in battle. Edward must have been haunted by the fact that his father, the ill-starred Edward II, had suffered a catastrophic military defeat at Bannockburn a generation earlier. There can be no doubt that one of the drivers of Edward's career as a war leader was his desire the recoup what had been lost by the previous generation.[1]

As a pointer to his thinking, in the year of his coronation young King Edward borrowed a book from his late father's library in the Tower of London – a copy of *De Re Militari*. This book, written by the Roman general Vegetius, had become the leading textbook of warfare in medieval Europe and we can guess that at this early stage Edward was preparing for his life's work by reading up on military strategy. Certainly, as a war leader Edward put much of Vegetius' advice into practice. He was a master at applying such advice successfully:

> Good generals are acutely aware that victory depends much on the nature of the field of battle. When you intend therefore to engage, endeavour to draw the chief advantage from your situation.[2]

Edward's great victories were gained by his application of this simple rule.

Edward was impatient for power and he was only eighteen when he and a group of his friends of the same age seized power from Isabella and Mortimer by creeping into the royal residence in Nottingham Castle using a secret tunnel. Edward then broke into his mother and stepfather's bedroom and arrested Mortimer, who was tried by Parliament for usurping royal power and condemned to death by hanging as a common criminal. His naked body remained on the scaffold for four days.[3]

At an age when many young people today are just embarking on their university careers, Edward had already shown that he had the energy, determination and, when necessary, focussed cruelty needed to succeed in the fourteenth century. For as long as he was physically capable during his fifty-year reign, he was engaged in warfare. Unlike most of his peers in other kingdoms, he tended to lead his armies in the field from the front, not just on horseback, but also on foot.

Not surprisingly, almost as soon as Edward was comfortably settled on the throne of England he turned his attention to recouping the military defeats that his father as well as his mother's lover had suffered at the hands of the Scots. By 1333 Edward was in Berwick with his armies and in no time he was leading his forces from an area of high ground that gave its name to Edward's first great victory – Halidon Hill. The nine-year-old David II of Scotland was no match for him. The farming adage, 'the best fertilizer is the farmer's footsteps' also applies to the presence of Edward's foot on the battlefield. The victory over the Scots was overwhelming and thousands of soldiers were slaughtered by the English in a bloody action.[4]

Edward was to lead his army again and again against his foes in the coming years but by the end of his reign, the decades of warfare had achieved little and at great cost. Edward did not understand what a much later military theorist said, that war is the 'continuation of politics by other means'.[5]

The French incursions onto English territory, which came about as a result of Edward's aggressive military presence in Europe, were an unintended consequence. The impact that these incursions had upon the ordinary working people who happened to live near the English coast was very great in terms of the lives disrupted, homes destroyed, possessions taken, violent death, and sexual violence.

Edward III's victory over the Scots at Halidon Hill did not stop the ongoing violence on the Scottish marches, nor did it make Scotland into an English possession. Instead it destabilised the relationships between France, Scotland and England, which led to decades of attacks upon the English mainland. Since the end of the thirteenth century, Scotland and France had been partners in a long-term relationship – 'The Auld Alliance' as it became known – by which the two nations could call upon mutual support against English aggression. Edward unwittingly provoked this moribund alliance to twitch back into life again.

After Halidon, nine-year-old King David of Scotland and his wife Joan were holed up in the ancient fortress of Dumbarton, sandwiched between the River Clyde and the precipitous Dumbarton Rock, effectively isolated from the rest of Scotland which was controlled by the English army. In May the following year of 1334 Philippe VI of France, not prepared to let an ally down, sponsored the Scottish Earl of Moray to pick up the boy king, his wife, and their (literally) tiny court and carry them away to France for their own protection.

From now on they were guests of the French Crown, living in the almost impregnable magnificence of the Chateau Gaillard that loomed 300 metres above the Seine Valley. Built by English King Richard 'The Lionheart', while he was also the Duke of Normandy, it was taken out of English control after a long, bloody and brutal siege in 1204. Thus the message to the English was clear: King David and his little queen were not to fall into English hands again.[6]

As a result of the exile of David II, the earliest naval attacks on English territory during this period were carried out by Scots, supported by the French. Judging by the ferocious response by the English Crown, from the first the Scottish naval threat was perceived as real. However, a party of Scottish warriors descending on English territory did not have the same news value as a French fleet. As a result, many episodes in this campaign did not make it onto the pages of the official accounts of the time; so much of this campaign has to be put together from (sensible) guesswork.

The earliest Scottish action in which we know the location for sure appears in a Parliamentary edict issued after the Scots invaded Kirklees, near Lowestoft on the Suffolk coast, in the same year that young David II was settling into his new home in Chateau Gaillard. Lowestoft was at that time a middle-ranking fishing settlement, isolated from much of the East Anglian mainland by the shallow arms of the sea, making it virtually an island. While Kirklees is now no more than a suburb of Lowestoft, now known as Kirkley, at the time it could have been an attractive location for a raid. Its waterways led to East Anglian pasture with flocks of sheep and cattle, and the Scots would have been attracted by a river port trading between the coast and the agricultural hinterland. The Scots managed to capture some English ships from Kirklees, and must have spent time on dry land ranging the hinterland, when they captured 'catella' – a word that refers to moveable goods such as cattle. In this era the Scots often rustled cattle in English territory and no doubt the raiders thought that cattle were a reasonable economic return for the effort involved in the raid. In later years when the invading fleets were from France, cattle were not the focus at all; high-status French leaders were more interested in barrels of Gascony wine, fine woven cloth, gold and silver coinage and, best of all, Englishmen for whom they could arrange ransom payments.[7]

A successful raid requires a number of features. Firstly, the raiders should be able to withdraw intact with little if any loss of the crew's life, or damage to shipping and equipment. The raiders should leave behind a significant amount of disruption, in the form of buildings and ships torched, and valuable ships captured and taken away. A number of local people should have been killed, assaulted, or, if of high enough economic value, ransomed. There should be the removal of valuable goods such as wine and wool, enough to make the raid self-financing. Maybe one-third of the raids that took place in our narrative could be considered successes by these criteria, but many were not.

In the armed incursions, the everyday inhabitants of coastal regions included men, women and children; rich, poor and middle-of-the-road, were confronted by the mercenaries often without warning or time to prepare. However, the professionals did not always win the day, despite inflicting huge damage. Local people had become surprisingly effective at fighting back. England had been at war with its neighbours for nearly a century, and the English people had lived with generations of battles, invasions and incursions across the borders of Scotland and Wales and over the water from Ireland. This helped to create a bellicose society; according Edward I's Statute of Winchester of 1290 everyone, with the exception of the clergy, between the ages of sixteen and sixty was obliged to own and to carry arms.[8] Throughout the period when foreigners invaded the English coasts, the local people retaliated and in many cases drove the invaders back to their ships. Sometimes after the risky landing phase of an invasion had passed, and the force was ready to fight on land, the locals turned up looking for a fight and they either beat the invaders back to their ships or killed them before they reached safety.

The type of arms that were carried varied. In a similar way that in the twenty-first century motor vehicles are often accurate markers of economic status, a fourteenth-century knight with a suit of armour, hauberk, sword and well bred warhorse displayed a superior position in the pecking order. So important was such a range of weaponry that knightly families that were not rich would put themselves heavily into debt to acquire the necessary equipment. Farther down the social scale, armaments became simpler and more basic. At the lowest level a fighter would possess a bow, a set of arrows, a knife, and maybe a pike. He might possess a quilted leather tunic, and if he were from a slightly higher social level, a steel helmet.

England had a fighting culture and 'leisure battles' between armed and trained Englishmen of all classes were common in the fourteenth century. The high-status pastime of jousting and tourneying is well described in the literature of the time. Less well known is the fact that lower-status archers and pike men would have spent much of their leisure time practising their skills.[9]

The very fact that so many adult and adolescent males were armed and trained encouraged violent criminality, and the sparsely settled population, well supplied with uninhabited forests, deserted farmland, and abandoned dwellings, was a perfect environment for criminal gangs, for criminal families, and for outlaws. The words *conspiratours* and *confederatours* are to be found in many Parliamentary edicts.[10]

Coastal settlements were especially prone to another sort of violence, and the seas around England were a lawless realm. For much of the time, the entire community was on its own against whatever the seas would deliver. In the years while the Anglo-French political landscape was steadily darkening, the coastal population quickly adapted to the habit of fighting back against the unwelcome Scots or Frenchmen. There was a related belief that foreigners in English waters were interlopers and, having no right to be there in the first place, were fair game. It was quite normal for fishermen, for example, to supplement their income by raiding passing boats that looked like easy targets. Indeed, mariners who lived in coastal communities with plenty of inlets to hide in would supplement their income by engaging in part-time piracy.

The fact that the local people were able to hold their own against the battle-hardened Scots may give us a hint that the local people had necessarily been forewarned of their impeding arrival but it also demonstrates that they were ready to retaliate. Chaucer's *Canterbury Tales* gives us a portrait of a Shipman, or Captain. He travels on his pilgrimage to Canterbury carrying a concealed weapon under his armpit,

A daggere hangynge on a lass hadde he
About his nekke under his arm adoun.

He was dishonest:

Of nice conscience took he no keepe

He was a skilled fighter:

If that he faught, and had the higher hond

The most telling statement in Chaucer's portrait of an English seaman at this time is the following – he was aware of how mariners dealt with his enemies whenever there was a battle at sea:

By water he sente hem hoom to every lond[11]

By this Chaucer means that he drowned his enemies. Chaucer is giving us a well-observed portrait of a type who would have been instantly recognisable to readers or to those who heard the *Tales* read aloud. This shipman surely would have been able to look after himself if he had to defend his home port from a group of raiders – provided he could rely on plenty of people like himself.

As relations with France deteriorated, Edward's administration started to collect information from their spies that the French were planning to help the Scots.[12]

News had also been received that at the Parliament of Paris held on the Octave of St Mary Magdalene [22 July] last, the King of France had announced by word of mouth that he desired to aid the Scots with a thousand men-at-arms and a large number of other troops, and a suitable escort of ships, pretending that he was bound so to do by virtue of a perpetual treaty of alliance between the two kingdoms. Writs had immediately been issued to summon the bishops and others to London to discuss the contents of the writs and other matters, which would be laid before them by the King's messengers.

Despite the lack of information in the records, there was plenty of indirect evidence of French-supported activity in both the North Sea and the Irish Sea. Wales saw action by marauding Scots and the English were not able to make the Irish Sea into an English lake, which is why, for example, keepers of the maritime lands

were appointed in South Wales in July 1335 to counter the Scots
and their Scottish confederates:[13]

> To Philip of Calanowe and others assigned to the defence of
> the ports and shoreline of Wales, in relation to arresting ships
> in these ports and impressing men, to the capture of Scottish
> ships invading England.

This information suggests not only that Scots were active in the
North Sea, but suggests that they were in touch with French
support coming into the area from the south-west. And the threat
was not just in the Irish Sea area. Here is a message from King
Edward addressed to the Constable of Dover in the same year:[14]

> King Edward, fearing invasion by Scots and other foreign
> people, whether in Kent or in nearby areas, orders the
> Constable of Dover, that he defends the castle with armaments,
> supplies of food, and whatever men are needed for defence.

Actions that we know something about include an attack in
1336 by the Scots on the Channel Islands, when the Keeper of
the Channel Islands was ordered to organise a defence force
for the strategically important English islands. The islands of
Alderney and Sark paid no tax for several years after this raid took
place, indicating that the two smaller islands had been entirely
devastated.[15] This action confirms the picture of a Scottish force,
supported by the French, active all around the coasts of England.

4

THE CONFLICT ESCALATES – FRENCH ATTACKS

In the following years the conflict escalated. The French acquired allies around Europe, the fleet expanded, and well-organised attacks became more frequent. Up until the 1340s there was a period of relentless French pressure upon English coasts and coastal waters. Lying behind everything was young King Edward III of England and the fact that he had made a claim to the throne of France. This dynastic dispute takes us to the heart of fourteenth-century politics. It is a complex question, related to the fact that the French feudal state was an amalgam of disparate territories, some directly ruled by the King of France, some ruled by other leaders who owed allegiance to him.[1]

The King of England was also the Duke of Aquitaine, in South West France. Edward III had inherited the French province of Gascony from his father Edward II, not as part of the Kingdom of England, but as his own personal property as a fief to the French monarch. Gascony was a valuable possession, a major wine producer and a source of much of England's trading economy. What magnified the effect of the Franco-Scottish crisis was an extraordinary twist by which it was possible for Edward III to argue that he was the true king of France, and that Philip VI was actually a usurper.

The Capetian kings had ruled France for hundreds of years, but in the early years of the fourteenth century bad luck had resulted in three of King Philippe's predecessors dying within thirty years of each other. The male line of the House of Capet became extinct, and Philippe Valois, a cousin of Charles IV, and Charles' nearest male relative, was pronounced king. But the deceased Charles's closest relative was his sister, Isabella, Queen of England, eventually to become known as as the She-Wolf of France, Edward's mother. Although it was generally accepted that a woman could not become the ruler of France, meaning Isabella could not reign, maybe the nearest male relative in the direct line of descent via a woman was – and that person was Edward III. The French legal experts had decided that this was not possible. Edward, not surprisingly, thought that it *was* possible. As a warrior king, Edward was not prepared to pass up the opportunity to use this genealogical and legal quirk as a *casus belli*.

This claim to the French throne bedevilled Anglo-French affairs throughout Edward's reign and beyond and was the cause of much violence, death and destruction. For Edward and the kingdom of England the Gascony question was not an issue of national survival. From the point of view of the French Crown, however, the issue was of existential importance. The French state was a ramshackle amalgam of different feudal entities tacked together by means of feudal oaths. If the King of England chose to pick and choose where his loyalties lay, others might follow – it could not be permitted, as the entire structure of the state required obedience to the underlying feudal principles.

The Franco-Scottish alliance obliged France to support the Scots if Scotland was attacked by the English. The fact that King Philippe VI was giving hospitality to King David II and his entourage strengthened the obligation that the French were under to take on the English – especially Edward III.

Sometimes just one statement made at the right time can change the political weather. Four years earlier, in 1334 the Scottish royal family were on their way to France. Edward was in Roxburgh, escalating the war on the Scots. Scottish ships were in the North Sea, and Scottish forces were receiving supplies from the French via the Irish Sea. In May 1334 ambassadors arrived from the court of Edward III in Senlis, north of Paris. They were there to negotiate a solution to the Aquitaine problem, and Edward's claim to the French throne – at the same time that Edward was creating mayhem in Scotland. While the talks were possibly reaching a conclusion, news of the arrival of the Scottish royal family in France came to King Phillip. The negotiations ceased.

Philippe's words to the ambassadors resonated in the coming years, contributing to the sense that war was inevitable. 'There would never be friendship between England and France until the same man is king of both.' Later English opinion was that Philippe had said 'There will be no perfect Christian peace until the King of France sits in the midst of England in judgment over the three kingdoms of England, France and Scotland.'[2]

What exactly was said at the meeting is uncertain, and can never be settled for sure. But the words of the French king resonated. Over the coming eighteen months France and England drifted further into a war situation without actually having declared that hostilities had commenced. Meanwhile, the papacy was urging the two monarchs to put aside their differences and join together in a crusade to expel the Saracens from North Africa. But this plan was never put into effect, and much diplomatic energy was expended to little effect. For King Philippe his focus was upon Scotland, and upon the English coasts.

Over the winter of 1335–1336 the French Parlement agreed to Philippe's request for money to strengthen the naval force.

It was destined initially for Scotland with the intention of supporting the return of King David from Chateau Gaillard exile, but the plan grew. In what was to become a typically French style of operation, an invasion plan was put together slowly and with a great many resources. It was to be one of the most ambitious naval projects for a very long time, and required a huge amount of logistical support. There were to be 1,200 men-at-arms, 5,000 crossbowmen, and 20,000 infantry. They were all to be packed into maybe 200 transport ships. Sixty fishing boats were needed just to carry food supplies, and 100 galleys were to escort the fleet and provide defence against attack on their way through the North Sea. Once a landing had been secured in Scotland, the French navy was to transport King David and his retinue back to Scotland, and replace him on the throne as the rightful ruler. This was an audacious plan and there had never been an equivalent project carried out in Western Europe since the time of the Crusades in the previous century.

England was a trading economy, with wool exports and wine imports both of importance. Consequently England's merchant classes were rich and the coastal communities were hubs of shipping, warehousing, shipbuilding and fishing. But the English state had very few naval resources. For the French, trade was of much less importance, so shipping in France was to a great extent financed by the state. The French Crown ran a naval dockyard in Rouen, which was becoming the meeting place of the Mediterranean shipbuilders and those of northern Europe – and indirectly the source of the Genoese, Monegasque and Catalan marines who would figure in many attacks in the coming years.

At the same time, reports were arriving at Edward III's court that an invasion of Scotland was planned. The French force would put David II back on the throne and provide Scotland with the necessary materiel and support for an attack on northern England. It would be carried out by the Scots, with assistance from the French. Two members of King David's court in Chateau Gaillard were sent on ahead of the expeditionary force to make preliminary arrangements. The expedition was to be mounted from existing naval resources in Clos des Galées in Rouen and elsewhere. Two thousand sailors were gathering in the port of Harfleur, in the mouth of the Seine, to board thirty copper-plated galleys ready for the expedition. Crossbows were being manufactured, and so were the shields that crossbowmen used. The purpose of this expedition was serious – nothing less than support for an invasion of northern England by a Franco-Scots army once King David was safely ensconced on the throne of Scotland.

The efforts on the ground were a lot more modest. A small force of French soldiers set out to Scotland to prepare the way for the big invasion force that was to come later. This was the start of a long story, and the idea of a Franco-Scottish alliance destroying English power was a long lasting one.

As was usual with King Phillippe, plans moved slowly and steadily, maybe uncertainly, and the results of the naval strategy were not apparent until the following year. But the warfare that ended 1336 demonstrated how effective sharp, fast, pitiless action on the ground was, compared with the slow development of policies. In other words, Edward versus Phillip.

In terms of logistics the planned French campaign in Scotland was a risky one. The Scottish environment was in terrible shape and possessed little surplus food, for example, to support a huge field army. Twenty years earlier the Great Famine had hit Scotland hard, as much of its farmland was on marginal climatic areas. The area that was farmed in Scotland had shrunk, as had the population. The wave after wave of English armies that had devastated post-famine Scotland had further reduced the country's ability to support an invasion by 25,000 hungry fighting men. Sixty fishing boats for 25,000 men and one fishing boat of supplies for about 420 men! The army would soon be scouring the countryside in a desperate search for sustenance.[3]

At this point the issue was resolved an example of Edward's firm and energetic leadership. By a process of elimination it was easy to guess that a French invasion force would need to land north of Edinburgh, via the North Sea. In a very poor country with a limited number of large ports available, and needing to be supplied from ships travelling up the North Sea there were only a limited number of landing areas available to the invaders. Edward's strategic guess was that Aberdeen would be the key location. Apart from the fact that Aberdeen and other north-east coastal towns had harbours of sufficient size for a large landing, the area was where a sizeable chunk of Scotland's farmland was located, much of Scotland farther south having in recent times been devastated by English forces.

Edward decided on a technique of warfare that was cheap, quick and effective, and totally destructive to the lives of non-combatants. With a small elite force of 400 horsemen he left his Nottingham Council in mid-June, and by July he was in Eastern Scotland, ready to waste the entire lowland area, making it impossible for the French to survive without supplies.

In a brilliant lightning campaign in July 1336, the sort of campaign that Edward was best at, he brought his forces into just the area where the French were planning to land, and via a scorched earth campaign destroyed all supplies. The towns of Elgin, Forres and Aberdeen were burnt. All stores of food were taken by the army, all livestock was killed. Reportedly 1,000 pigs were massacred on one July day in 1336, in a sort of porcine genocide. The only building left standing in Elgin was its cathedral. The campaign finished with Edward personally inspecting the remains of Aberdeen, to make sure that nothing was visible above ground. He was reportedly satisfied.

After Edward's return from Scotland a second punitive invasion was launched, and South West Scotland was burnt and destroyed in the same way, not by Edward this time but by one of his close entourage. Was this second campaign carried out in order to forestall a French attempt at a landing by way of the Irish Sea?[4]

At about the time that Edward III was carrying out the type of land operation that he was best at, that is, spreading death and destruction around the location of his enemies in lieu of carrying out a land battle, the French were creating an important new strategic plan. King Philippe and his advisors called in the resources of the Mediterranean to the troubled English Channel. With a bigger and more skilled navy based along their Channel coast they would be better able to withstand the coming English onslaught. In the coming decades the Mediterranean ships were to become very visible indeed around English shores. The very phrase 'galley from Monaco' would strike terror in the hearts of many a citizen of an English port. While Edward's bloody campaign was going on in Scotland, news came to the English court from the king's spies in France. The French Mediterranean fleet had arrived in the English Channel and there were reportedly twenty-six Mediterranean galleys at King Philippe's disposal, high-quality elite fighting ships, some armour-plated with copper sheathing, ready to catch the sunlight and strike terror in the hearts of the English townspeople and sailors.

At the start of 1337 representatives from towns around England were summoned to Westminster and given what until then was an unprecedented order by a senior counsellor to King Edward. They were to return home and pass on the command of the king. Ships were to be made, and fencible men were to be available for three months – ready to go out and face down the French enemy, without pay or compensation. The provincial magnates refused such an outrageous order. A week later, writs were issued demanding service without compensation.[5]

England was now on a war footing, but as always there was room for diplomatic negotiation. What better time for Edward to use the services of two leading churchmen to meet the French monarch one last time in an attempt to find some form of peaceful solution to the problems that were largely the result of Edward's own reckless leadership? The Bishops of Durham and of Winchester, with a very small number of companions, were charged by Edward's grand council in Nottingham with a mission to parley with the King of France himself. They left Dover at the end of July and spent much of the first part of August in the royal residence in the Bois de Vincennes, near Paris but well separated from the violence and hubbub of the capital itself. Originally a hunting lodge, the Bois de Vincennes was deep in the forests of the Isle de France, surrounded by ancient oak trees, and the deer would approach the walls of the residence when not chased into the woods by royal hunters. However, it is unlikely that the clerics representing Edward took advantage of this leisure opportunity. The French king had summoned his council to meet with the English ambassadors and reportedly the atmosphere was less than friendly. The two sides were wrangling in the Gothic gloom of the Bois de Vincennes council chamber when King Philippe dropped his diplomatic bombshell – he did not want to talk any longer. He had already assembled a huge fleet, and a large body of fighting men. He had the means to invade both England and Scotland simultaneously – and he intended to do just that. Negotiations were at an end.

The astonished English clerics thought this information should remain secret until it was given to King Edward, so it was not committed to paper. Instead a clerk of the party, William Tickhill, and a companion, presumably chosen for their fitness and horse-riding skills, set off immediately for England. They were in Dover by 23 August and, in a mammoth feat of overnight riding, Tickhill was in Nottingham by 24 August. Edward was away in the north, still fighting the Scots. The permanent councillors immediately started to do what was necessary to call a full council meeting, and Tickhill was sent on his way to find Edward.

Tickhill returned to the road – it was more than 260 miles to Berwick, on the edge of the war zone. Edward was farther north, many days ride through dangerous territory. Conditions in Scotland were such that any well-dressed English emissary would have had little chance in a meeting with impoverished and enraged survivors of Edwards's destructive campaigns. It was not until late September that Edward heard that invasion was imminent. He immediately turned south. What state William Tickhill was in by this stage we do not know.[6]

Edward's style was always to act fast. The war in Scotland was abandoned and by the end of September the king was in Nottingham, planning a new campaign in response to Philippe's challenge. In the four weeks since Tickhill's departure from Bois de Vincennes, the French had begun the first steps toward a French invasion of England. Between then and the end of 1340 there were at least twenty-four French naval attacks on England. As we now know, the English were ready and organised to fight back at least some of the time.

The first attack in late August was on the port that Edward would remember very well from when he was a boy – Orford. The raiders were in luck because when French warships descended on the harbour, a large merchant cog, the *Caterine*, was there. The ship was boarded and the crew killed. Although the chroniclers do not go into detail, the simplest method was simply to throw the unfortunate men overboard assuming that they were not able to swim well enough to save themselves. When the wind was right, the captive ship was sailed out of harbour, heading south-east across the North Sea to Sluys, in French Flanders.

Next the flotilla followed the flat Suffolk coast towards the south and, just a few sailing hours away, they descended on another soon-to-be vanished harbour, Walton. Another day, another top-quality big merchant cog – the *Paternoster*, also carrying a valuable cargo, was at anchor. As before, the crew was disposed of and some of the invaders sailed the ship off across the North Sea to French Flanders. Just a few more hours sailing time and French and Monegasque ships would have been in the Thames estuary, ready to descend on London itself.

Philippe IV received 50 per cent of the haul. The fleet that carried out the raids included ships from Genoa and Monaco. This was the first time that the Mediterranean experts appeared around English shores. They were to remain in English waters for much of the following decades.[7]

An even bigger flotilla made its way out of the French harbours and along the South Coast of England in the summer of 1336. This was a more serious and threatening array of vessels, and included some of the fearsome Genoese galleys whose purpose was so specialised – interception, landing, ravaging, killing, looting and burning. They made for the Isle of Wight, the key to the entire south coast. In an era before compasses and accurate timekeeping, experienced sailors made their way along the coast, following landmarks and geographical features – part of the intellectual property of a professional sailor. Much of the Isle of Wight was surrounded by low chalk cliffs, and Carisbrook Castle at the highest point of the island would have been manned with young lookouts, those with the sharpest eyes.

The French fleet would have been arrayed in its finest gear, and the ships brightly painted. The royal standard flying from each ship signified that they meant business and that much blood would be shed. The same design would have been sewn into the sails, and the highest status warriors with iron helmets or breastplates would have burnished their armour so that it gleamed in the sun and any copper plating on the galleys gleamed and reflected light onto the waves.

When the fleet was first sighted the galleys would have been moving under sail but as they approached the shore, the sails were lowered, ready to move seamlessly into landing mode. As the galley had under oar a speed of maybe 5 miles an hour, the inhabitants of the Isle had a couple of hours at least to prepare to meet the enemy.

It is impossible now to reconstruct the exact events of this raid, but it would appear that there was little resistance. The ships probably followed the north coast of the island, with Portsmouth and the Solent in view. The big natural harbour of Cowes was full of merchant ships that were boarded, the crews were disposed of, and the valuables were loaded onto the merchantmen. The less valuable ships were destroyed and sunk, and the others were sailed off to France for sale. This was one of the more successful self-financing expeditions and it would have helped to secure the loyalty of the Genoese and Castilian allies.

* * *

Raids such as that carried out on the Isle of Wight were to have a profound effect upon English society in the coastal regions. England's well-oiled government machine had whirred into action almost as soon as Edward's government understood that the coastal lands were under threat from Continental invaders. In the coming decades the populations around the English coast were recruited into a highly regimented defensive system, which placed a serious burden on inhabitants and which, in the long term, was to create widespread dissatisfaction among the people who were most affected.

Although the feudal system in which every subject of the Crown was required to carry out obligations to their liege lord without any payment had largely died out by the middle of the fourteenth century, the pressure from French attacks led to its revival. The *posse comitatus* system of obligation dated back to Anglo-Saxon times and it had been revived during grave national emergencies. On this occasion, however, the system was in operation for a lengthy period and at times of especial crisis it was imposed in a draconian way. Keepers of the maritime lands or commissioners of array had power to recruit able-bodied males between the ages of sixteen and sixty into defensive forces. They were obliged to train, maintain and keep them in a state of readiness. This system continued in operation until the 1380s.

Landowners in coastal counties were expected to contribute to the defence of the realm, according to income. A landowner with lands worth £10, for example, might be expected to contribute a single footman. Whenever danger threatened, edicts would be sent out instructing all landowners with coastal lands to return to their estates and to organise their forces. Edward's government machine continually issued edicts aimed at landowners who were not fulfilling their duty, with severe penalties levied on those who did not oblige.

All through this period the defenders of the English coast struggled with a major problem. It was relatively easy for enemy shipping to slip through the very rough-and-ready defensive net along the English coasts. Many major raids were carried out on settlements that had no inkling that they were to be singled out. So on many occasions French landings were made unopposed until, after a time lag, a force of defenders appeared and a fight ensued. However, in the course of a multiple raids, as the news travelled along the coast, the attacking force found it harder and harder to find an undefended location for a landing.

A successful English response to a French raid could pass through a number of stages. On many occasions English spies in France were able to forewarn the English administration that a raid was on its way, in which case Edward's warning system would move into operation and send out warnings around the kingdom, which should have alerted the commissioners and ensured that each area was for action. It would be rare for the early warnings to state exactly where a raid was going to take place but as soon as a hostile fleet was sighted by the watchers on the coastline, the defenders should be alerted and made ready for action. The next step would be lighting the warning beacons. All along the coasts the Crown had ordered each stretch of coastline to set up '*communa signa, quae per ignem super montes et alio modo*'. So the lighting of the beacons would be passed along the coast ahead of the enemy fleet, making it hard for the French forces to land anywhere. At least, that was the theory. In effect, on many occasions, the system seems to have broken down. A final form of communication was the church bell. One of Edward III's edicts required churches to signal divine service by single strokes of their bells, while continuous peals of bells were by law reserved for an incursion.[8]

The coastal towns were of especial importance within the system and locations of key importance, which might well have fortified structures in place, would be permanently manned by full-time soldiers, in receipt of regular pay. For example, during the 1340s Carisbrook Castle defending the Isle of Wight had a small defence force consisting of six men-at-arms, four mounted soldiers and eight archers.

In a time of crisis there was no escape for citizens. The wealthy and the poverty-stricken were all expected to contribute what they had available to the national defence against the French. Wealthy knights would have shown up to the array on horseback, in full armour, armed with high quality ironware, with heraldic devices on their shields, accompanied by squires to tend to their needs. In the lower levels there would be many people with stout leather jerkins and maybe simple iron helmets, armed with spears and knives. The poorest peasants would have little more than poleaxes. Every man according to his means. After presenting themselves, the fittest looking men were selected to serve their king and country – the unfit men in each community were required to contribute a cartload of food supplies for the active soldiers.[10]

The English nation was responding very well to the invasion. England was led by a king who had the energy, focus and determination to take measures fast. And he was lucky that he controlled state machinery that allowed him to raise money quickly.

There were French ships active around the south and east coasts of England all through the summer of 1336. It is quite likely that information about some raids was not picked up by the chroniclers of the time. Some raiding would have involved low-status craft such as fishing vessels and small-scale traders and did not make sufficient impact to be documented. There is no doubt that the French threat was dramatic and for the time being resulted in a wave of national pride – a determination to stand up to the Frenchman.

The action at sea moved along the English Channel as the French navy started to harry English merchant ships in the sea lanes to Gascony. England was swept by rumours of French spies, of Scots working on behalf of the French king plotting acts of sabotage. Any French people still in England were liable to arrest. Meanwhile, English traders in Flanders – of whom there were many, engaged in the wool export trade – were arrested. And any English traveller in Normandy was treated as though he was an enemy and arrested.

The French, acting with their Scottish allies, invaded the Channel Islands in 1336. In the years to come there would be plenty of ongoing work on the Castles of Gorey and of Jedburgh which were repaired, strengthened, and manned with men-at-arms and archers. This was prescient, as there was more conflict on the way.[9]

By October every ship in any English port was potentially liable to serve the king. Many were ordered to congregate at sea, near Sandwich and the horn of Kent, waiting to intercept the French fleet as it was, supposedly, returning to home ports for the winter. None of the French fleet appeared. Mutiny and bad morale became apparent among the English. A large contingent of ships from

Great Yarmouth decided to seize the moment, slipped away and carried out a brutal raid on Winchelsea, in retaliation for some supposed past offence! It was realised by the authorities that large numbers of idle seamen waiting together was not a good idea. By November the entire sea defence force was disbanded. The ships owners were able to go back to what they did best – trade. Then it was the turn of the home defence force to disband.[12]

After the defence forces were formally ordered to disband Edward focused his mind on what he was really interested in – the Scots. As soon as he could get away from Nottingham he was back in Scotland, recapturing Boswell Castle in its strategically important location at a crossing of the River Clyde. Then he was hard at work undoing the damage done to its fortifications during the Scottish occupation.

By Christmas Edward was back in England, doing what he did not do very well – trying to minimise the diplomatic fallout that his hyperactive and aggressive policies had created on the other side of the English Channel.

5

ACTION UP TO 1340

At the end of April 1337 King Phillip took another step to escalate the Franco-English conflict, and the ancient feudal military summons of *arrière-ban*, requiring the whole French nation to present themselves in arms ready to fight, came back into use. The phrase comes from the German Frankish world of the Dark Ages. By harking back to an earlier period of heroic warfare, the *arrière-ban* was designed to stimulate patriotic sentiments and it was a dramatic way of declaring that formal hostilities between France and England had begun.

Every able-bodied male between the ages of sixteen and sixty, from the wealthiest magnate to the poorest peasant or member of the city proletariat had to present himself to his feudal lord, armed and willing to go off to fight.

Except – there were exceptions. If the feudal lord agreed, it might be possible for the military service to be commuted via a monetary payment. In general the chivalric classes of French society were eager to see action against the English. Indeed, even before war was officially declared some young French knights were gaining fighting experience by serving in Scotland. But in the case of the bourgeoisie, the merchants and traders for example, a generous cash payment, to be used to finance ground and naval forces, was a vital part of the preparation for war.[1]

Edward had enraged the entire French ruling class by claiming the title of 'King of France'. By referring to the real French King in Paris as 'my cousin Philip Valois who calls himself the King of France' Edward seemed to be inviting the King of France to retaliate, which he did. Philip had to be seen as getting tough on this young, energetic monarch.

Edward held Gascony as a fief of his feudal lord King Philippe. As Edward had renounced his allegiance, it was only reasonable for King Philippe to invade Gascony and reclaim his possession. It was clear too that Edward was planning to fight the French on French soil. English forces had been actively fighting in Scotland on and off for years, which meant there was a battle-hardened English war machine ready to move into operation. France had far less experience of serious warfare and did not possess the same fierce fighting spirit that England had.

When the *arrière-ban* was declared, Edward's war machine was already in operation for the forthcoming expedition to the Continent. The planning involved amassing military supplies such as armour, longbows and arrows. Quantities of supplies were being stored, mainly in the Tower of London, in readiness for action. For the huge number of longbow arrows a gigantic number of feathers were needed – which involved plucking tail feathers from geese. Every goose in the whole kingdom of England was expected to contribute!

At the same time Philippe's ministers were getting ready for full-scale warfare against England. Armies were summoned, the French alliance with Scotland was strengthened and the Scottish court in Chateau Gaillard was kept in touch with the Scottish loyalists using French naval assistance. It is likely that many shipments for Scotland slipped up from northern France to

Scotland without being intercepted by the English, but one episode has been logged into the history books.

The *Cogge de Flandre* was intercepted by armed ships from Yarmouth on its way to Scotland. It was one of the largest cogs in the French fleet, and it was loaded with a treasure trove of 30,000 silver livres, jewellery and armour. Maybe of even greater value to the English royal machine were chests full of secret correspondence. The ship was full of dignitaries, with the Bishop of Glasgow in attendance – a stalwart of the court of King David. There were many soldiers aboard and although none of the chroniclers tell us so, we can guess that some at least would have been young French aristocrats seeking the essential battlefield experience of any young man wishing to be a respected knight. Where better than Scotland to get it, so that when the big invasion actually happened, with their new knowledge and experience these young knights would form the core of a cadre of leaders?[2]

However, as the implications of the *arrière-ban* became obvious English attention switched to operations near the English Channel. After all, if King Philippe raised an invasion fleet in Clos des Galées it was only a short trip to the English ports of southern England. Commissioners of Array had been active all over the south, from Kent to Cornwall, from early in the year, and all ships of over 30 tonnes capacity were liable to arrest and impressments. If Philippe planning a big invasion, the English had to be prepared to fight it off. So during the coming months while Edward was preparing a military expedition to the European mainland he was also making preparations to fight off French invaders, not to mention Scottish! Edward's poor diplomatic skills had led him potentially to wars in Scotland, in Gascony and on the seas.

Not surprisingly, during the spring, summer and autumn of 1337 the entire south and east coasts were in turmoil. Merchant ships were confined to port, unable to go about their usual business. Most ports were closed to commercial traffic. Soldiers and sailors who had been called up for the forthcoming invasion of France were billeted in various ports, waiting for action. Inevitably there was a breakdown in law and order as idle soldiers caused trouble. As was to happen on many occasions with Edward's foreign invasions, the logistical difficulties of obtaining suitable shipping, getting it arrayed in a suitable port while also organising supplies and fighting men, created long-term chaos for the compulsory hosts. Hosting the King's army for an entire trading season was nearly as bad as being raided by the enemy.

Not until November of that year, in a cold and rainy autumn, were Edward's armies and ships able to assemble in the ports of Sandwich and Orwell, bound for Flanders. The nobility of England were there, and archers and men-at-arms from as far away as Wales were arriving ready for battle. An advance force landed in Flanders in November and using the territory of Edward's kinsmen in Hainault as a base was getting ready for battle. And naturally the French military was preparing to defend themselves against the English. At some time in the near future war between England and France on Continental territory was looming.

While Edward was slowly assembling his invasion force it was not surprising that Philippe Valois should seek to create a northern diversion. Any tactics that forced Edward to switch military resources away from the Flemish battlefront would make the forthcoming Anglo-French showdown more manageable for Phillip's armies. So while Edward's forces assembled in the cold and wet autumn months of 1337, the French were ramping up the Auld Alliance. More and more materiel and advisors shipped up the North Sea from France to Scotland, while the English royal attention was on the European mainland.

Flush with French supplies and confident in the expectation of direct physical support, the independence-loving Scots launched a series of attacks across the border into England. The fortress of Carlisle was besieged and the castle's Cumbrian hinterland was burnt and wasted. This created a dangerous situation for Edward. Scottish King David and his tiny court were guests of King Philippe, and it was surely not unreasonable to expect that once Edward was enmeshed in operations on the French mainland some sort of French invasion of Scotland in support of King David would follow. Having come close to the classic strategic error of fighting on two fronts simultaneously Edward was forced to divert valuable and scarce supplies to the north. A cohort of soldiers travelled the more than 300 miles north from Kent to the Scottish Borders to beef up defences against the marauding Scots. There would have been much grumbling from them, as service in Scotland, a country stripped bare by continual English marauding and suffering badly from the onset of the Little Ice Age, did not offer the same opportunities as in France.[3]

Edward had over-extended himself and his army was now short of money needed for his multiple campaigns. As a cold and wet autumn rolled into winter more forces were needed in the north, and the troops waiting impatiently in Sandwich and the East Anglia ports were suffering food shortages and were unable to get out of their ports. The English weather had turned against Edward in the form of contrary winds, pinning his navy in port. At the end of November the entire expedition was abandoned. The soldiers who had already sailed returned home to England from Flanders, never having seen action.

* * *

The *Chronicle of Lanercost* reports that early in 1338 there was a big attack upon the Solent by a fleet assembled by the King of France with the assistance of the King of Bohemia. While the King of Bohemia might appear to be an unlikely English foe, as King of both Luxemburg and Bohemia he was part of the network of family and dynastic alliances that made up the leadership of

Western Europe. John, Count of Luxemburg, although from the family of the German emperors, lived for much of the year in Paris. In the coming years John of Luxemburg was to serve King Philippe faithfully, until his life ended on the killing fields of Crécy.[4]

On this occasion John of Bohemia helped his royal cousin King Philippe by loaning him an invasion fleet that was to cruise round the coasts of England and carry out small-scale raids. The plan was, according to the Lanercost chronicler, to

> ... harass the southern parts of England in the cause of the oft-mentioned David de Brus, who had done homage for the Kingdom of Scotland for the King of France, in order that the King of England, hearing that his country was invaded by foreigners in the South, should desist from molesting the Scots in the North.

This early campaign should have left more traces in the historical record. A force of several hundred and an alliance between monarchs aimed at supporting Scotland by opening hostile actions in the south of England is a significant move. In fact, in this case we have very little to go on and the chronicler's account is sketchy. The *Chronicle of Lanercost* describes just one raid carried out probably in 1338 soon after the fleet first appeared in English waters.

> There appeared very shortly the aforementioned ships near Southampton, of which eight ships took possession of the harbour, the men who were in two ships entered onto dry land, and burnt two settlements whose name we do not know.

But the men of the country, having been forewarned about the invasion, killed the men, took the ships and seized everything they could. That left six ships still on the high seas.

After this the story becomes confusing. Only one ship appeared in this area again; laden with 300 armed men, it took control of an area near Portsmouth and carried out some burning near the landing area. The Lanercost Chronicler says, 'none of those three hundred men every saw their homeland again' – which is difficult to understand. During the entire narrative there is not a single case of local defence forces wiping out an entire foreign army. But it is reasonable to guess that the local people did retaliate. The sight of ships arrayed for war moving round the east coast of the Isle of Wight and sailing along the north coast of the channel of the Solent, spying out a suitable location for a landing and then sailing towards Southampton looking for same thing, was to become far more familiar in later years.

When the Lanercost Chronicler tells us of 'two settlements whose names we do not know' he could be referring to Portsea, Gosport, or Southsea – in the fourteenth century they were all tiny waterfront communities. Lanercost does not tell us what sort of ships the Franco-Bohemian force were using, but it is possible at this stage they were still using ordinary merchant vessels, such as cogs, and they may well have had no special modifications in order to make them into proper fighting vessels.

We can guess that the people of Southampton were not overawed by the men who landed. The Lanercost Chronicler does not tell us, but we can guess that the fighting crew were not arrayed like knights, more likely they would have been lightly armed foot soldiers with leather jerkins. It is clear that the writs and edicts coming from King Edward's court machinery were already having an effect in encouraging the major ports along the south coast to increase their security. It is quite possible that local traders took the law into their own hands to protect themselves from danger from the sea, as they would have done so often in the past against pirates. They would have been ready with bows and arrows – deadly weapons for anyone who can aim straight.

And the higher-status fighters would have been as well armed with pikes, swords, and daggers as anyone in the landing force, as appropriate to their status.

By the end of that day in March many a body would have been floating near the shoreline, buffeted by the waves. And if there had been any Continental knights in the raiding party wearing breastplates and with aventails covering the entire head, a knife slipped through their armour plates to deadly effect followed by a slip over the side meant they would have been dragged down to the seabed and finished off by the equipment that was designed to make them impregnable.

It appears that while this raid was being planned and carried out, King Philippe was making different plans. Over the winter of 1337/1338 King Philippe appointed an admiral to lead his newly strengthened naval force. Admiral Nicolas Béhuchet stands out from most characters of this time as he was not of aristocratic background, and was not a trained fighting man. He had little hands-on shipping experience, but was a competent administrator, who knew how to do accounts. Described as being 'short and fat' and apparently unpopular, he would have instantly stood out among the highly battle-trained aristocracy. He was brought in to carry out a specific task, which did not require naval expertise but did require efficiency and strategic vision. Although he had never done this himself, Admiral Béhuchet understood the importance of brutal mass killings, looting and destruction by fire, and he had the organisational skills to quickly and effectively put together large fleets. He advised Philippe to focus on a strategy by which the island enemy would lose control of its coastal waters and sea routes to Flanders and Gascony – and thus ruin an English shipping and trading economy that depended on these waters and these routes. Unlike Edward, he knew how to put invasions together fast. He was appointed in February and just a few weeks later, in March 1338, the first of his expeditions took place.[5]

It was the first of many. For the next two years there would be more than twenty landings on British soil by enemy feet, and there would also be plenty of all-naval action taking place far from land. There would be tit-for-tat invasions of northern France by the English. From this time on, Scottish naval action takes a back seat and the action is generated by the French and their other allies.

This first expedition was a high-quality operation. The battle-hardened Mediterraneans, including the Monegasque contingent, were there. The landing created a landmark in the history of warfare. Béhuchet introduced a product of the metallurgical operations at Clos des Galées – the pot-au-feu. This was the very first weapon that was able to fire out projectiles powered by gunpowder in Europe. The first raid from the newly assembled French attacking force used this revolutionary new weapon.

* * *

On 24 March 1338 a fleet of thirty ships flying English flags appeared in the Solent opposite Portsmouth, after having rounded the eastern part of the Isle of Wight from the south. Some of the ships were cogs, the workhorse of both peacetime and wartime northern seas. Despite the flags, the fact that many of the fleet were galleys should have raised an alarm. England had few galleys, and the thirty ships must have found it difficult to find anchorage in the 200 yards or so which was the medieval Portsmouth waterfront. Possibly the English flags did the trick and the ships entered the Camber unchallenged. The Camber is a natural harbour that is now the home of the Royal Navy. Once near the quayside the citizens of Portsmouth must have guessed that something was not right – the ships were filled with soldiers, largely of Mediterranean origin.

At this point it is likely that the pot-au-feu was fired. We do not know where its dart-shaped projectile landed, not do we know what if any damage it did. It is recorded the attackers didn't bring enough gunpowder to do any serious damage but the noise must have terrified the people of Southampton nevertheless. It was the very first time that the noise of a gun being fired was heard in England. It was the start of a long story.

The citizens of Portsmouth did not yet know that the crews were elite troops, able to row for hours and go straight into action on dry land as necessary, which is what they did when they drew up at the Portsmouth waterfront. Heavily armed and ferocious, they were immediately ready for action. It took just a little light slaughter for the entire surviving population of Portsmouth to turn tail and run, leaving the port's entire stock of goods and raw materials open to looting. The enemy started to ransack the waterfront warehouses.

This attack was carried out under the personal supervision of Béhuchet, and Portsmouth was a good first target. A relatively new settlement, Portsmouth was built around the fine natural harbour still known as the Camber. So then as now Portsmouth No was a naval port, and its shipbuilding and repair facilities were commandeered whenever necessary to support English invasion fleets, and naturally it had among its citizens not just merchants and sailors, but specialists in naval technology.

Béhuchet chose the site for his first attack carefully and effectively. Portsmouth was home to a select group of rich traders whose taxable profits helped finance royal wars – and whose ships and crews in wartime were commandeered by the Crown, to carry out the heavy logistical marine work that every English army needed.

Hidden from the open sea behind the Isle of Wight, yet close to the French coast, where better for a strategically important window on the dangerous world on the other side of the English Channel? And where better for the French to trash as part of the opening salvo?

The settlement at this time was tiny, little more than a couple of hundred yards inland and, north to south, with no fortifications or defensive walls. But it was wealthy and its warehouses were full of valuable commodities.

Once Béhuchet's men started looking in the quayside cellars they found them full of hogsheads of French wine, imported by the Crown, and ready to distribute around England. So Behuchet's haul in March was a good one – valuable raw materials to sell on in France and Flanders, and many barrels of French wine, waiting to be commandeered and returned to their home territory. After, that is, the consumption of some as part of the victory celebrations.

The Franco-Genoese operation was a perfect raid. Being unopposed because of a simple stratagem the attackers suffered minimal losses. And the rich haul of wine and wool meant the raid was a self-financing one, very important in an era of when governments were chronically short of money. The participants could return home covered not only in glory, but in possession of large amounts of valuable booty and perhaps suffering from hangovers.

The chronicler Froissart, always an admirer or military prowess, passes on to us a scene of unrestricted violence:[6]

> They came on a Sunday in the forenoon to the haven of Southampton while the people were at mass. And the Normans, Picards and Spaniards entered the town and robbed and pillaged the town and slew divers, and defiled maidens and enforced wives and charged their vessels with the pillage and so entered again into their ships.

Béhuchet's fleet took off round the Isle of Wight and across the Channel southwards towards the Channel Islands. They landed on Jersey, occupied and wasted the eastern side of the island and besieged Castle Gorey. But the castle resisted the invaders and the

French gave up and sailed on. The English had got wind of the expedition and had even sent out a naval force to try to intercept the flotilla but in vain. As so often was the case the navies failed to meet up and the enemy ships continued unchallenged.

* * *

In July of 1338 Edward's Flanders force finally set off from ports in East Anglia – Yarmouth, Ipswich and Orwell. There were 350 ships assembled in these three quite small ports, and they held 1,400 men-at-arms and 3,000 archers ready to do battle. Edward was taking a risk in crossing the English Channel at a time like this when England had no control of the seas. It could have been a disaster – but King Edward's luck held and the army landed safely. Once Edward was landed on the European mainland he set about trying to activate a network of allies and create an anti-French coalition based in pro-English Flanders.

During that fateful summer an ambassadorial meeting with the French king had failed to create a truce. This was hardly surprising – Edward's representatives took with them a set of peace proposals using the Edwardian expression designed to infuriate Philippe – 'Philip of Valois, he that calls himself King of France'.[7]

Edward was determined to spur the French monarch and his advisers into action. Edward was sure that if he took on the French in a straight land battle that he would be victorious. If he was victorious he would be able to take the title of King of France that he so much desired. But if the French avoided battle, much as the Scots had learnt to do when the English were in their territory, then Edward might be in trouble.

For the rest of 1338 Edward's troops and those of his allies tried to bring the French troops onto a battlefield. If the French had only agreed to fight it out on the battlefield Edward's military genius would have assured an overwhelming victory. But the French did not oblige and the English troops were until the beginning of the following year bottled up in Flanders, desperately short of finance.

Philippe's immediate response to Edward's provocation was a symbolic one. King Philippe, accompanied by a group of his closest court confidants made a pilgrimage to the Church of Saint Denis, a short distance to the north of Paris, to take the oriflamme. This banner had a legendary origin in Roman times when it was said to have been dipped in the blood of the Christian martyr Saint Denis. Emperor Charlemagne had used it while destroying Saracens in the Holy Land. This numinous banner was only raised in times of great national import, and was designed to strike fear into the hearts of the enemies of France. On a practical level – if the oriflamme was flying no prisoners were to be taken. Death or victory![8]

Shortly after the unfurling of the oriflamme, the Genoese under Ayton Doria carried out a whole series of attacks on coastal settlements and inflicted damage after each landing. It is likely that there were more raids than we know about, but the locations that were recorded are of secondary importance. It appears that Doria returned to the Solent and Isle of Wight area and found that in the aftermath of the big action earlier in the year it was well defended. There would have been watchers all along the cliffs, beacons burning on hill tops, possibly peals of bells indicating danger.

Portsea was one target. Although close to Portsmouth, it is possible that the raid was made on minor coastal locations on the south side of Portsea Island away from the defenders. More than one day's sailing to the west is Swanage, which was also raided. In the fourteenth century Swanage was a stone quarrying settlement, exporting Portland Stone around England for use on high-status buildings. To a raiding fleet with limited local information the sight of Swanage with a working harbour and possibly large cogs waiting to load up with building stone might have indicated a good site for a raid. It is unlikely that they found much of interest, however. The final raid was on East Dean, 60 miles eastwards in a break in the cliffs known as Birling Gap. Doria's fleet may have had access to local knowledge as the entrance to Birling Gap is remote, but a few miles inland there was a sizeable aristocratic estate.

After they had finished on the English mainland, the same ships, now led by Marshal Robert Bertrand, descended again on the Channel Islands. The fact that this time the fleet was led by an Admiral of the Fleet himself, and not by a mercenary, indicated the importance that the French forces placed on these islands. At their closest they are only 10 miles from the coast of Normandy and 30 miles from Brittany. Alderney, the northernmost in the archipelago, lies opposite Plymouth. If the French had been able to take control of the islands it would have had a disastrous effect upon the English position.

Since the raid at the start of the year the English had reinforced their garrison in Castle Gorey, but not their presence on Guernsey. The small force on Castle Cornet, the large island castle in Guernsey and former tidal island, was taken by surprise, and all of the 65 defending soldiers were killed. Jedburgh was defended by 12 archers – they were disposed of and the castle was taken. However, before the whole island could be occupied by French allies, the local fishermen put up a strong resistance. Two of the galleys were taken and probably burnt.[9]

It is perhaps not surprising that the Guernsey sailors were able to best the marines given the right opportunity. Life for a humble fisherman at sea had always been a risky affair and since Edward's aggressive politics had made the English Channel into a war zone, Guernsey fishermen had to learn how to look after themselves when strange galleys hove into view and they were as ready as anyone to resort to violence if necessary. Several years earlier the islanders had complained to the English Crown that they were 'In full view oppressed and impoverished and in danger of being forgotten ... for they are surrounded by the great sea and away from every other nation'.[10]

The islanders fought bravely against the invading Monegasques, but they were beaten. The island of Guernsey was captured and held by the French for several years, although such was the lack of English presence in the Channel that the news of the taking of Guernsey took two weeks to reach Edward's council. Admiral Bertrand himself stayed on the island for some time, no doubt to strengthen its defences and train defenders – testimony to the effectiveness of the island forces.

The invasion fleet then moved on without the Admiral and took on more routine tasks, such as accompanying a convoy of French vessels to La Rochelle. The ships under the command of the Grimaldi went on into the Gironde estuary, and captured Bourg and Blaye in the territory of English Gironde.

One practical response to the fact that Edward's armies were now uncomfortably close to French territory was an ambitious attack on one of England's key ports. Behuchet's fleet descended upon Southampton in October of 1338 – did the earlier unfurling of the oriflamme lead to an increase in violence? The Southampton raid seems to have been especially brutal.

Southampton was the leading port in all of England, and its location was at the northern end of the Solent, even better tucked away than Portsmouth but much bigger, all of 300 yards north to south along the waterfront. This put it in the midst of much of England's greenest and most productive farmland, and richest estates. Situated at the junction of the Itchen and Test rivers, it offered easy access to Sarum, Salisbury, and Winchester – key English centres of wealth and consumption, especially Winchester, shortly to become the focus of Edward III's courtly life, with architecture to match.

Southampton's strategic location made it a favourite military naval base, and it grew rich from the importation of luxuries such as wine and the exportation of raw materials. It was the focus of the very lucrative trade with Italy. There were merchants from Genoa and Florence here in the midst of the English realm, dealing in small-circulation luxury products as well as in the staple English commodities.

This time the French pulled out all the stops. Their joint Franco-Genoese force, aided by a contingent of Scots, was made up of 50 ships including, as before, plenty of galleys in addition to cogs – and a pot-au-feu.

Did the fleet fire off the pot-au-feu as they arrived so as to scare the citizens of Southampton? We do not know, but the invading force had an easy landing. According to Froissart the fleet attacked on a Sunday morning while the population was at mass, while John Stow says that the townspeople simply ran away in panic at the sight of the invaders when they landed at about 9.00 a.m.

Froissart says that the invaders slew many of the men, raped some of the women (the usual outcome whenever soldiers met with the general population) and sailed away on the next tide, which in Southampton would be just a few hours later. But the Stow narrative is slightly different, making the citizens rather more proactive. According to this version, the citizens must have regrouped after their panicked flight and spent the day raising a posse from the hinterland of Southampton:[11]

By the break of the next day they which fled, with the help of the country thereabout, came against the Pyrates & fought with them: in the which skirmish was slain to the number of three hundred pyrates together with their captain, a young soldier, the King of Sicils son ... whereupon the residue of these Gennowaiese after they had burnt the Town afire quite and burnt it up quite, fled to their galleys and in their flying certain of them were drowned. And after this the inhabitants of the town encompassed it about with a strong and great wall.

Note how Stow has belittled the status of the invaders by calling them pirates. And how he emphasises the fact that the citizens later returned and, by his account, gave as good as they got so that in the end the invaders do not just run off but seemingly are in such a panic themselves that some of them fall in the water and drown. Note too the implication that the citizens of Southampton took speedy and appropriate action in order to build strong fortifications against future raids. This suggestion is an exaggeration, as will be seen later. This theme emerges time and again – how the French and their Continental allies were rarely a match for the stout-hearted English! Sometimes it was true.

Stow casually tells us that they had 'burnt it up quite' which surely indicates that the entire town of Southampton was destroyed. Recent archaeology confirms that many of the fine stone houses belonging to the merchants of the town situated alongside the quayside were totally destroyed and they would have been entirely looted of their valuables. Whatever wool the invaders were unable to carry away with them was added to the great fire.

The invaders found in the house of the Mayor of Southampton, Richard Sampson, a strongbox containing what was essentially the archives and instruments of government for the entire port of Southampton, known as the 'common chest', and carried it off. This was a serious loss, an essential part of a Mayor's responsibility, and contained the seals of the town without which official documents could not be issued, plus its charters and, very important, actual money, in gold and silver coins. What is more, across the street from Richard Sampson's house was the Weigh House, another key instrument of local government. Scales, authenticated weights and weigh-beams and customs seals were also carried away, an act that struck at the very foundations of the emerging bureaucratic English state.[12]

Thus Béhuchet was achieving his objectives. By attacking a second key economic centre in Edward III's England he had inflicted on behalf of his royal master more fiscal damage on their enemy. There is ample evidence that Southampton, which was England's key strategic city after London, never recovered during the fourteenth century. Many of the houses that had been wrecked by the invaders remained unrestored, and the Italian and Genoese merchants that used Southampton as a port upped sticks and moved to Bristol – away from what may have looked too much like a war zone for comfort. The extent of the very well focussed destruction of the port is testimony to the leadership of Nicolas Béhuchet.

When the French invasions took place, Portsmouth and Southampton should have been fully prepared. But they weren't. By an extraordinary act of carelessness Edward's attention was taken up with launching his new campaign with his own hands-on involvement; this time in Flanders where Edward was trying to put together an anti-French coalition with the intention of invading French territory, while launching a complex financial deal aimed at providing the necessary funds to equip and pay a large army.

How could the English have been so lax? We know that many coastal communities took their defensive obligations very seriously. Not surprisingly, Edward's reaction to the attacks on Portsmouth and Southampton was immediate and angry. To make matters worse, after the Franco-Genoese invaders had left, locally grown looters moved in and took what they could: cowardice on the part of local citizens, their militias, and of local forces, corruption and theft. What could be worse?

A Robert fitz Alan was appointed by the king to investigate and find out 'through whose default the town of Southampton was taken, how the keepers bore themselves when the galleys came into sight ... the names of the men of Southampton and others who fled from the enemy...' The aim of the enquiry was clear: 'punish such as are most guilty by imprisonment in the Tower of London or elsewhere as may be expedient'.

Fitz Alan was to discover who, 'both before the king's enemies, and after they entered the town, carried away his wool there'. (The wording of this proclamation indicates a more complex story than the one we hear from Froissart and Stow).

Nicholas de Moundenard, the Collector of Customs in Southampton up to the time of the invasion, ended up in the Tower of London. It appears that Mr de Moundenard's management style was what you would expect from an inefficient and corrupt government official in a slack regime: allowing goods to be loaded without paying the full export tax, selling ships to official enemies of the crown, stealing goods from the Crown, appropriating to his own account money raised in order to build fortifications for Southampton. All of this emerged during his trial.[13]

There must have been many episodes of local corruption getting in the way of strong and effective defensive action during this period – but only on occasion does it get reported. Perhaps it is surprising how rarely this appears to have occurred.

The Crown took the French threat very seriously indeed. In 1338 a Royal Mandate was issued instructing the citizens of London to fortify their city against the imminent French threat. The words of the proclamation, which would have been read aloud in public places in London, gives a flavour of the mood of the time:

Edward by the grace of God etc. to the Mayor, Aldermen, and Sheriffs, of London, greeting. Forasmuch as our enemies, collected in galleys, in no small multitude, have in hostile manner entered our kingdom in divers parts, and purpose shortly to invade our city aforesaid, if they can, and there to perpetrate such evil and wickedness as they may.... do command you, strictly enjoining that with all the speed that you may, you cause the City to be closed, and fortified against such hostile attacks towards the water, with stone or with board, that you cause piles to be driven across the water of Thames, for the defence of the city aforesaid.[14]

What can be called the 'Béhuchet Strategy' was not just to disrupt life in coastal settlements in England. The really important objective was to inflict economic damage to an upstart enemy that was proving to be very troublesome. A key role for the multiple naval forces that the French crown controlled from 1338 onwards was to disrupt the marine communications that the economy of England depended upon. A large proportion of England's world-class raw woollen exports went to Flanders.

In 1338 the entire Atlantic coastline of France was occupied by five highly professional and aggressive naval fleets, ready to disrupt English trade. The growing French naval threat to England led to the gradual introduction of convoys, where a group of merchant vessels would be escorted by an armed ship provided by the state. The Scottish attacks upon English shipping in the North Sea and the Irish Seas led to the use of state-sponsored military escorts for groups of merchant vessels. As the war progressed merchant ships would themselves become armed and remain in convoy even on short journeys, to Calais, for example.

Although the attention of the English fighting machine was for much of the time focussed on land warfare in Europe and upon reactive responses to French attacks, there were certain defenders who went out into enemy territory in order to take the war to the maritime enemy. The most effective such defender was perhaps Sir Robert Morley. He had been appointed by Edward III as Admiral of the north.[15]

Rather like Nicolas Béhuchet in France, Robert Morley's past experience was confined to administering his family estates in Norfolk, but as in the case of Béhuchet, it was thought that the practicalities of running a fleet could well be left to such an administrator, as long as he was able to plan and lead. This Morley showed himself able to do. He was lucky to have a right-hand man with a fascinatingly chequered career – John Crabbe. Crabbe was Flemish by birth and early on in life he had taken up piracy. Pirates often had short and adventuresome lives but luckily Crabbe had abilities that attracted the attention of Robert the Bruce, who was looking for capable and aggressive naval commanders who could be used against the English menace. This Crabbe did. He also showed a bent for military engineering. Then while working in Southern Scotland, he was captured in a skirmish. Crabbe could have come to an unpleasant end at this point in his life but his captor Walter Mauny was also of Flemish origin, and was able to spot talent when he saw it. As someone who started out as a soldier of fortune, Mauny organised a complex sort of ransom arrangement and sold Crabbe to Edward III for 1,000 pounds!

Now in the service of Admiral Morley, Crabbe's natural aggression created results. Working in the routine job of accompanying a large North Sea convoy of English ships bound for Flanders, they came upon a big French fleet of merchant ships and Genoese galleys. They turned on them, chasing them along the coast to the key Flemish harbour of Sluys.

Sluys was a key strategic location east of Calais. Being handy to survey traffic between the North Sea and the English Channel, and being at the mouth of the Scheldt River, which is a branch of the Rhine, gave the harbour good connectivity with both French and German states. It is located close to the key cloth cities of Flanders, as Ghent and Bruges are no more than 25 miles away, French territory was no more than 35 miles away and Antwerp and the start of the German states was less than 40 miles away.

Today, although the old town of Sluys is well preserved, the remnant of what was such an important harbour is no more than a set of drainage ditches and scrub known as the Groote Gat, and the sea is some 5 miles away to the north. In the fourteenth century the harbour of Sluys was busy with trading vessels, seamen and merchants from all over Europe. It was linked to a complex system of wide shallow rivers, with low-lying islands such as Cadzand scattered between them, shielding the port from the North Sea.[16]

In fact, from a military point of view the harbour was a trap. If a fleet took refuge from attackers in the inner waters of the harbour it would be caught if the wind was onshore. Not realising this, once the Genoese vessels had taken up what was thought to be an impregnable position behind the narrow harbour entrance, they had put themselves in jeopardy.

Morley and Crabbe led ships that pressed into the harbour, presumably with the wind behind them, and we have to guess that the English then started fighting battles on the decks as though they were on dry land – coming up to one ship at a time, holding it with grappling irons, landing on the enemy ship and battling it out. One ship after another was plundered by the Morley fleet, but perhaps Morley should not have placed quite so much trust in his ex-pirate second-in-command. Ships belonging to the Spanish allies of England were also attacked, and even an English ship carrying English treasury money was set upon. And in typical pirate fashion, once the ships returned to their home East Anglian port of Harwich there was a falling-out over the division of the spoils – leading to a mutiny.[17]

* * *

Edward was engaged in highly ambitious campaigns, and his first-class track record in Scotland, which included brutal and ruthless responses to any threats, indicated that the French leaders should take him seriously, even if his realm was so much smaller and poorer than that of France. But by now he was struggling.

Not the French however. By 1338 King Philippe's court had assembled a fine array of armed forces, especially after his fleets had been strengthened by the arrival of those from Castile. He now had the use of three entire fleets, in addition to the French Atlantic and Mediterranean ones – that is, Genoa, Monaco, Castile – plus thousands of soldiers recruited via the *arrière-ban* who were ready and willing to fight for their country. In addition, payments in lieu of service gave Philippe a sizeable war chest.

In the circumstances it was only reasonable for King Philippe and his advisors to plan something on a very large scale, a knock-out blow perhaps, aimed at the very heart of the English nation, which, if successful, would permanently remove the source of so many of France's problems – the pugnacious English monarch. After all, it was little more than a century since French warriors had taken Normandy away from English King John. In 1216, the future French King Louis VIII nearly swept the board. The Normans were now French – but almost 300 years before the Normans had carried out a very successful attack on England! King Edward was struggling at present so a well-timed, committed attack might be enough to permanently remove him. King Philippe was thinking big! In addition, he and his advisors could reflect on the fact that France was the fount of chivalry. The very idea of chivalry was French. The very kingdom of France as it existed at this time had been won by force of arms. France had been at relative peace for some decades at this time, and now was the moment to revive the warrior tradition.

6

THE BIG RAIDS OF 1339–1340

The following year, 1339, was to be the one when the English would be dealt with by nothing less than a full-scale invasion. King Philippe VI's plan was to put together an army of 24,000 – including 6,000 horsemen, 4,000 archers and a huge array of foot soldiers. The massed ranks of multinational navies currently occupying the Channel ports and the Rouen naval dockyard had ample carrying capacity to ferry these warriors to their various landing sites. The Franco-Scottish alliance was to be rebooted. King David would be able to regain his throne, and the many French agents who had been active in Scotland in the last two or three years would assist. An invasion of England from the north would hopefully be launched at the same time as the one from the south. Gascony was to be invaded too.

This force was to be led by the King's own son, the Duke of Normandy – which historically, thinking of 1066, seemed appropriate. A timetable for operations was drawn up. A force of 24,000 was thought adequate for a full conquest of England in ten to twelve weeks.

The campaign was not only self-financing, it was also audacious. The entire landed wealth of England, including that of the Church, would be confiscated and distributed to the combatants. Maybe most audacious of all, the Crown lands held by Edward III were to go to the Duke of Normandy himself. It was to be a second Norman Conquest! A meeting with the Norman leaders was held in the Chateau de Vincennes on 23 March 1339 and the scheme was approved; the invasion would start that year. Detailed planning now went into the practicalities: how to organise convoys, signalling, orders of battle, and procedures when action started. Everything was being considered.[1]

As usually happened, news of the projected French invasion soon reached the ears of King Edward. It was an undertaking which, if successful, would change history. At the start of 1339, England was in a state of turmoil and foreboding. The danger of a full-scale invasion, another Norman Conquest, was serious and it needed strong leadership to combat it. Each part of the English coastline was by now under the supervision of a nobleman – namely the Dukes of Oxford, of Huntingdon, Surrey, and Arundel, who were all close friends and relatives of the king. Inland levies were raised in readiness, under the nominal control of Prince Edward, eldest son of Edward III – who was at the time only nine years old. Clearly, King Edward planned for his son to live the same kind of life as himself. Troops were gathered at the places of most importance – Southampton, Portsmouth, the Isle of Wight, and Porchester.[2]

On that exact day in March when a full-scale assault on England by the Franco-Scottish alliance was formally agreed with the Norman lords, what was to be another raiding season opened with a fleet made up of French and Genoese galleys. Led by Ayton Doria they sailed across the Channel from the Flemish port of Sluys on the Rhine Estuary, and stopped off on the way at the East Anglian port of Harwich.

Harwich was East Anglia's most important port, and the most secure anchorage between the Thames and the River Humber. It was a wool port so it had close links with Flanders. The medieval settlement was on the peninsula at the southern entrance to the estuary, less than 400 yards across, overlooking the estuary entrance. The galleys landed unopposed, but this was 1339 and England was prepared to act. After the French and Genoese had beached their vessels and were began to take action, the local militias appeared, ready to resist the invaders. The attackers tried to fire the town but the English weather assisted the locals; strong winds from the west blew the flames away from the houses and the fleet retreated, with most of the settlement of Harwich surviving undamaged.[3]

Later in the month a similar fleet of 40 French ships and 17 galleys led by the Monaco prince Carlo Grimaldi arrived in Jersey to find that Gorey Castle, the main fortification on the island, was occupied by 300 local and English troops. The English made it clear that they would put up with a siege, indefinitely if necessary, so the French gave up and sailed on to Guernsey, which was still occupied by the force that had captured the island the previous year. Leaving behind some forces to strengthen their garrison, they went on to Gascony where they were needed most because Edward's army was on French soil.[4]

* * *

In France invasion preparations were continuing apace. The various squadrons of ships scattered over the Bay of Biscay, the English Channel and the North Sea were gathered together in readiness. Transports and barges for the movement of horses and equipment were waiting in the Channel ports. The Mediterranean and French squadrons arrived in the Channel and commenced a campaign of harrying the English coast.

By May 1339 the Genoese fleet consisting of 20 war galleys was ready for action in the English Channel. Doria's southern fleet sailed up Southampton Water looking for a suitable landing. Since the earlier landing in Southampton, about which there is doubt, the sea port should have acquired fortifications against any future landings. These had not been built in stone, as they should have been, although there were some temporary wooden defences. Maybe more importantly there were many new levies ranged all along the coastline. It was, in fact, impossible to land in Southampton itself, and it would have taken just a few English ships in the entrance to the Solent for Doria's Genoese feet to be trapped.

Instead, Doria's fleet took off to the more open waters around the Isle of Wight, but levies were similarly arrayed all along the island coast. The chronicler Adam Murimuth says that they 'did not dare to land on Wight, being very well defended, they took themselves off to other more rustic locations and there carried out many acts of brigandage'.[5]

Moving west took them away from defended coasts. Once they passed the border between the southern and the western regions, we can assume the presence of coastal levies ceased. Then Doria was able to cruise along the undefended coastlines of Devon and Cornwall, boarding any fishing boasts unfortunate enough to be in their way, taking the fish and the boat and throwing the crew overboard. Murimuth says that the fleet rounded Land's End and entered ports in Devon and Cornwall, going as far north as the environs of Bristol.

It is possible that Grimaldi's ships had tried to enter Fowey harbour, the biggest in Cornwall. The mariners of Fowey had a piratical reputation and doubtless the galleys would have nosed their way into the spacious estuary of the Fowey River with caution. Maybe they would have been warned off by the fact that the entrance to the town of Fowey itself was guarded on each bank by a castle, and that the two were just 220 yards apart – the range of a crossbow arrow. Dangerous waters.

The landing in Plymouth was by no means a failure, but it is unlikely that Doria and Grimaldi felt much satisfaction once they were out at sea again. Although larger than other ports along the south-western peninsula, Plymouth was still a second-rate target; its warehouses, for example, would not have been as big as the ones on the Solent, nor as full of valuable goods. The invaders had been unable to destroy the settlement to enjoy the further opportunities that offered for taking loot from the richer Plymouth homes. Worst still, some of the Genoese crew had been killed while trying to escape the ferocious English attack.

After being expelled from Plymouth by Hugh Courtenay's force, the attackers were in mid-Channel on their way back to the Isle of Wight. The twenty Genoese galleys attempted a landing but failed again. The Isle of Wight was a well-guarded location, Carisbrook Castle was heavily manned, and coastal lookouts and beacons meant that an unopposed landing was very unlikely. Much of the coast of the Isle of Wight consisted of low chalk cliffs, giving the advantage to defenders lined up above the beach. The flat areas suitable for landing were limited.

Thus they proceeded down the south coast, searching in vain for a suitable place for a landing. Dover, Folkestone and the Isle of Thanet were all failures, where they were chased off by determined defenders and forced to abandon their landings. All the way along the coast from the Solent to the Thames Estuary the defenders were ranged, waiting for action.

Only in Hastings was a landing finally achieved. Hastings had been one of England's leading ports earlier in the Middle Ages, but by the fourteenth century it was in a state of decay. The castle on the clifftop was virtually unoccupied, and the town was no more than a small settlement under its ancient walls and around the small inlet of the sea (which, since the fourteenth century, has disappeared). The ships that used Hastings would have beached on the foreshore, and there may not have been much high-status shipping to plunder. The galleys from Monaco, led by the indomitable Carlos Grimaldi, achieved just what a fleet of mercenary fighters most hoped for, namely an unopposed landing, rowing up to the cliff-side settlement, loudly proclaiming their arrival with war cries and trumpets. Their exotic liveries and their use of an uncommon ship associated almost entirely with aggressive warfare would have terrified the inhabitants, who mostly fled. As can happen in such circumstances, some of the sick and the old who had limited mobility were left behind, and the raiders killed them, either by hanging or in more brutal ways. Then the invaders ranged through the town, burning and looting. All three of Hastings' ancient churches were wrecked and the valuables were removed. The castle was occupied and everything of value was taken. It was considered a successful raid by the Monegasques, and before taking off for the temporary home port of Calais, Carlos Grimaldi took a number of the bodies of the dead with them. The naked and mutilated corpses were displayed to the inhabitants of Calais alongside the booty. Was this a public relations exercise by Grimaldi? It seemed to be a brutal attempt to deflect attention from the fact that the raid had not been a great success – and was perhaps not very profitable.[6]

Although the 1339 raids had a big impact on the settlements of southern England, and should have been followed up by a full-scale invasion, the alliances with the Castilians, Genoese and Monegasques began to fail. On the borderline between allies and high-class mercenaries, the Mediterraneans required a quick payback after risking of their lives to support the French. A raid in which the mercenaries were driven away was worse than useless. Over these months they had seen some of their comrades-in-arms being ignominiously killed by amateur local levies, and this without the reasonable compensation of plunder and loot. At the end of the raiding season, some Genoese ships simply gave up and sailed home to the Mediterranean. Other Genoese leaders took their grievances to King Philippe, only to find that he was less than sympathetic – actually commandeering the ships belonging to the troublemakers. Carlos Grimaldi of Monaco stayed loyal longer than his fellows, but by the end of the fighting season the Mediterranean allies had left and surely the chance of a serious invasion of England had passed, at least for that year.

In the late summer of 1339, England Robert Morley and John Crabbe took a leaf from the French book and tried raiding the French coast. This was the first time that an English force had tried to turn the tables on their enemy. In a series of raids that continued into 1340, they followed the example of the French incursions on English territory. Their ships sailed across the English Channel, following a coastline whose chalk cliffs looked similar to the Sussex coast, looking for suitable locations to land.

The English lack of control of the sea lanes in the North Sea, vital to the English war effort in Scotland, meant that movement between the French ports and the east coast of Scotland was unhindered for the burgeoning Franco-Scottish alliance. By May the Scots formally renounced the truces that had been agreed after the exile of David II in France. Meanwhile, the Scots were making huge inroads into the territory that was controlled by the pro-English Scottish forces, so that rather like in twenty-first century Afghanistan, the official pro-English Scottish government's writ extended little further than heavily garrisoned towns such as Perth, Stirling and Cupar. The seasoned freedom fighter William Douglas was running a brilliant guerrilla campaign against his enemies and safe English territory was shrinking. Perth itself was now besieged by the Scottish army.

The French supplied the Scots with oared barges built in their naval dockyard of Clos des Galées. These were used to harass English shipping in Hull and Kings Lynn, thus disrupting English supplies in what was now to Edward an irritating side issue. William Douglas was now in France, greatly improving

French intelligence about the situation in England. His request for ships and materiel was granted by a sympathetic Philippe Valois, and in midsummer he and a pirate Hugh Hautpoul led a party of five oared barges all the way along the North Sea coast of England as far as the Tay Estuary.[7]

Among the mariners were exiled Scots from King David's retinue in Chateau Gaillard, and French knights with their followers. It is not clear whether the French knights were playing the role of military advisors to the Scots, in order to strengthen their military strategies, or whether they were simply young knights in search of military experience.

The flotilla made a clever strategic decision. The besieged garrison in Perth was being supplied by sea via the Tay Estuary – a mere 1 mile wide at its entrance from the North Sea. The fleet of heavily armed knights and foot soldiers and, doubtless, archers, was powerful enough to cut English supplies. By August the garrison was starving and the commander, Sir Thomas Ughtred, surrendered to an army that included a number of French knights. At the very time that Edward was launching himself as a military leader on the Continental stage the architecture of his policy of controlling Scotland through puppet monarchs was collapsing behind him. The naval supremacy at this time enjoyed by France and her Mediterranean allies was a major factor in this weakness in Edward's military and dynastic ambitions. The vitally important sea lanes around the English coast, and between England and Flanders and Guyenne, for example, were not secure.

7

SOVEREIGNTY OF THE SEA AND BATTLES ON LAND

There is a serious disconnect in our period between the idea that the English nation possessed of itself, and the reality of England's relationship with its Continental neighbours. It was widely believed in England that she was either the supreme power in the northern seas, or that she should be! This idea goes back at least as far as Edward's grandfather – Edward Longshanks, the 'Hammer of the Scots'. Here is what he thought:

> Whereas the Kings of England by right of the said kingdom … whereof there is no memorial to the contrary, have been in peaceable possession of the sovereign lordship of the sea of England, and of the isles within the same … affording safeguard in all places where need shall require … and equity among all manner of people … passing through the said seas … heretofore Kings of England have been in peaceable possession of the said sovereign guard.[1]

For Edward III, activity by any non-English vessel that was not clearly involved in trade and commerce was suspect. But during his reign there was little action to back up this belief. Edward had no interest in naval affairs, and had never spent money on the development of a professional navy – despite being a free spender by nature. Edward's warrior culture revolved around armour, swords, bows and arrows, and for him naval affairs were not the preserve of a 'gallant knight'. Unfortunately, the effect of Edward's constant warfare put the maritime community on the front line. Take the case of a merchant who carried on overseas trade, and who owned one or more ship. In medieval society the ship was one of the most costly investments that there was. A large ship would use up a huge acreage of oak forest, perhaps in the Sussex Weald. The cost of cutting, transporting, and working the wood was enormous, not to mention the manufacture of iron nails and fittings, the ropes and the fabric for sail making, and the huge, heavy iron anchors. Profits from international trade were recycled not just to the royal government in the form of taxes but also in to pockets of ordinary people who built, assembled, manned and owned ships. In fourteenth-century England a very large proportion of the moveable wealth of the kingdom, that is, apart from buildings and land, was tied up in its ports in the form of ships and shipping; and in warehouses, as well as the goods they held, goods that were ready to distribute around the kingdom or send abroad. Taxation – on imports as well as exports – was essential to the running of a highly militarised state.

In a parallel campaign to attacks on English coastal settlements, French galleys were active in the North Sea and the English Channel concentrating upon harassing shipping and capturing merchant vessels. The earliest direct attack upon English shipping that we know about was in 1336, the raid on Orford, when the cogs *Caterine* and the *Paternoster* were captured while indentured. The Crown had taken the ships from their owners without compensation, requiring the ship to stay in port until used to transport the army to Europe. The owner would have spent the better part of the spring and summer unable to use his ship, thus losing an entire trading season. When his most valuable possession was lost in an era before the invention of insurance, the state had no obligation to reimburse the owner for his losses. The owner could maybe have consoled himself with the thought that he had carried out his loyal duty to his king and those of his knightly caste whose job it was to fight with their lives if necessary against the enemies of England – but then he might not have seen it in that way.

In August ships were attacked around the Isle of Wight by the new generation of French warships – some were scuttled, and the more valuable ones were taken off to the ports of Normandy as valuable prizes. The Safeguard of the Sea did not protect valuable ships. Over the coming years when the French naval threat was at its height we have to assume that many incidents were not recorded for posterity. We catch glimpses of what went on by looking at the large-scale raids and attacks at sea.

For example, in the summer of 1338 a fleet of Castilian galleys based in the French port of La Rochelle, no more than 100 miles from the strategic key English-held port of Bordeaux, was harassing English shipping passing to and from English Gascony via Western Brittany. At the end of August two ships, possibly with a cargo of valuable wine, were taken out of the convoy – indicating that the English were no match for their foes in sea warfare.[2]

In the years up to 1340 when the English Channel was certainly dominated by Mediterranean allies of the French, the Channel Islands were a strategically important English location in the Channel. Removing the English from these outposts of English power, roughly 100 miles from Southampton on the south coast, would have further lessened the ability of the English to keep open their routes along the Channel to the Western Approaches and down south to the Bay of Biscay. The Channel Islands had (and still have) an anomalous status in relation to England, being well-guarded English possessions without being part of the English or British state. These remnants of the English possessions in Normandy were close to the enemy coast of that province, so they occupied a strategic position close the Channel sea lanes and were coveted by the French. The Channel Islanders were used to living under threat of attack. The French had raided Jersey at the end of the thirteenth century, for example, killing perhaps 1,500 islanders. Jersey and Guernsey both had coves that were suitable for enemy landings, so were defended by powerful castles: Castle Gorey in Jersey and Castle Cornet in Guernsey loomed over the main settlements and danger points.

The islands had been targeted on a number of occasions. In 1337 a combined Franco-Scottish force under David Bruce landed on the small island of Sark, killed many of the local inhabitants, burnt many properties, and then occupied the island.[3] It is not clear whether or not the island was recaptured by English forces in the following year.[4]

In March 1338, after Béhuchet's Southampton attack, his convoy sailed south 100 miles farther on to the Channel Islands. The Béhuchet forces landed on Jersey. Gorey Castle, on a peninsula on the east of the island, was impregnable and the defenders held on to it. Despite this, the French carried out a savage and thorough chevauchée on the little 10-mile-long island. It is said that during the action churches were desecrated, the host was struck down from altars, images were burnt, and holy vessels were taken away. Women and children who had taken refuge in churches were led away and up to 1,500 men and women were massacred. Everything of value was taken away.

In September the Béhuchet fleet returned and made another attempt on Castle Gorey and consolidated the French hold on the other islands. They were now in control of all the islands – Jersey, Guernsey, Alderney and Sark – while Castle Gorey alone held out against all odds. This territory was given by King Philippe to his son – who, as mentioned, with a real sense of historical irony had the title of Duke of Normandy. Although they stayed French for only a few years,[5] from now on French domination of the English Channel became a fact of life.

Edward's army had crossed the Channel to Flanders in 1338 and spent the coming months waiting to start the action. While Edward tried to put together an anti-French coalition of the willing, assisted by mercenaries, ready to take on King Philippe of France, once he was on the Continent Edward was effectively trapped by the French naval forces and her allies in the Channel. Edward could not have retreated to his island kingdom even if he had wanted to. To give an idea of the English mood of the time here is a proclamation that came out of Edward's Chancery in Westminster in 1338, warning that all English shipping was at risk from the Franco-Genoese forces, whose intentions were to

> ...proceed from port to port and place to place along the coast, wherever ships may be found, to sink, burn and destroy the shipping of the kingdom; and then to attack, occupy, plunder and burn the ports and other towns on the sea or its inlets, perpetrating every evil that man can work.[6]

One month after Grimaldi's triumphant and grisly display in Calais of the dead bodies taken from Hastings, the French admiralty put together a return visit. Ships from most of the usual sources, namely Genoese warships, French galleys from Rouen, Norman barges, plus Grimaldi's battle-hardened crew, all set out on a major attack on the Cinque Ports. There were 65 ships in the fleet, including 32 galleys. One supposes that as a result of the action of that campaigning season, there should have been quite a lot of information available about the current disposition of the various settlements and possibly about the likely level of their defences. The expedition was led by Admiral

Béhuchet, a sure sign it was of key importance. It was planned to start with a raid on Sandwich.

The port of Sandwich was located on the Cassel, which at that time was a waterway of maybe 100 yards width. Its location just south of the Isle of Thanet meant it was a port in its own right, but also it acted as an entrepôt for London itself. Large unwieldy cogs would unload in the harbour and go on their way rather than attempt the difficult and dangerous journey up round the Isle of Thanet and along the Thames. Smaller river boats then loaded up cargo, went north into the Thames and then turned west towards London.

Edward's Flanders army has spent months in Sandwich gathering the muster, and by the late summer of 1339 the town's commercial life must have been badly damaged. Many Sandwich ships were by now in Flanders and the merchant community itself would have suffered greatly because of the damage to trading that the military takeover of Sandwich had already caused.

As the Franco-Genoese fleet approached the port they found, not surprisingly, the same picture as they had seen earlier in the year – huge numbers of defenders (complaining no doubt about it being 'just one thing after another') lining the clifftops to the south of the port, along the flat lands to the south of Sandwich, and arrayed along the entrance to the harbour. They were ready to pounce on the sailors as they landed. Sixty ships slid along past the cliffs, flying pennants, the Admiral's ship with the oriflamme stating its message of total war. The Admiral's ship would have had the French royal standard sewn into its fabric – a clear signal of threat. There was the sounds of trumpets – both for traffic control and in order to strike terror into the watchers. The French war cry of '*Montjoie – Saint Denis!*' was supposed to terrify the local defenders, but they were ready for an assault. As the fleet turned away to the south, they would gradually have understood they had succeeded in scaring off the invaders. The beacons would have done their work and there would have been watchers all the way along the cliffs, past Dover. The fleet did not attempt landings in Hythe, or Folkestone for example – both of which were significant coastal settlements but they might well have been well defended.

Twenty miles further on, Rye and its twin Winchelsea were built on the edge of the estuary of the River Rother, at that time a spacious natural harbour extending inland as far as Bodiam. Today what was Rye Bay has turned into grassland, and the last trace of the sea is the narrow but tidal River Camber, leading to open water a mile away. The medieval bay was dominated by the twin settlements of Rye on the end of a low peninsula jutting into the north of the bay, and Winchelsea built on top of a 90-foot hill to the west, looking rather like a French hill town – which in fact it was, as a recent and rationally planned town following Continental planning guidelines. These were two prosperous, thriving fishing and trading communities with economic links to the English south-west France, including the key wine trade.

In fact over the next fifty years Rye Bay became one of England's most invaded places. When Winchelsea was laid out with a geometrical grid of streets some fifty years earlier, the founders had big plans, which are evidenced by the fact that the town was laid out to be comparable in size to the City of London itself, approaching London's 1 mile in length! The next fifty years of threat and destruction meant that Winchelsea never did get to mature and grow. Perhaps if its economy had not been so badly damaged in these decades, Winchelsea in the twenty-first century could have been an important location, and not a tourist one.

The ships slipped into the harbour, potentially a risky place for a big invasion fleet if an enemy appeared at the harbour entrance. The citizens of both towns must have been watching with apprehension to see which way the ships would turn. It is very likely that the rude health of Rye's trading economy was visible to the leaders of the invasion fleet in the form of ships moored at the quayside, and maybe activity on land. Perhaps in contrast Winchelsea was quieter, lacking such a well-defined commercial area.

The 65 ships would have been at this stage signalling by trumpet and drum to each other in order to coordinate unloading the hundreds of rowers from their galleys. So the landing area must have been congested with ships – one galley's oars would have got in the way of others – the actual landing quays would have been thronged with several hundreds of armed men trying to get out onto dry land and to the fighting.[7]

The landing however was carried out without opposition and the invaders had started their work of looting, killing, but they had not yet reached the stage of extensive burning and they never did. Morley and Crabbe yet again showed what could be achieved by a vigorous and aggressive naval coastal defence force. They showed up in Rye Bay and in a panic the attacking force, afraid of being bottled up in the harbour got back into their ships and out of English waters as fast as possible. Morley and Crabbe's fleet chased after them. They met up near Cap Gris-Nez, near Wissant, but decided not to do battle, and went their separate ways.

In March 1339 the French followed up on the incomplete occupation of the Channel Islands in the name of the Duke of Normandy. They put together an invasion fleet, including seventeen Genoese galleys and many other ships and sailed to Jersey to carry out the final step in the occupation, that is, to remove the English from Castle Gorey. The leader Marshal Robert Bertran landed, we suppose, near the castle and summoned the defence force to parley. He threatened the entire English company with death if they refused to surrender. But the English refused. The French force roamed the island burning and looting. Then the English force descended upon the French and killed forty of their company. At this the French ran back to their ships and returned to France, while some of the Genoese galleys went on to Guernsey for more raiding.[8] The Morley Crabbe fleet continued with the ideas from their French counterparts in the previous session, and started out on a set of successful raids along the Channel coast of France. They travelled about 50 miles south-west, past chalk cliffs reminiscent of those of Kent and Sussex. The naval port of Le Crotoy on the Somme Estuary would have been a prize, but presumably it was too risky. The small settlement of Ault was their first prize even though it was well-hidden behind its white cliffs (which probably extended several hundred metres further north than today) so it did not have an inviting landing place. Presumably Crabbe enjoyed the excitement of attacking the enemy on their home ground, and then moved on. Le Tréport was only 4 miles further along the coast, and it was a much bigger prize. The English force landed unopposed, as the local people did not realise that they were being attacked by a ferocious enemy. A full-scale fully formed raid took place. The town was largely destroyed, many innocent people were killed, and looting took place. Morley and Crabbe's men left the immediate vicinity of their ships and fired villages within a couple of miles radius of the port. The local militia was stationed in the village of Eu, just 3 miles away. But they did not show up until the English were back in their ships and away farther down the coast. Emboldened by their successes, the ex-defenders, now raiders continued down the coast, rounding the Breton peninsula, and started to attack harbours to the south. No doubt encouraged by reports of the English successes, Flemish ships started to raid the Channel towns of France.

By the end of the 1339 fighting season, the French naval alliance was failing. Ayton Doria was facing a mutiny among his men, who were risking their lives solely for generous pay. Doria had not received all of the money that had been promised, which included the agreed percentage of the proceeds of looting. Worse still, what he had received he had quietly trousered and not passed on what he owed to his crews. When some of the crew complained to King Philippe, they were thrown into prison. Not unexpectedly, the rest of the crew upped sticks and started the long and arduous journey back home through the Straits of Gibraltar and the sunny Mediterranean to Genoa after a not entirely successful eighteen months in northern waters. It was no doubt good to get away from northern Europe, suffering as it was from the effects of global cooling. But soon after Doria returned to his home state, a revolution occurred which led to his group of magnates losing power. Times were hard.

* * *

The year 1339 ended badly for Edward III. The twenty-eight-year-old had overreached himself and was still in Flanders hoping to land a knock-out blow. He had literally pawned his crown jewels plus the value of an entire year's wool export revenues, in addition to one whole year's tax revenues, to finmance his hoped-for invasion of France. What Edward had been aiming for was to meet with the French army at the head of his anti-French coalition, beat them roundly and extract large amounts of cash from the French system. Given Edward's reputation for winning battles in Scotland when he was leading on the ground, it is hardly surprising that the French seemed determined not to meet with Edward.

Edward used a technique that had sometimes worked with the Scots. His armies ranged about the countryside destroying everything in an attempt to make the enemy strike back in desperation. The town of Origny was looted, burnt and destroyed. A nunnery was looted, the nuns raped. Over two or three days, as many as a dozen settlements suffered the same treatment, and fugitives were hunted down in the woods and ruins and put to the sword.

Philippe cracked under the strain and agreed to meet in battle in La Capelle, flat open ground ideal for a 'fair fight'. Edward's plan was to wait for the French to charge and then to mow them down by intensive barrages of arrows. The armies waited and waited. Much advice was given to Philippe, none of which he took until his ally the King of Jerusalem sent a message that he had consulted the stars and that the prognosis was that in no circumstances should he do battle with Edward's forces, as he would always lose. Advisors close to the French king argued that it would be dishonourable to fail to do battle after ranging his troops on the battlefield. Philippe took the advice of the stars and ignored the stain on his honour.

Edward was now in trouble. At the end of 1339, out of money and maybe out of luck, many a leader would have been considering ways of lowering the temperature, of maybe finding a diplomatic way out of his mess. That was rarely the way of Edward III. This was when Edward returned to the dispute that had started the war – his claim to the throne of France – and declared that he was King of France and England. His Flemish allies recognised this title, but in France and elsewhere it was met by puzzlement and fury. Even the Pope was critical. At the end of the year Edward issued a declaration inviting the French people to recognise his title, circulating his Great Royal Seal, on which the panthers of England were quartered with the French fleurs-de-lis. Edward spent the winter of 1339/1340 in Ghent (or Gaunt, the English form of the name at this time) with his pregnant wife. Despite being technically bankrupt the royal couple lived lavishly. Edward organised a royal tournament in November of 1339 which brought together knights from countries that were not part of the French alliance. It was reportedly a great success.[9]

One small event from the fighting season of 1339 remains: the French who still occupied the Channel Island's mounted another attack on Castle Gorey in order to remove the last vestige of English domination of the archipelago – and failed again. It was a bitter, hollow occupation. The taking of the islands had been so destructive that there was little to occupy. For years Alderney and Guernsey paid no taxes because there was nothing left to tax.

8

THE BATTLE OF SLUYS AND AFTERWARDS

Soon Edward was back in England, after an absence of a year and a half, trying to raise money and bolster support for the continuing war. His wife and baby son were in Flanders and his crown jewels were still pawned. He was trying to put together yet another invasion force, after the failure of the coalition of eighteen months ago. From February 1340 the long, complex process of raising levies, commandeering merchant ships for transport and producing the materiel for the forces started. We can imagine that if the process had continued unhindered it would have taken months, and Philippe's second Norman Conquest would have gone ahead.[1] It could have been a terminal disaster.

Edward's luck came into operation at this stage, and changed the direction of the conflict. As part of the new-found English active fight-back a group of Cinque Ports mariners captured a French ship on the high seas. Before ransoming the officers, Cinque Ports leaders subjected them to some desultory torture and extracted the information that that most of the French galley fleet was beached for the winter on Boulogne beach. Considering that galleys represented the attacking spearhead of the force, it was valuable news. A fleet of Cinque Port ships was assembled as fast as possible. It arrived outside Boulogne harbour in a thick mist, allowing ships to slip into the harbour undetected – another stroke of luck. There were defenders in the area, but as so often happened it took some time for them to get organised and by the time they met the invaders, the damage had largely been done. The galleys were torched. Houses in the waterfront area, warehouses filled with naval supplies such as oars, sails, and crossbows, 'such as were needed in order to arm and supply the number of men needed to crew the nineteen galleys' were all burnt.[2] After they had finished their work, the defenders showed up and a fierce battle followed. 'While many on both sides were killed, more of the men from Boulogne were slaughtered.'[3]

The loss of the galleys was very serious to the French plans for the imminent raiding season. Taken in conjunction with the loss of the Genoese fleet and Doria's leadership, the French were now unlikely to put their Norman Conquest plan into operation. Also, encouraged, the English started to raid France. Immediately after the Boulogne raid, there were others – Dieppe, Le Tréport and Mers again.[4]

Philip's caution was in complete contrast to Edward's boldness. Having been given a bloody nose by a small flotilla of lowly Cinque Port mariners, in the shadow of the loss of most of his galleys, his main weapon of naval offence, Philip pulled in his horns. The French navy – what was left of it – was consolidated into what was called the 'Great Army of the Sea'. The French followed a strategy, perhaps borrowed from the English, of arresting and forcing civilian ships into service to make up the losses. The entire fleet was moved to what seemed to be the ideal location, on the fringes of French territory near the Flanders war zone.

The harbour of Sluys, where Morley and Crabbe had carried out their raid the previous year, seemed to be a perfect location.

The shallow estuary, spacious inside, with a narrow entrance, seemed to be ideal. Putting their entire fleet in this one apparently safe location would pose a maximum threat to the English enemy with the minimum danger. Or so they thought! Edward was planning something big in Flanders – the French navy was in Flanders, ready for him. It seemed a good idea.

In May Edward was engaged in one of his favourite pastimes, jousting, in the grounds of his castle of Windsor. A messenger arrived, bringing urgent news from Flanders. Two of his closest associates – the Earls of Suffolk and of Salisbury – had, after a bloody battle with the French, been captured and were being held hostage. The French army was in Hainault – the home of Edward's father-in-law – and had already destroyed two towns, Haspres and Escaudœuvres. Now they were besieging Valenciennes itself.

Edward's own dear wife Philippa was still in Hainault and she was pregnant. Could Philippa end up as a guest of the Valois family, as a hostage? It was unthinkable. Yet with the French fleet in Flanders in support of their ground operation, what alternative was there? The alternative was to get to Flanders as soon as possible, with a force, to ask for help from his brother-in-law Count William of Hainault, and to use Hainault as a base from which to attack France. There were the makings of a disaster. The whole of Edward's Flanders policy was at stake.

Meanwhile, further news was coming in from English spies in the French court. There was a strategy behind the massing of a huge fleet behind the barrier islands of Sluys. The troubles of the past years boiled down to one person only – King Edward. Take Edward out of the picture and relative peace might well ensue. A wall of ships was ready for Edward. Just one effective sea battle would be enough, with a modicum of luck on the part of the French, and Edward could be captured – remove the man, remove the problem.

Edward was forced to raise a fleet to transport him to Flanders as quickly as possible. No months of painstaking preparation this time. The French were settling into their anchorages with a total of 202 ships, with 19,000 fighting men on board. This works out at about 100 fighting men per ship, which suggests that most ships would have had their decks crammed with armed men.

Edward knew that he had to act fast and he was prepared to sail with just a skeleton fleet of 40 ships, and a small force of just 400 men. Edward's advisors were horrified. Edward's Chancellor, the Archbishop of Canterbury, advised Edward that attempting to cross the Channel was currently too risky. Edward rejected the advice, and the Archbishop resigned. More buccaneering advisors with a hands-on track record of daring deeds were the redoubtable Robert Morley and his right-hand man, John Crabbe. They also advised the king that he should not sail.

At this point Edward's exceptional leadership qualities came to the fore. He was able to persuade his fighting men that they would not be sailing across the Channel to oblivion and failure – if he had not succeeded, many of his force would have deserted. Realising that the coastal levies assembled to protect the English coast from French attack were, for the year 1340 at least, irrelevant, he used his authority to persuade the Cinque Port ships and the seamen of Yarmouth and the other east coast ports to join the expedition. By June Edward had managed to put together a fleet of maybe 130 ships, moored near Harwich at the mouth of the Orwell Estuary. So when Edward sailed just before Midsummer Day from Harwich he had at his disposal perhaps 9,000 men – most of whom had fighting experience. As luck would have it, the wind favoured his fleet.

When Edward's fleet arrived off the coast of Flanders, they were able to see the entire French fleet at harbour in the Zwijn estuary – their total number was 213. They could see a forest of masts. The wind was still to Edward's advantage, blowing inland off the North Sea, limiting the movement of the French fleet. With the wind behind them, the English navy had a distinct advantage. The internal channels were no more than a mile wide and all around there were settlements so we can imagine people standing all around the coast watching what was going on. Béhuchet and Hugues Quiéret were in charge. They were neither of them naval experts, and their instincts were to play it safe and stay in harbour. The leader of the Genoese ships, who was an experienced fighting seaman, warned the two French admirals that there were mistaken and told them to go out to sea, turn so that the wind was behind them, and attack.

The entire Zwijn estuary was spacious but broken into channels and the entrance was narrow. If the attacking force were to come at them with the wind behind them, the French fleet would be trapped while just a few ships at any one time would be able to face the enemy and the English would be able to pick off a few ships at a time. The English soldiers packed together on the decks were hardened veterans of Edward's past wars. The French were not. Edward decided to use longbows as a strategic weapon and to act as though they were carrying out a land battle on the ships' decks.

The English moved against the French with grappling irons. Once an English vessel had taken a French one in its grip, the soldiers came at the French with all the weapons of land warfare. The fight commenced with men-at-arms, murderous wielders of the sword, backed up by longbow men who kept up a continuous rain of arrows 'like hail in winter'. The French did not use longbows and their crossbows were slow and unwieldy. The French were outclassed.

This type of naval battle was carried out as though it were a land battle. Grapple and bring the enemy ship alongside and invade it. Fight hand-to-hand on the deck. Dispose of the dead by throwing them overboard.

The English soldiers were avenging the raids that they had suffered over the years at the hands of the French. The French, looking west at the English ships, were dazzled by the afternoon sun, and as the afternoon wore on the Flemings, who were not friends of the French, came out of their harbours and moorings in the surrounding area and joined in with the English.

The hundreds of archers on the English ships did not need to be in the front line of English boats to make their presence felt. The arrows rained down on the French, and there were many casualties caused. The chronicler Froissart, always an admirer of deeds of bravery and arms, observed:

> Seafights are always fiercer than fights on land, because retreat and flight are impossible. Every man is obliged to hazard his life and hope for success, relying on his own personal bravery and skill... the English were hard put to it to hold their own, since they were opposed by hardened soldiers and seamen, who outnumbered them four to one.[5]

The result of the battle was astonishing: 280 out of the 300 ships in the French fleet were destroyed and burnt, 16,000 French soldiers were killed. Froissart said that the very fish in the Zwijn started to speak French!

Admiral Béhuchet was captured by the English. On Edward's orders he was hanged from the yardarm of an English ship – a form of execution more suitable to a pirate than to a French admiral. The French side blamed him for the failure, the experiment of using people of non-aristocratic background for key posts was abandoned and the French retreated into their traditional roles.

Froissart vividly describes the victory celebrations. As an uncritical supporter of the chivalric ideal he glories in their exultation:

> After winning this victory, the English King spent the whole of the night, which was Midsummer Eve, on board his ships

at sea, amid such a banging and blowing of cymbals and trumpets, drums and cornets that God's own thunder would not have been heard above it.[6]

This was a turning point in the war against the English mainland. In just one day, the French fighting machine had lost many of its ships and a large proportion of its fighting men. Of the 25,000 casualties reported in Sluys that day, maybe 18,000 were experienced soldiers and mariners who would be difficult to replace. In something similar to the effect of the First World War on civilian populations, the French ports along the English Channel were denuded of their productive, experienced seamen and instead acquired a population of men badly injured in battle. And long after the battle, corpses of dead fighting men were washed up all along the Channel coast.[7]

Edward had a lucky day –23 June 1340 could have spelt the end of his war against the Valois. If the seasoned Genoese captain had been listened to, the French navy would have been outside the Zwijn Estuary and the superior numbers of the French would have made a French defeat much less likely. If the wind had on that day been blowing away from the Flemish mainland, the English ships would have found it hard to approach the entrance of the harbour. If the battle had gone in the other direction, Edward III might have been captured and ransomed and the second Norman Conquest would have been a possibility. Although Edward was wounded in the leg by an arrow, bravely he continued to lead. But if the arrow had landed just a few feet further up Edward's body, history might have been very different. If his wound had become infected he could have died.

After the battle, Edward duly gave thanks to God for His assistance by visiting the Shrine of the Holy Blood in Bruges, an appropriate choice. From there he went on the see his wife Philippa and their new baby – the future John of Gaunt – for the first time.[8]

Then he went back to trying to make war against France from Flanders. Within one month he was in action again, besieging the almost impregnable city of Tournai. But the action was badly planned, Edward had no money, Parliament in England was not prepared to vote funds, and Edward was forced to abandon his campaign; although he believed that he was close to taking the city. Near to Tournai at the end of September, the French and English representatives met and in a matter of two days agreed a truce which was supposed to hold for at least one year. Edward was virtually bankrupt and the French state was suffering too. For the time being there was a period of relative peace.

During August of 1340, before the failure of the Siege of Tournai but after the naval disaster, a group of French mariners carried out a final set of raids on the English coastline.[10] A new naval leader was appointed – Robert Houdetot. He gathered together the few ships that had survived Sluys, three galleys and seven armed barges. Some Spanish merchantmen were hired. The English had assumed that French raiding would cease, the coastal defences were abandoned, and the armed convoy system stopped. So when Houdetot appeared in the Channel, his fleet was able to slaughter the crews of 30 wool ships and capture each ship, bringing them and their cargos back to port in Normandy – a welcome addition to the depleted French stock of ships.[9]

The fleet went on to the Isle of Wight, and managed to land. The defenders led by Sir Theobald Russell fought back but the knight was killed, the force was decimated and had to retreat.

The fleet moved along the coast to the west – and when the Houdetot fleet saw the Isle of Portland they stopped. Maybe they saw ships in the harbour? Most of the island is quite unsuitable for raiding, being rocky and precipitous.

The fleet sailed on to Teignmouth in Devon, at that time second only to Plymouth. It was raided but we know little about those events.

The fleet sailed on to Plymouth, but the defenders were fully prepared for the attack and the French fleet had to withdraw. There are two final twists to the story before we enter a period when there was much less action.

At the end of July Sir Thomas Ferrers set out from Southampton for a re-conquest of the Channel Islands. The English were able to take back control of Guernsey, but Castle Cornet remained in French hands for the next five years.[10]

By the end of 1340 there had been fighting between England, France and Scotland for at least six years. There had been many land battles, and in most cases Edward was the victor. The French had carried out more than twenty-five incursions onto English territory, some profitably, but they lost an entire fleet and also an army. The English had won many land battles in Scotland but not in France and they had not won the war.

At this stage of the conflict the endemic problem underlying the war trumped all plans – finance. The medieval European state was always short of money. In normal times the revenues of the French monarch were sufficient to support the expenses of the court and little more. The traditional manner of waging war was to raise armies via feudal obligations involving knights carrying out their duties as vassals of the king. By the fourteenth century these obligations had declined in importance. So the *arrière-ban* had largely ceased to be a call to arms and had turned into a method of extracting payments from the wealthy.

Although Edward was able to raise money directly by means of taxation agreed by Parliament, by 1340 England had been drained of funding and Edward was technically bankrupt. He has staked his entire reputation and the wealth of his kingdom upon his claim to the throne of France but he did not succeed in taking the title of King of France from the Valois.

His kingdom's coastal towns had been damaged by war, and the merchant class has been badly affected by the disruption that naval warfare had created in its ports. England was more highly taxed than any other country in Europe, which made everyone poorer. The disruption in trade caused by the French presence in the Channel had led to economic decline in the maritime areas of England while the economic disruption to the wool-exporting industry that Edward's Flanders campaign had created impoverished the ordinary rural workers in the sheep-farming regions of England.[11] At the end of 1340 Edward's life was a mess. If he had been less lucky – if he had been a little less skilful at leading people, at persuading people to follow his commands, to talk himself out of trouble, he might not have survived the crisis. Once he had signed up to the truce, Edward was not free to return to England. As a bankrupt in a foreign country, he was not free to flee his creditors; his debts should be repaid.

He stayed on in Ghent, and tried to make a deal with his creditors – but they rejected his offer. He wrote to the pope, hoping that he would intervene in his favour – but the pope was not on his side. Finally at the end of November, Edward did what a gentle and valorous king should not ever do. He ran away from his palace in Ghent in the dead of night with just a few trusty companions.

From Sluys the party took a ship to England. The weather was against them and they spent three days in a winter gale in the Channel and round the east of Kent into the Thames estuary. It was said that Edward nearly drowned before the ship reached the safety of the River Thames.[12]

When he returned to England he found what often happens to charismatic leaders when their big plans go wrong – the knives come out. It would appear that there was a plot afoot to remove Edward from power. The Archbishop of Canterbury was leader of the plotters. Edward confronted them, and in a testimony to his skills at knowing how to be a king, he managed to put the coup down and survive.

In the early part of 1341 Edinburgh was taken by the Scots. By midsummer of that year King David arrived back in Scotland after seven years in Chateau Gaillard.

We could describe 1340 and 1341 as Edward's 'Darkest Hour', when the damage caused by warfare had not produced any return, he had spent years in Flanders and failed. But Edward was a stayer. He found ways to reschedule his enormous debts and he was impatient to go back to his wars against the Valois kings. By the end of 1341 he had found the right vehicle. A disputed succession in the Dukedom of Brittany, part of the Kingdom of France but effectively autonomous, gave him the chance to support anti-Valois parties. While still bound by the terms of his truce, Edward was involving himself in a proxy war.

9

ALL QUIET ON
THE HOME FRONT

Over the next twenty years Edward bounced back from this low point in his career. There was a lot of action, mostly on land in France, involving English armies, and Edward's military and leadership genius underwent its full flowering. This two-decade period was one of relative peace for England's coastal communities although the action on the Continent did result in some incursions and naval activity that had an impact.

By 1342 Edward was fighting a proxy war in Brittany, which, although it was officially a fief of France, was ruled as an independent dukedom. His intention was to put a pro-Edwardian leader in power there. Edward, his magnates and Parliament supported an English invasion force to give real teeth to this policy. The fleet was to sail from Southampton and Portsmouth, making its way to Brest. As so often happened with Edward's expeditions, the process of arraying shipping took much longer that it should have, and the French, who had royal ships available at any time, very sensibly put together a fleet to blockade these two ports and stop the English fleet sailing. It was a good idea but the timing was, from the French point of view, unfortunate. By the time the Isle of Wight hove into view the English were on the high seas on the way to Brest. So the French burnt Portsmouth yet again, just four years after the previous raid. It is reported that the fleet stayed some time at the entrance to the Solent, terrifying the people of the area, but with the Court's attention elsewhere, they were not challenged.[1]

Three years passed without any recorded action on English territory involving the French or French allies. However, the French occupation of Castle Cornet gave the French an excellent base from which to harass English shipping in the Channel. The communications from Edward III concerning collaboration with the French occupation after the recapture in 1340 give a hint of the uncertain situation in the Channel Islands.

> Seize all lands and goods of traitors in the islands, as he is informed that diverse men having land in the islands [have] absented themselves in time of war staying among the king's enemies of France ... and returning in times of truce and peace.[2]

The opening of Edward's involvement in the Breton war put the Channel Islands in the spotlight again and an expedition was set up to dislodge the occupiers. In the summer of 1345 the English governor of the Channel Islands led a fleet of galleys from Bayonne, in the English possession of Guyenne, in order to reclaim his territory. They were manned by only about 100 fighters but in the small space of Jersey that was enough, the entire French garrison was massacred, and the Channel Islands were again free of French control.

* * *

The English were at war in one location or another for the next couple of years. The next great victory was in 1346 in Crécy,

Normandy. In another example of Edward's luck, it followed a campaign involving sieges and battles that all went wrong. When the English finally met with the French in Crécy, the great victory that resulted in the death of as many as 1,500 French noblemen was devastating to the French state.

Never one to dither, Edward went on the exploit his victory by turning on Calais the following year. There are very few examples during the Hundred Years' War of successful sieges of important towns. They usually failed because the besiegers were unable to bring in sufficient supplies, so the aggressors frequently found themselves suffering from food shortages. The key factor that allowed the English forces to starve the citizens of Calais into surrender was the English domination of the English Channel, largely as a result of the victory at Sluys. The surrender of the burghers of Calais to King Edward is one of the most celebrated scenes in medieval history. In 1347 the inhabitants of Calais were starving. Six representatives came out of the city to speak to King Edward. They were so weakened that some could hardly walk. When they presented themselves to Edward, each petitioner had a hangman's noose around his neck. They asked Edward to accept their surrender in return for the lives of the people of Calais. An enraged Edward rejected their plea and threatened to massacre the whole town in retaliation for having resisted his attack for one whole year. His wife Isabella apparently pleaded for mercy – and it was granted. Many historians question the veracity of this part of the story, with good reason. The leader of the burghers was Jean de Vienne, a minor noblemen from a family of fighters from the French Alpine region. He was taken into captivity and held for many years before his friends and family raise the money for his ransom. His name will recur in the person of his nephew and namesake, who will play a leading role later in the century.[3]

Most of the events in this book took place against a background of English aggression against France, and two great victories made

Edward III into an international player. The Battle of Crécy and the successful siege of Calais between them changed the balance of power between France and England – Edward was no longer the challenger of the continental superpower, now he was a major power himself. The mass slaughter of the French knighthood at Crécy was a turning point for Edward's ambitions. And from the point of view of the security of the English mainland, the capture of Calais was of huge importance. With England holding both coasts of the Straits of Dover, the French space for manoeuvre was greatly restricted.

There was a third great victory that year, when the English army – led by a cleric with a military bent, the Archbishop of York – defeated the Scottish army at Neville's Cross and took the twenty-two-year old King David II captive. He was promptly moved to the Tower of London, and demands for a ransom were started.[4]

* * *

All of the events of the narrative up to now took place against a background of cold weather, rain, periodic famine and population decline. In this most unfortunate of centuries the entire Asian and European world now entered into one of the greatest existential human crisis in recorded history. The Black Death appears to have originated in Central Asia moving out of its Central Asian homelands during the early fourteenth century as a result of the desiccation of central Asia, the same climatic disturbance that caused the Little Ice Age – a result of the same climatic shift causing the great famines at the start of the period.[5] For some reason a species of blood-sucking flea that had until this time lived on the bodies of rats jumped species and moved to the human being. The jaws of the flea carried the bubonic plague bacterium, *Yersinia pestis*, which, once it entered the bloodstream of a human being, almost always killed its victim terrifyingly quickly. The illness moved relentlessly through Europe from the Black Sea, and arrived in the Channel Islands before it jumped to the English mainland.

It arrived in England in the summer of 1348 and it spread throughout England rapidly at a rate of 10 miles a day. By the end of the first year up to 60 per cent of the population was wiped out. Whole villages were emptied of their population. Entire families caught the sickness at the same time. Monasteries and abbeys where members lived communally died out together. People's view of the world changed. Surely it was the will of God that the human race should be doomed? Flagellants and penitents roamed the roads. In England the first epidemic was accompanied by cold and rainy weather, and the populations of animals such as cattle and sheep died in the fields. Landscapes and cityscapes changed. Abandoned farms and deserted villages were visible in many areas. In ports empty houses and warehouses were in evidence. Over the years the landscape would change with abandoned fields reverting to scrub and woodland.[6]

It was noticed at the time, however, that the highest classes of society were less affected than the lower orders. Within the royal family, for example, there were no deaths as a result of the plague. After the Crécy and Calais victories, the court style became ever more extravagant, regardless of the atmosphere of existential terror that was gripping the whole world. As the Black Death was moving over southern England in the summer of 1348, after the baptism of King Edward and Queen Philippa's eleventh child, Edward held a great tournament in Windsor, to which his high-status French captives from Calais were invited, all dressed at Edward's expense in elaborate colour-coordinated velvet costumes. The Christmas festivities of that year were especially bizarre and outré. Guests were dressed as elephants, wild men of the woods, in drag, while the king himself appeared on horseback, man and horse dressed in full body armour, spangled in gold, with a shield bearing the motto – 'Hey hey the White Swan, By God's soul I am Thy Man!'[7]

By the start of 1349 the pandemic was abating but law and order was breaking down and prices were falling as demand in the economy was disappearing. As Henry Knighton observed:

> And there was a great cheapness of things for fear of death, for very few took any account of riches or of possessions of any kind. A man could have a horse that was formerly worth forty shillings for less than seven shillings.[8]

Over the whole of war-torn Europe, the Black Death resulted in a pause, an emotional numbness took hold, and for a period little fighting took place. But gradually, as so often happens, the disaster became incorporated into the emotional landscape, and life went on, changed forever for many of the survivors, but continuing all the same. In the political world, the earlier patterns reasserted themselves in war-torn France and England, but the physical landscape was changed forever – the population would not recover until well into the eighteenth century, and after 200 years of agricultural expansion, farming was in retreat. The 1350s and 1360s were England's least-invaded decades in the period, apart from a single raid on Plymouth in 1350.

The temporary halt in hostilities in these years did not lead to a loosening of military obligations for ordinary people. It appears that in the aftermath of the Black Death the survivors lost interest in training to be archers. It appears that post-Black Death society saw an increase in the playing of games among the ordinary people. King Edward issued an order to his sheriffs forbidding this:

> The King to the Sheriff of Kent.
> Whereas the people of our realm ... usually practised in their games the art of archery ... now the people amuse

themselves with throwing stones ... or playing handball or football or pila calculis (cricket?) or hockey or cock fighting... We order you ... that in all places in your shire ... [they] shall use for their games bows and arrows ... forbidding all and single to toy ... with those other games ... under pain of imprisonment.[9]

It is the occasional document of this sort that gives us a picture of the profound effect that wartime conditions had upon daily life .

After the arrival of the Black Death, the next big event, in 1350, was the so-called 'Battle of Winchelsea'. This fight between Spanish and English cogs was something of an outlier because, unlike later centuries, battles at sea where two sides line up close-to and fight it out either hand-to-hand or by the use of ships' guns was very rare in the fourteenth. The combination of the lack of manoeuvrability with the single-sailed cog's inability to sail close to the wind made it very hard for two opposing fleets of cogs to come near each other in order to do battle.

As a result of the post-Sluys French lack of shipping, Castilian ships were patrolling the English Channel on behalf of the French, attacking English shipping and disrupting their trade routes. The Castilians were closer to the more advanced Mediterranean shipbuilding traditions than either the French or the English and when they appeared the Castilian cogs created a sensation. They were much bigger that their northern counterparts, towering over the relatively poor English models; as the chronicler put it – 'like a cottage to a mansion'!

The naval intelligence was that the Spanish ships were armed merchantmen on their way to Sluys, where they would buy their shipment of wool and then set off back down the Channel to the west, on the way looking for English ships to attack. The main target was said to be the annual English convoy carrying wine from Gascony – economically an essential shipment. If allowed to operate in the Channel unchallenged, the Spanish fleet was clearly a threat.[10]

The Spanish ships were prepared for action armed with the sort of projectile throwers that were at the time used during sieges, plus a plentiful supply of stones. The extreme height of the Spanish ships meant that they would be throwing the stones downwards onto the smaller English vessels, a dangerous situation for the English.

Edward hurriedly arrayed a fleet to watch out for the Spanish ships, fixing upon Winchelsea as his base as he expected that the fleet would pass nearby. Edward's luck certainly held that day as the wind was blowing down the Channel from the east. The Spanish fleet of giant cogs, so unfamiliar along the southern English coastline, was moving fast, following just the course that Edward had expected. This again demonstrates his ability to choose the right location for battle.

We are fortunate to have a detailed description of this naval battle written from the point of view of Jean Froissart, the writer of the period most full of admiration for the aristocratic and regal warrior ideal. In Froissart's description we see a picture of war as something to celebrate, to go into with feelings of joy while celebrating beauty, colour and pride. There is no hint of the post-twentieth-century notion of war as something entered into with feelings of fear or foreboding, as the result of policy failures. Froissart's description of the Spanish fleet as they sailed out of Sluys harbour is a marvellous evocation of the aesthetics of warfare. The fourteenth-century merchant ship was the high-tech moveable object that used the most resources of anything in its era.

There were forty big ships all sailing together, so powerful and splendid that they made a beautiful sight ... on the masts also there were streamers bearing their various colours and emblems which waved and fluttered in the wind.[11]

In the meantime Edward was in Winchelsea with his family. His wife Philippa was there with their eldest son the Prince of Wales, twenty years old, and little John of Gaunt, just ten. All his close supporters were there too, all the dukes and earls, and whichever of the aristocracy could make the journey in time after being summoned. The cliffs to the west of Rye Bay were reportedly crowded with spectators. Philippa and her entourage were in an abbey just outside Winchelsea. Edward introduced his two sons to warfare by taking them with him on board his ship, rather as his father Edward II had done when he took his young son to the Battle of Boroughbridge. Including those aboard other vessels, Edward's force comprised 400 ordinary knights, and plenty of longbowmen. They waited, says Froissart, at sea.

> Edward stood in the bows of his own ship, wearing a black velvet jerkin and a black beaver skin cap which greatly suited him. On that day, I was told by some that were with him, he was in a gayer mood than he had ever been seen before. He told his minstrels to strike up a dance tune which Sir John Chandos, who was there beside him, had recently brought back from Germany. And out of sheer high spirits he made Sir John sing with the minstrels, to his own vast amusement.[12]

While this banter was going on Edward was listening to the lookouts at the mast tops. Eventually they called out that they could see a ship appearing. When asked how many there were they started by counting – two – four. Then they said that it was impossible to count them – although it appears that the Spanish fleet was made up of forty ships. It was now necessary to get ready for battle. Wine was passed around, and armour was put on; for the highest ranking members of the fleet, this included wearing the pig-headed bascinet that was so typical of the period.

The huge ships were moving so fast that more timid commanders on both English and Spanish sides would have decided to suspend hostilities – to let the Spanish sail on, while the English sailed back into port. But as the Spanish fleet got close to the English lines, Edward gave the eccentric order, 'Steer this ship to that Spanish one – I want to joust with it.' It has been suggested that Edward was now drunk and acting recklessly, but the order opened the real battle.

The battle was closely matched. Crossbowmen on the giant Spanish ships were able to rain down bolts on the English ships and the English did suffer losses, and the huge rocks hurled down in the decks killed many. But archery is not really suited to the lurching decks of ships in choppy Channel waters, and the battle was won by Edward's ability to lead his forces into fierce close combat, as at Sluys. The English ships came close to the Spanish ones and pulled them in by grappling irons. Then the English fighters boarded the Spanish ships.

What ensued was, as had happened at Sluys, a land battle carried out at sea with close hand-to-hand combat, and the Spaniards and Flemings were no match for Edward's battle-hardened troops. The English remained supreme at close-fought combat, hour after hour, and systematically destroyed the Spanish and Flemish enemy. Dead and wounded were thrown overboard, and once enough of a ship's company were disposed of, the ship itself was taken. The English count at the end of the day was perhaps as many as twenty-four Spanish ships captured – no English ships taken by the Spanish. Not all the Spanish had joined the battle; the survivors made a run for it westwards to safety.[13]

Edward returned to Winchelsea with his two sons safe and sound, and ready to be returned to their mother. Froissart says the end of the day was an Edwardian mix of domesticity, extravagance and high spirits.

(Philippa) was overjoyed to see her lord and her children, for during the day she had suffered great anxiety. ... the night was passed in great rejoicings by the lords and ladies and in conversations on arms and love.

The moment when Edward gave the command to charge the leading Spanish vessel near Winchelsea, it could be argued, was the moment that the tide in his affairs started to turn. By challenging the Spanish ships, who were acting on behalf of the French navy, he was making it clear that it was going to be difficult for King Philippe to fill the gap that the loss of the French navy had created. Over the coming years Edward took the fight onto French territory and by his putting the French forces into defensive mode, there were hardly any more raids for a period, until the next round of attacks on English territory started.

10

THE TRIUMPHS
OF EDWARD III – 1363

In the next few years when there was little action on the coasts of England, there were many invasions of France by English armies. While not all English attacks were successes, there were a number of victories that were of huge importance.

At the Battle of Poitiers on 19 September 1356, six years after the victory at Winchelsea, the Prince of Wales captured King Jean of France, and a large proportion of the nobility of France. Jean II had succeeded his father Philip VI, being crowned on 26 September 1350. Poitiers marks a high point in the trajectory of King Edward's life, for his large family, for his friends and supporters, for the ruling classes and, to a certain extent, for the English population at large. After Poitiers Edward III's two great enemies, France and Scotland, had been well and truly bested in battle and their kings were in English captivity.

At Poitiers the English were able to kill or capture many of the French ruling classes, and with most of the upper echelons of the French aristocracy, from the king down, in captivity, the French state had ceased to operate. The Regent, Charles, usually known as the Dauphin, was a teenager and Paris was controlled by mobs. The countryside was infested with irregular armies of unemployed soldiers, wannabe knights and chancers – generally supported by the English as a way of neutralising France as a security threat. So it is not surprising that the arrival of the French royal prisoner on English territory in May 1358 opened a year of celebration in England. The lavish series of events that were staged in the coming months was aimed at commemorating victory in the wars that had turned out, for the present at any rate, far better than anyone could have anticipated, which had validated Edward's concept of chivalry, and which had brought unheard-of wealth to those close to the royal court, if not to most people in the lower levels of society.

When the royal flotilla arrived in Plymouth from English Guyenne it was led by the king's son Edward, the Prince of Wales, known as the Black Prince, bringing to England and gilded captivity the highest status prisoner of the century, perhaps of all time – the King of France himself, Jean II. The triumphal procession on horseback through England, via Salisbury, Sherborne and Winchester – more than 250 miles – was a lot more than just a journey to Jean II's future quarters in London. It was a celebration of English valour triumphing against the greatest power on the European continent. The party processed slowly, as was fitting, and it must have taken two weeks before the VIPs arrived in London. The members of the party – including fifty court companions to Jean, maybe a similar or larger number for the Prince of Wales, plus an unrecorded number of knights and men-at-arms, would have caused a sensation in the towns and villages that they processed through.[1]

The people of England had been in a state of euphoria ever since the news of England's total victory at Poitiers had arrived in the country. It was unprecedented to be able to stand on the roadside to see the English royal party and their royal French prisoners pass by. Not just the king of France himself, but also his younger son Philip, who, too young to fight, had seen has father captured and led away from the battleground at Poitiers. There were crowds all along the route and for many of the rustics who saw the royal party pass it would be the finest parade that they would ever see. Warfare in Edward's England meant display. Rather than dressing down for combat, twentieth-century style, Edward's armies were finely turned out. Iron breastplates, bascinets, arm and leg pieces were all burnished so as to gleam in the sunlight, on occasion dazzling the enemy when the sun was in the right quarter. Surpluses and shields were painted with family colours, in the brilliant hues of the world of heraldry. The English leopard would have been very much in evidence – and the St George's Cross. The drums and bugles of the party must have been audible before the procession came into view. There might even been chanting of favourite battle cries, such as 'St George and England!' The sounds struck fear into the breasts of their enemies and pride into the hearts of friends.

In the midst of this military triumphalism Jean and the rest of the French contingent were dressed in austere black as though they were priests rather than failed warriors. If there was cheering when the Black Prince came into view, his magnificent armour covered in a black surplice, which there must have been, can we guess that the sight of the Frenchmen elicited jeering? Or the fourteenth century equivalent of thumbs down, or two fingers up? Unfortunately our chroniclers do not tell us.[2]

Edward's love of display, of dressing up and of extravagance was to the fore and from his residence in Windsor he arranged for an army of 500 men-at-arms dressed like Robin Hood in green and armed with bows and arrows to stage a mock ambush for the hapless French king. Apparently once the joke was explained to him King Jean understood it. It was a cruel joke against a monarch whose armies had been bested by English archers over and over again.

The arrival of the triumphal party in London was even more over the top. They were met outside the limits of the city by the mayor and the aldermen dressed in elaborate costumes and escorted through streets decorated with coats of arms and armour, and jammed with cheering people. The water conduits along the royal route ran with wine. Beautiful young women occupied human-sized birdcages along the route, strewing gold and silver leaves upon the passing royalty.[3]

It had taken Edward more than twenty years to reach this pinnacle, to become Europe's dominant warrior king. In the early days of Edward's leadership the picture looked very different. At the start of his career as a warrior king Edward was little more than the youthful and inexperienced leader of a relatively minor country. His threats to overthrow the balance of power with England's great neighbour must have seemed incredible. France, a country central to European culture and having maybe four million inhabitants and an economy to match had surely little to fear from Edward. Ignoring normal diplomatic niceties after the start of his reign, Edward had turned upon his feudal lord Philippe Valois, claimed on dynastic grounds the very crown of France which belonged *de facto* to Philip, and set about trying to create an alliance with the intention of toppling the Valois family from power. A combination of luck and military genius had led to this. Edward was waiting to meet with his captive fellow monarch in Westminster, surrounded by his ecstatic subjects, while holding another monarch captive nearby. King David II of Scotland, who at the Battle of Neville's Cross had been taken into similarly although slightly less comfortable captivity, thus extinguishing Scottish independence for a few years at least.

The triumph in Westminster was followed by a grand tournament at Smithfield to the east of the City of London. Edward, watched his followers, engaged in mock but sometimes bloody and highly realistic battles, dressed in all the finery that he could muster.

He was seated between Jean Valois, still dressed in black, on his right and, on the left, the lesser position, King David of Scotland, similarly dressed down. They were both totally in his power, and both up for sale back to their subjects, each, of course, for a king's ransom. Near him also was his wife, whom he genuinely loved, and his many children, including Edward, his eldest, destined for the throne upon his father's demise, now having proved himself in the international arena of war as an equal to his father.

Edward at the age of forty-seven must have felt that he had created a great legacy for his children, and that he had created a family worthy of that legacy. Edward was not given to introspection, but it is possible that his mind strayed back to that dark night when, a bankrupt fleeing his creditors, he nearly drowned on the passage from Flanders to London, and was met with a near coup.

11

THE FRENCH RETURN
TO ENGLAND

After the courtesies had been fully completed Edward escorted Jean II of France to his quarters at the Savoy Palace, probably the finest townhouse in all of England, overlooking the Thames in the area of Westminster This was a much finer residence than Odiham Castle in Berkshire, which was to be the quarters for David II of Scotland, reflecting Jean's exceptional status in the royal pecking order. At this stage the diplomatic manoeuvring commenced. The objective for the English was to extract as much gold from the French as they could as a ransom, thus recouping the costs of the war, and also to add as much territory as possible to the English possessions in France, strategically drawing frontiers to inflict as much economic damage on the French state as possible. Like many negotiations between the insular and Continental powers even in the twentieth century, negotiations were slow and frustrating. It has been demonstrated in later European history that it is usually a mistake to treat a defeated nation too harshly. 'Make them pay!' is often seen as a national humiliation, giving future leaders *carte blanche* to extract revenge on the perpetrators. Edward fell into this trap.

At this stage of the story Charles Valois, the eldest son of King Jean, enters the picture as heir to the throne under the title of the Dauphin. His character and personality will be one of the forces driving future developments.

The Dauphin and the English king were opposites in some ways, alike in others. Edward was physically powerful, Charles was frail, and suffered from chronic illnesses such as an abscess on his left arm, which a doctor of the time sagely cautioned would cause his death if it healed.[1] Edward was an instinctive leader, open and magnetic. Charles was complex, hidden, inclined on occasion to treachery. His slight frame, pointed, weasel-like nose and intense but hidden eyes are well captured by contemporary illustrations from manuscripts (see the plate section for an example).

Like Edward, Charles became acting king prematurely, while still a teenager, and like his English rival, he came into power under challenging circumstances. Before being thrust into the limelight, Charles had anything but an unblemished record. For example, as an impressionable teenager he had appeared to support Charles of Navarre's bid to seize the throne from his father, an act of foolish treachery that his father forgave.

Charles was in charge of one of the battalions that made up the huge French army at Poitiers. When the French defence began to fall apart and chaos broke out, Charles' loving father, seeing a military catastrophe in the making, told Charles to leave the field of battle and save himself. The sight of the Dauphin with his followers galloping away from the field of battle had a disastrous effect upon morale and, arguably, contributed to the military catastrophe that was Poitiers. The story spread around France that the Dauphin had run away from battle, and when Charles arrived in Paris intending to take up the reins of power he found that he had little power to hold. While the Prince of Wales was getting ready to take King Jean to England, the Estates General –the nearest thing to a national assembly that France possessed – met and, after due deliberations, the 800 members presented Charles with a list of demands, which he almost certainly was not prepared to accept.[2]

The diplomatic process in London dragged on over the coming year. Perhaps relations between Edward and Jean deteriorated a little – who knows – or maybe security concerns gained traction. Whatever the reason, Jean and his entourage were moved away from their original location near the centre of affairs to the isolation of Somerton Castle in Lincolnshire. Somerton Castle, which is still occupied as a private residence, is a comparatively modest building, close to Ermine Street, the main road from there to London, and at least 30 miles from any suitable landing place on the River Humber. For a French king it would have been a comedown, and a signal that the extreme degree of respect with which Jean had been treated by his fellow monarch Edward was not open-ended.

The negotiations led to a draft agreement between Edward and Jean in which Edward abandoned his claim to be King of France in exchange for a ransom of four million écus; this was the equivalent of £667,000 and an immense sum in the fourteenth century. A part-payment of 600,000 écus was to be paid in advance of Jean's return home, and 40 hostages were to be taken from the ranks of the French aristocracy to guarantee that the balance would be paid. In addition, parts of south-west France and territory along the Channel coast were to be ceded to Edward as his exclusive possession.[3]

These terms were rejected by the Estates General, and the Dauphin was forced to move out of Paris for his own safety. From May 1358 groups of peasants turned on their local aristocracy, committing savage atrocities, and the violence spread all over the Isle de France. Aristocratic dwellings were attacked and burnt, whole families were massacred.

While the English court continued to celebrate over the coming months, life in France deteriorated. While Edward's Orders of

Saint George and of the Garter held glittering festivities and carried out mock battles dressed in the most luxuriant costumes, law and order broke down in most areas of France. Whole stretches of country lost all their buildings to burning, fields were not farmed, entire local populations either fled or were massacred by psychotic bands of bandits.⁴ Armed bands made up of ex-soldiers, impoverished knights, and members of families that had been ruined by the peasant uprisings joined in, looting and destroying everything they could lay their hands on, and although Edward III officially did not lend his support to this type of brigandage, it is quite certain that he secretly approved. This was just one more way of ensuring that France would not pose a military threat to the English Crown in the foreseeable future. Ever since his early days in Scotland, Edward had understood the benefits of brutal wall-to-wall destruction of an enemy's assets.

At the start of 1359 Jean capitulated to Edward's demands and the Treaty of London was sent to the Dauphin and the Estates General for ratification. Having failed to get his treaty ratified the previous year, Edward had made the terms even worse for France. Perhaps Edward and his advisors thought that because the process of societal breakdown in France had gone further than the previous year the possibility of total capitulation was greater – or maybe he had another plan altogether.

The territorial demands were increased to a ridiculous extent. Now Edward and his ambassadors were asking for the whole of Brittany, Normandy, and all the Atlantic provinces between Brittany and Aquitaine. The royal party, desperate to get King Jean out of captivity, capitulated and the complex formalities were completed. King Edward's emissary went to Paris to address the Estates General. The answer was no. It is possible that Edward always had hoped that the terms of the treaty would be rejected. Maybe he wanted an excuse for going to war again. In June of 1359 the writs and proclamations began to flow out of the Edward's government machine.⁵

The darkest hour is always just before the dawn. It is the year after Poitiers. King Jean is still in captivity and peace negotiations are under way. But the English terms are so tough, requiring big transfers of territory and huge ransom payments that they are moving glacially slowly. France is in a state of chaos.

* * *

In May of that year a strange proposal came through via the diplomatic system – about the same time that the French Ambassador was on his way back to England with the news that the representatives of the French people would not accept the punitive Treaty of London. Ambassadors of the King of Denmark had a remarkable proposal for Charles. The King of Denmark wanted nothing less than to lead an invasion of England.

Waldemar III of Denmark was a warrior king who won battles. He was one of the founders of the modern state of Denmark and he unified his kingdom, more or less within its modern borders. We can guess that he did not want his northern state to be a small political entity on the fringes of European affairs. Nor had Denmark always been on the fringes. Under King Cnut the Great, Denmark had been part of a North Sea empire that included England and Norway as well as Denmark. Waldemar's ancestors had been a power in England when Duke William invaded. Indeed, on two occasions after 1066 the Norman hold on England was threatened. During the anti-Norman rebellion in Northumbria a Danish fleet was stationed in the Humber estuary waiting to help the rebels. And, more seriously perhaps, in 1085 King Cnut IV put together a huge army of mercenaries for an invasion of England via East Anglia – a move that panicked the Normans and which might have brought the Normans down if King Cnut had not been murdered in a court intrigue. It appears that Waldemar still had hopes of creating a 'Greater Denmark' that would be a significant

European power. And he had never been happy about the Norman takeover of the English state.[6] In his own words,

> ... the King of Denmark wishes to do this for three reasons.
>
> He says and maintains in truth that the Kingdom of England belongs to him ... and that his predecessors were disinherited badly and without reason
>
> The next – to avenge the losses and wars that the kings of England have done to him
>
> The final one – for the love that our king has for the French crown.

The impossible English demands of 600,000 gold écus from a France whose economy and infrastructure were badly damaged, and whose population was shrunken as a result of the Black Death, gave him his entrée. The Danish Ambassadors met with Charles just after the Estates General had rejected the English ransom proposal. For a French subsidy of 300,000 gold écus Waldemar would assemble a huge army of 12,000 fighters. He knew a lot about assembling armies as he had taken part in 'crusades' against the pagan Baltic peoples. He also asked for the hand of one of the French royal princesses in marriage. He would assemble an army, hire the shipping and organise the logistics. The 'Auld Alliance' between Scotland and France was to be revived. After all, they shared one thing, a king in English captivity. The army would land in Scotland and fight its way south through Northumbria to the city of Lincoln, less than 200 miles from Berwick on the Scottish border. There they would capture the French king, return him to where he belonged in France and, in the meantime, deal a huge blow to English pretensions. Who can say what more Waldemar might have achieved? The total destruction of the English ruling classes? A second Danish dynasty in England? At the very least a useful dynastic link to Europe's leading kingdom.

All sides were keen on the idea, with some reservations. The representatives of the regions of France, such as the assembly of Languedoc were, in theory, interested – but they had no money. They could only provide some fighting forces, and a much smaller sum of money, provided every region was prepared to do the same. The Scots sent ambassadors to meet with the royal leaders in Paris, but they too had no funds at their disposal. Like France, the Scots had a king in captivity, and they too were asked to pay a huge ransom to get him back. The Chamberlain of Scotland, Robert Erskine, arrived in Paris where he spent time with Charles. They agreed to work with the French for a fee of 50,000 écus. It was the turn of Charles and his ministers to raise the fee from his subjects, who had been bled dry by the disasters of recent years.

Despite having made promises, none of the bodies that the Dauphin's agents approached actually raised any money. The Scottish Ambassadors returned to Scotland without any promise of action. Waldemar's project never got off the ground and the King of Denmark disappeared from English and French history.

This episode may seem peripheral in our history, and the Dauphin, inexperienced and overwhelmed with crises as he was, may have been naive in giving his support to Waldemar's project. But from this time onwards, a strategy was emerging whereby the France could rid itself of the menace of an aggressive and militarised England, turning the tables by taking the war across the English Channel. And Waldemar and his armies reappeared in later years.

In October the Scottish delegation wound up their deliberations with Erskine returning to Scotland, while his companion joined the French Queen's forces in Burgundy, ironically only to be captured by a group of routiers.[7]

While the Waldemar project was doing the rounds in France, Denmark and Scotland, Edward had thrown himself into action again. The negative response from the French Estates General was a danger signal. We can guess that English spies in France might also have picked up whispers of the Dano-Franco-Scottish invasion plan to sidestep the punitive Treaty of London.

The year 1359 was another of climatic disturbance at the start of the Little Ice Age. All over the Northern Hemisphere temperatures through the 1350s were low. In the summer of 1938 rain fell continually on English and French alike and 1359 was a particularly cold year. The chronicler Fordun says of heavy rains in northern Britain:[8]

> ... such a great inundation burst forth ... that from the time of Noah until the present day the likes had not been known ... crops also and cut stubble ... were with damage ... dragged away from the use of men to places far and near.

During the winter 1359/60 the Deputy Marshal of France (his chief was with the king in captivity in England), Jean de Neuville, with the assistance and support of the Comité de Normandie and Dauphin Charles himself started to put together a re-run of the Waldemar operation. It was far more modest and would not involve Scottish friends. It would be more in the nature of a daring raid. A quick landing, a cross-country raid and a fast getaway having been never more than 30 miles from the coast.

Neuville planned to transport a force of about 2,000 troops from northern France in 200 ships. Over the cold wet winter work went on assembling the ships, men and materiel needed for the well-focussed raid. The port of Le Crotoy at the mouth of the River Somme was the mustering point. The incursion could only have a chance of success if the plans were kept secret. It was difficult to keep secrets in the fourteenth century. In the case of these two enemies, France and England, countries whose upper classes were so closely linked by language, and aristocratic and chivalric culture, not to mention marriage and generational family histories, it appears again and again that plans that should have stayed top secret were far from that, thus thwarting, in many cases, the purpose of the operation that was being planned.

De Neuville's plan was an example of this. Edward's council had ships reconnoitring the Channel coast of France as a routine precaution and very early in the year they must have noticed a build-up of ships in the broad harbour of the Somme estuary. The English response to this undefined threat was to put into operation the system that had been created in the early years of Edward's war with France. It is a tribute to the efficient and responsive fiscal system that Edward had created to fund his wars that this system seems to have been working, although the shores of England had not been threatened for more than ten years. All along the south and east coasts, ships were arrested. The entire population of fencible age were arrayed, and the right to tax was devolved from the Westminster parliament to the costal county courts, at the same rate as had been used when Edward was raising his armies to fight on the Continent. Cash raised was deposited in safe boxes in local cathedrals, to be used when needed.[9]

When he bade farewell at the start of the expedition, it appears that Neuville had announced his intention of rescuing King Jean from his captivity in Lincolnshire, but we can guess that word had got around even earlier. Before the arrival of the fleet in English waters the defence forces were concentrated in East Kent, especially Sandwich, and the Thames Estuary.[10]

Tellingly, the King of France himself was moved from his residence in the Lincolnshire Wolds to Berkhamstead, north west of London, further from the sea than Somerton, and unlike Somerton Castle on Ermine Street, his new abode was a fully defended and defensible motte and bailey castle, built originally by Edward's ancestor William the Conqueror. Both Edward III and his son the Prince of Wales had used Berkhamstead Castle as a residence, so we can assume that the accommodation was of regal standard, which might have been a form of compensation for the indignity of Jean's sudden removal, and that of the more than fifty people in his entourage.

The next part of the story is hard to interpret. It is said that de Neuville intended to land on the East Anglian coast and move inland to Somerton but he did not know where Somerton was, and landed in Sandwich instead. This is highly unlikely. For a long time there had been close maritime relations between the French and the English, despite the ongoing fighting. Walton and Great Yarmouth were both major ports at the time. The Isabella and Mortimer invasion of England had been via Walton and it is surely unlikely that a major naval expedition was being launched by the French without some basic knowledge of where to go and what to look out for while following the coasts. In our opinion it is far more likely Neuville's intelligence network and spies had told him that the aim of the expedition had been discovered and that King Jean would be moved away from Somerton. In this case, it seems likely that Neuville decided to continue but to switch to the type of expedition that the French had carried out in the 1330s and '40s.

Neuville's invasion fleet sailed out of Le Crotoy at the end of February. The same cold rains that fell on Edward's army fell on de Neuville – but the weather pattern that brought the rains came from the Arctic, meaning winds from the north-east. We can guess that what was now a French revenge attack might well wish to descend on the port that had been used by the English as a base for operations against France – Somerton. They struggled for two weeks to round the East Kent Peninsula, in vain. They were beaten back by cold, wet winds from the north-east. As would be natural, the fleet veered away, following the white cliffs that stretched along the coast for 20 miles. The Monegasque-Genoese 1339 invasion had followed the same route that had led them to the Rother Valley and the twin towns of Rye and Winchelsea.

The coastal areas around from the Kent coast northwards had been put on alert by Edward's deputies as soon as news of the forthcoming raid got out and it is quite possible that watchers on the coast could have followed the movements of the fleet as it went west along the Channel – and perhaps the uninhabited area of Romney Marsh was a gap in the coastal defence system, so that once the fleet was beyond the shingle beach and into Sussex, the coastal watchers were not operating, and this made an unopposed landing a possibility.

As previously mentioned, Winchelsea's hilltop location gave it a commanding position. It had been laid out a hundred years earlier by Edward's grandfather, with a regular grid of streets so that it looked like a bastide in south west France, such as Montségur. Winchelsea was one of England's wealthiest fishing towns, alongside Great Yarmouth and Hull, made rich by the incredibly plentiful North Sea and Channel herrings. It was also a key port dealing with the importation of Gascony wine and its merchant houses all had huge cellars for the storage of wine barrels. It appears that many of its inhabitants spoke French. At the start of the fourteenth century the relatively new town was on its way to being a leading coastal settlement – but the Hundred Year's war had not been good to Winchelsea.

We can imagine the scene from Winchelsea, overlooking the harbour. The ships would have been highly decorated in the usual style of military vessels of the time. The cogs would have had forecastles and after castles, probably brightly painted in livery colours. There would have been heraldic devices a-plenty. There could well have been French fleurs-de-lis devices on the sails of the ships. And the horses, knights, men-at-arms and archers would have been pressed close together on the decks, as packed as a football crowd.

As the fleet approached, the sound of imminent warfare would have terrified the local people; drums, cornets, war chants – all designed to disorientate and thereby increase the impact of the massed ranks of iron-clad knights.

At the same time the routine to be followed in case of invasion would have been in operation, including the continuous ringing of church bells. By the time the fleet drewn up along the foreshore and the soldiers disembarked, the entire population would either have run away to raise the alarm, or hidden in the nearest fortified stone building, namely a church. There is no record of any organised resistance. A large number of the townspeople were massacred – men, women, children. The operation that had started as an attempt to free the French king from captivity degenerated into a bloodletting.

One young woman was raped repeatedly by soldiers until she died or was murdered, then the group turned on another, older woman. Others were 'exposed to even more hideous atrocities'. Apart from any individuals who seemed to have some monetary value and were held hostage, many were tortured in order to extract useful information. The raiding party went through the town cellars and removed barrels of Gascon wine. Also waiting to be exported was wool, and tin from Cornish mines. Everything was removed, ready to be loaded onto the cogs. Next morning the raiders set fire to the town, as was to be expected.

It has been said that the invaders had received word from some of their prisoners that levies were on their way. This is difficult to understand. If the citizens of Winchelsea had known that levies were on their way to the landing point, why did they not organise themselves to oppose the landing the previous day? It is more likely that the prisoners would have told the French that people in the surrounding villages, once they saw the fleet landing, would have spread the alarm, possibly by lighting beacons, and by riding as fast as possible through the cold and rain to spread the news. The passage of the French fleet along the coast of Kent and Sussex must have been watched by many people, including the population of Rye and Winchelsea. But when the fleet sailed into Rye Harbour the leaders of each town would have conferred, and sent messengers to their nearest

Commissioner of Array in order to get help. The Abbot of Battle was located about 12 miles away, maybe one-and-a-half-hours' journey over waterlogged tracks. As soon as the Abbott received the news, the well-oiled call-up procedures would have moved into action, and by the following day the response was ready. It is a tribute to the efficiency of the Edwardian war machine that the following day the Abbott was able to organise such an effective response.

The following morning the militias arrived, while the looting was still going on. They were able to enter the town and kill as many as 160 of the soldiers – but too late to save many of the inhabitants, too late to stop the removal of Winchelsea's entire moveable wealth, too late to stop the burning of the town and of its ships. The French retreated, and made their way in marching order along the foreshore to their ships, followed by the English. Their ships would have been moored as close inshore as possible, but the waters of the estuary were shallow so the French, wading through the water and weighed down with loot and weaponry, made it easy for the English to pursue them into the water. As many as 300 of the raiders lost their lives at this last moment, some killed, and some drowned.

While the English had good reason to be proud of their retaliation, the fact was that the French had inflicted real economic damage on their enemy. From now on England had to stay to a greater or lesser extent in a state of readiness, devoting resources to defence. Three years later 409 properties are recorded as being in ruins – and seven years later, in 1370, only 36 of these had been rebuilt.[11] Winchelsea lost almost all of its population during that raid and the town was only effectively repopulated in later years.

* * *

Let's return to Charles – the young Dauphin. Few royals in history could have assumed power under less auspicious circumstances than Charles Valois. He was only eighteen years old and although he had been close to royal power all his life, his life experience was gained in the chaos of France while Edward was in the process of demolishing it as a state. His father Jean had not been known for his political judgement, and Charles had shown himself to be easily influenced by unworthy role models such as King Charles of Navarre.

Meanwhile in England, King Edward's future looked bright. For as long as Edward III was able to lead his armies into battle he was almost always successful, emerging the victor. During the whole of Edward's entire career as an on-the-ground fighting man there was not a single occasion when he led an army to defeat against an enemy in a set-piece battle. But in the words of the nineteenth-century war strategist, 'war is a means to achieve diplomatic aims when diplomacy has failed'. Edward's overall strategy was to become king of France. In 1359 Edward embarked on an invasion whose climax would have been Edward III of England crowning himself king of France in the Cathedral of Rheims. Rheims was well-chosen as it was relatively near the English Channel, and close to both English-held Calais and Valenciennes, in the territory of his allies in Hainault. It was the ancient place of coronation of French kings, and Edward was a descendent of many of them. Once he was crowned king, then he could impose his will on the French and collect the ransom money that was owing to him. These war aims were designed to humiliate.

From May onwards the writs and proclamations flowed out from Edward's cabinet. Edward was back in action doing what he probably liked best, preparing for war and preparing to get out on the battle trail. If the campaign were successful, and why should it not be successful against an enemy that had already been routed, it would allow Edward to retain the territories that he considered he had won fairly in battle. Throughout the summer the preparations continued, in a kingdom flush with money this was to be the biggest and best-equipped army ever.

As was usual in Edward's England, although the decision to put together an invasion force had been taken in spring, it was not until October of that year, while it was still raining, when the failed harvest would already have been and gone and the average rustic would already be suffering from the effects of a dearth of food, that the 1,100 ships were ready to go. Significantly, the fleet was well stocked with food supplies in the expectation of there being none available in France. Although this does not get a mention in the chronicles, the presence of Edward's suppliers scouring the countryside for rations would have exacerbated the serious food shortage.

According to Edward's thinking, the fact that the French state had collapsed meant that France had no army, which meant that the timing was perfect. There would be no opposition to his forces so he would easily take control. Edward could not have been more wrong.

The plan was to land in English Calais and join up with other troops waiting there, then to march through the French countryside some 130 miles to Rheims (about the same distance that Waldemar had planned to cover between Berwick-on-Tweed and Somerton Castle) on the river Marne, where Edward intended to have himself crowned king of France. Then he would move on to Paris and assume the reins of power.

The English were not planning on taking part in a set-piece battle. What they were hoping for was the chance of a good chevauchée – ransack houses, steal moveable wealth, take all portable food, and destroy the non-portable kind; then wait outside Rheims until the starved inhabitants gave in. Finally, go through the coronation ceremony and then move on, taking over the rest of France.

Meanwhile the Dauphin and his counsellors were using a tactic known to Edward from his wars with the Scots and since then applied in his dealings with the French, namely the scorched earth policy. And this time the climatic disruption was to Charles Valois' benefit. As Napoleon would discover retreating from Moscow through a Russian winter, the climate curse could be potent. In the fourteenth century, it had turned on Edward, the Pride of England. Orders had been sent out to the French citizens that they were to remove themselves from the area occupied by Edward's army. All dwellings and other buildings were to be vacated, stripped, and burnt. No supplies or goods of any sort were to be available. In autumn and winter, the weather got worse; after a summer of incessant downpours, the rain was turning to hail and sleet. Horses sank up to their bellies in clinging mud and developed sores under their saddles. The 9-mile baggage train was bogged down – the English army used to be lean and fast but as Edward was approaching the ripe age of fifty, his army was fat and unwieldy.

Each fortress they came to had been vacated and slighted. Each walled town was the same. Not even a farm building remained intact to be looted. It was all the army could do to move 10 miles in a day. Even Rheims was a disaster. By the time they approached it, soldiers had begun to die of disease – dysentery and typhoid in all likelihood. Their supplies were used up and hunger was wasting the army. The inhabitants of Rheims were on their own, without any assistance from the government in Paris and they had to defend themselves. They were lucky in that the city walls, the lower parts dating back to the Roman period, were in reasonable shape. Working parties had been quickly organised to mend the walls and to block up most of the city gates. Defensive trenches were dug, and a no-man's-land of razed ground was created around the walls. Any surviving supplies from the surrounding countryside were taken inside the walls. When the English arrived, the citizens of Rheims were better placed to withstand the siege than the English, who were now in terrible physical condition. The siege lasted less than four weeks and at the start of January Edward's army abandoned the attempt and moved on through a muddy desert.

Edward was now approaching Paris, and peace offers from the French were being rejected as Edward was insisting the French accept the terms of the Treaty of London, giving him the whole of Maritime Atlantic France. By 5 April Edward's army was outside the city. The sky of Paris was lit with the flames of war, the extra-mural suburbs were being burnt by the English, and there were skirmishes at the very gates of the city. Edward wanted an open battle but did not get one, so he and his army marched on to the cathedral city of Chartres. Again the French did not emerge from behind their fortifications, so a siege was his only alternative.

The date 13 April 1360 has gone down in history as Black Monday, and it marks the end of Edward's trajectory of success that had begun when King Jean was captured. That Easter Monday saw what may have been the greatest storm that occurred during the onset of the Little Ice Age. Darkness came on during the day, the temperature plummeted so low that ice started to fall out of the sky. The hailstones were so big that they killed both men and horses. It is recorded that up to 1,000 people in the English army died – and maybe 6,000 horses. Were the hailstones really so big that they actually killed upon impact? It is possible. A hailstorm in Bangladesh in 1958 killed as many as 90 people. But it is also possible that the icy storm was just the last straw, adding hypothermia and impact damage to men and horses weakened by months of inadequate nutrition and relentless exposure to cold, wet conditions.

By 2 May, in the nearby village of Brétigny, a treaty was signed between the French and the English ambassadors, returning to the terms of the Second London Treaty.[12]

In July King Jean landed back on French soil in Harfleur, but his journey to Paris was not a happy one. He was reportedly moved to tears at the devastation that he saw during his journey through Normandy. There was no trace of agriculture to be seen in the hundred miles south of the English Channel, and there was not a single building left standing, right up to the walls of Paris. In the areas of the north which had been most exposed to the depredations of war, in the wake of the loss of population in the famine and the Black Death, the depopulation was worst. It was said that many towns in the area of Bayeux had lost all their inhabitants. In the areas that had been most affected by the English, the inhabitants had simply moved away into the hilly regions to the south. In the Isle de France the situation was as bad, and the number of households in Argenteuil had dropped from as many as 700 to sixty or seventy. Over the following years Charles, the Dauphin and later the King of France, was to fight hard to restore order and to expel the mercenary soldiers who regularly plundered the country when not employed. Much of this fight was led by individual loyalist warriors, dedicated to the reconstruction of their country.[13]

* * *

After the Treaty of Brétigny had been signed, promising peace between England and France, as well as a huge transfer of funds from France to England, there were many signals that Edward did not consider that his war aims had been achieved. He was back home in England and the collapse of the French state meant that there was no immediate threat from France on the horizon. As an indication of his thinking, one project that took up Edward's attention in the following years, when he had more leisure and the cash to allow him to enjoy it, was the fortification of the entrance to the Thames Estuary. The fact that he undertook major defensive works when there appeared to be no foreign threat indicates that Edward did not believe that the peace would last. In the more than twenty years of war since the 1330s there had been thirty landings by France and her allies on English territory, but none nearer than the entrance to the Thames Estuary and as far as we know, no enemy fleet had ever approached London itself. As early as 1338 when England's defensive infrastructure was being set up, London had not been overlooked. The fact that Edward now took this opportunity to spend a lot of money to fortify the entrance to the Thames shows us that people in the know in Edward's court and government machine saw more trouble ahead. They were correct, there was.

Edward had been back in England only for a few months and in the spring of 1361 the royal administration commissioned works on the Isle of Sheppey, with construction of the only new fortified castle to be built in England since the early Middle Ages under way. The site was strategically well chosen. The entrance to the Thames north of the Isle of Sheppey would have been clearly visible from the top of the fortifications, and the location also commands the entrance to the River Medway. Shipping hidden in the River Medway would have been ready to intercept the invaders. This structure possessed living quarters for King Edward and Queen Philippa, and he seems to have had a special liking for the building as he named the settlement next to the fort 'Queenborough' after his queen. The castle was circular – a shape that did not become the norm until more than a hundred years later, when it was associated with the need to build walls that would resist the new gunpowder technology of heavy cannon designed to break down castle walls.

On the north side of the estuary on the Essex shore, on the top of some low clay cliffs, was its sister structure, Hadleigh Castle. It had been built more than 150 years earlier, but along with with the construction of Queenborough Castle Edward also started to improve this fortress, building the fine crenellated walls that fit on top of the natural mound that gives it such a commanding position. These two great structures on the Thames, near the entrance to the capital city, give us a hint of what the English defenders were afraid of. A great fleet, maybe an alliance of the French with others – Castilians, Danes, Navarrese, who knows? – appearing out of the North Sea, overwhelming local defenders, sailing onwards, landing on the shoreline of the estuary and fanning out across southern England until the French Royal standard flew in Westminster![14]

At about the same time that Edward was fortifying the Thames against possible future French incursions, his chancery was issuing orders that effectively put the civilian population of England nearly on a war footing. In 1363 archery practice was made compulsory for all adult males on Sundays and feast days. So called 'idle games' such as cockfighting, football, handball and quoits were formally banned. This was a reiteration of the ruling that had been issued in the relative peace after the Black Death running its course. People who broke this law could be imprisoned.[15]

It must have seemed at this time that the English campaigns in France had brought peace to the shores of England, but a change of leadership in France opened up the possibility of a new generation of threats to English security. The hapless King Jean did not enjoy his freedom back in Paris for long. His son Louis had been sent to England as one of the hostages to ensure the remaining payment of King Jean's ransom, but when his son escaped and refused to return to England Jean II himself returned to England and took up residence again in the Savoy Palace, trying to negotiate deals that never quite gelled. King Jean had never been a healthy person, and holed up in his London residence in a London suffering a resurgence of the plague his body gave up the struggle in 1364.[16]

The Dauphin Charles was now King Charles V. He had inherited the Valois sickliness, and he had been thrown into the political deep end after Poitiers. He was small, pallid, physically weak, and in an age when many kings led from the saddle of a horse he was unable to match the feats in arms of an Edward III or a Black Prince.[17]

When he was Dauphin Charles had taken on the task of resolving the revolution in Paris, of removing enemy bands from the countryside, and of imposing some sort of order upon the economic chaos of the French state. After the death of his father the king he continued in the same direction, and in a few years some form of normality was returning to France.

One example of the reconstruction was an event in eastern France, near the city of Besancon at the end of 1362 when a company of routiers, made up of mixed English and Gascon soldiers, were preying on the peasantry of the region, pillaging and burning. Then they attempted an audacious plan against the city of Besancon itself, with an attack followed by a pillaging of the entire city, tactics far more profitable than merely attacking villages and farmhouses. The attempt failed when a group of fighters led by Jean de Vienne, the nephew of the burgher of Calais who surrendered to Edward III, retaliated.

Early in 1363 the company of routiers was near the banks of the River L'Ognon, close the small town of Chambornay. They were continuing their usual business of looting, pillaging, raping and killing peasants and other defenceless inhabitants of the region. Jean de Vienne, a young knight and member of a well-known military family known as 'Les Viennois' was, at the age of twenty-three, riding out from Besancon with a group of friends and fellow warriors, most of them as young as he was. The Gascon leader, Guichard Monnet, was described as being *'grosse et grand'*. Jean de Vienne and his friends were *'moult esbais'*, very terrified, as they faced up to this group of hardened bandits, all multiple murderers who would kill without a second thought. We can guess that when the company from Besancon tracked them down they were not alone. Rather they were near the village of Chambornay and we can guess that they had already turned on the local people and were carrying out a reign of terror in the area.

At this point Jean de Vienne bravely challenged Guichard Monnet to single combat. They chose to fight on horseback, with lances. They charged each other and Jean de Vienne planted the perfect blow on his adversary, killing him instantly as his lance pierced his armour.

Then the entire company from Besancon went for the routiers, hammering them in fights, scattering and disarming them, and rendering them helpless. As a young aristocratic leader, fully signed up to the principles of chivalry, Jean de Vienne did not choose to massacre the broken company of defeated brigands. Rather he turned the troupe over to the local inhabitants to deal with as they saw fit. We can imagine that their hatred was given its full expression in a mass killing of knights by peasants and villagers in a variety of cruel ways.

Jean de Vienne's leadership in this battle came to the attention of King Charles. Jean was given the title of Constable. A small village in his native Franche-Comté provided an income for him. This engagement was the start of a distinguished career in the service of King Charles. Jean de Vienne was soon to become a leading figure in the history of the raids, invasions and incursions of the following period of the fourteenth century.[18]

Charles became known as 'Le Sage' (The Wise) in recognition that he had a strategic vision and that he was able to plan. He carried out a sweeping reorganisation of French military potential, making it easier to enrol fighters when necessary. Like Edward at the start of the 1360s, Charles ordered improvements to castles, city fortifications and ports. Fortifications were the dominant form of fourteenth-century architecture. The financial difficulties that Philippe had experienced in the earlier years of the war became a thing of the past, as the State took more money-raising powers to itself. Under the pressure of war, France was putting its old feudal complexities behind it, and was beginning to gear up to being a more centralised, active State.

At about the time that Charles was taking the reins of power in France his recently appointed military leader Jean de Vienne was on his way to Venice to carry out his Christian duty of fighting the enemies of the Church.

In the Eastern Mediterranean the Seljuk Turks were taking territory from the Byzantine Empire, and they had established themselves as a Mediterranean power. The Eastern and Western Christian churches had for a long time been split. The Byzantine Emperor John Paleaologus was related through marriage to the Count of Savoy, Amadeus – known as the 'Comte Vert'. When Emperor John was captured while on a diplomatic mission to the Bulgar King Shishman and taken into captivity, the patience of the Westerners reached its limit. Pope Urban called a crusade against the Turks and although the Bulgars were Orthodox Christians like Emperor John, they were also targeted. The crusade was led by Amadeus but knights came from all over Europe – from Germany, Provence, Genoa, Monaco and France.

Jean de Vienne had been fighting on the side of his king, trying to restore order, and squeeze out from French territory the bandits and irregulars who had been destroying his nation. It was hard, dirty work involving unpleasant small-scale brutalities day by day. Perhaps Jean de Vienne needed an adventure – to get away from the cold, rain, destruction and chaos of post-Poitiers France – and by participating in a crusade fighting the infidels he would gain credit in the afterlife. In addition, very important for his future, he would be able to advance his career by mixing with the international fighting elite of Europe.

The crusade assembled in Venice. The streets of the city were crowded with warriors looking for transport through the Adriatic, round the Peloponnese, to Constantinople and who knows how much farther? In an age when knights would dress up in their best attire they must have been an extraordinary sight with their burnished armour, heraldic surpluses, shields with matching motifs, powerful chargers, many with armour and surpluses matching those of their owners.

The logistics of matching hundreds of fighting men and their supporters with available shipping to launch the crusade were huge. The coordination of a huge fleet, passing commands around the flotilla, coordinating landings, coordinating supplies, all the aspects of the journey from Venice to Constantinople and beyond was complex. It is not surprising that the Grimaldis had joined the Crusades, and their knowledge and expertise was valuable in captaining ships on the 1,300-mile journey from Venice to Constantinople.

As chance would have it, Jean de Vienne travelled to Constantinople on the ship that was captained by Rainier Grimaldi. It appears that Jean de Vienne's abilities were recognised by the Monegasque prince, and as a result Jean de Vienne learnt about seamanship on this journey. He was forming a relationship with the Grimaldis that was to develop in the future, and between them they would leave their mark on England's coastal society.

The crusade of the Comte Vert achieved its objectives, each incursion onto enemy territory was a success and accompanied by a high level of violence. Possibly Jean de Vienne's experiences in the Eastern Mediterranean successfully taking part in incursions against a hated enemy recommended him later to his king, Charles 'the Wise', who wanted a leader who could fight and at the same time organise ships and fighters.

After the fleet had left the Adriatic and turned east towards Constantinople and the Black Sea, it stopped in the Venetian port of Coron, in the south of modern Greece, to meet up with the crusaders from southern France and Spain. It was possibly here that Jean de Vienne met with Carlos Grimaldi for the first time, and began to form his relationship with him. The next stop was Gallipoli, on the European shore of the Dardanelles, commanding the

A map showing all invasion sites mentioned in the text. There are two invasion fronts: one from the Continent, and one from Scotland. Scottish ships were active as far south as Sark. (Author's collection)

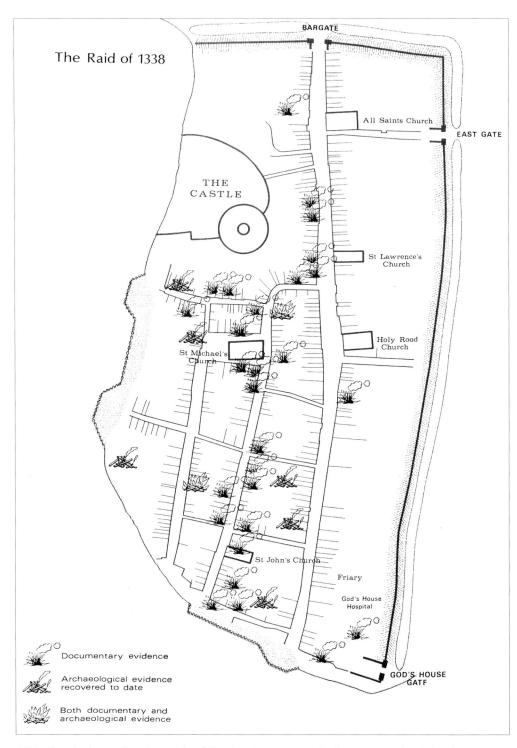

The Raid of 1338

BARGATE

THE CASTLE

All Saints Church

EAST GATE

St Lawrence's Church

Holy Rood Church

St Michael's Church

St John's Church

Friary

God's House Hospital

GOD'S HOUSE GATE

Documentary evidence

Archaeological evidence recovered to date

Both documentary and archaeological evidence

This sketch shows the aftermath of the Southampton raid of 1338. Much of the destruction would have been to high-quality but flammable merchants' houses, with valuable goods stored in cellars.

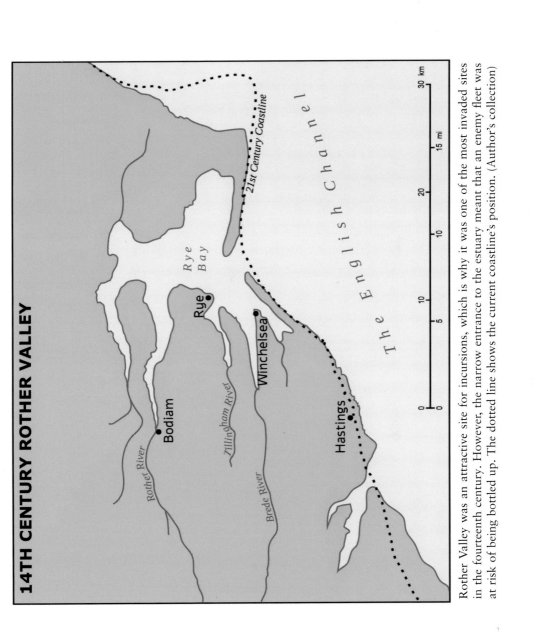

14TH CENTURY ROTHER VALLEY

Rother Valley was an attractive site for incursions, which is why it was one of the most invaded sites in the fourteenth century. However, the narrow entrance to the estuary meant that an enemy fleet was at risk of being bottled up. The dotted line shows the current coastline's position. (Author's collection)

The wooden-framed houses houses of Rye were often subjected to raids. (Author's collection)

The Bargate in Southampton, a fine defence against land invaders from the north. (Courtesy of Geni under Creative Commons)

Right and below: Living above the shop, fourteenth-century style. The contents of a cellar would help recoup the expenses of a raid, and its value was shared out according to an agreed formula. (Courtesy of Geni under Creative Commons)

The inside of a rich merchant's house with its cellar for storing goods.

Above left and right: The *Luttrell Psalter* (*c.*1325–1335) shows what ordinary people were doing during the period. Peasants are rarely portrayed, despite forming the vast majority of the population.

Below left and right: The woollen industry was one of the mainstays of the English economy, generating government revenue at each stage from live animal to finished cloth, as depicted in this set of images from the *Luttrell Psalter*.

Above: Archery practice was compulsory for many men for much of the period. This depiction from the *Luttrell Psalter* would have been a familiar sight in any English village on a Sunday.

Left: Sir Geoffrey Luttrell III was the lord of the manor of Irnham in Lincolnshire. War involved display, and the very highest-status leaders rode off to battle magnificently apparelled. For a poor knight, looting and hostage-taking could help generate the capital required to put on this type of display.

The cog, with its single sail and broad, capacious hull, was the workhorse of English trade and a familiar sight in England's trading settlements.

Once a cog had been converted to military use it had a very different appearance. Its castles fore and aft, and on the masts, plus the war pennants and shields, meant danger.

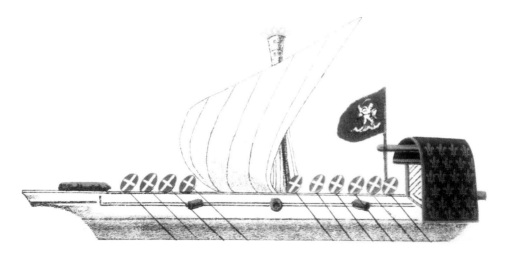

Mediterranean-style galleys were almost unknown along English coasts. A galley manned by sailors from the Mediterranean was not a welcome sight.

A fleet of ships ready for battle, designed to terrify. The Oriflamme flying beside the French fleur-de-lys meant that the King of France was at war. For those in the know, the many heraldic devices were a medieval 'who's who'. (Courtesy of the British Library)

Both a royal residence and a high-status prison, the Tower of London played a key role in Isabella's plot against her husband Edward II. (Courtesy of Dave Addey under Creative Commons)

A fifteenth-century manuscript illustration of Isabella of France with Roger Mortimer. Isabella is shown here at the head of an army with her non-royal lover. (Courtesy of the British Library)

Above: The three Edwards. Edwards I and III look like what they were – warrior kings who won wars. Edward II is portrayed without any fighting spirit, while Edward III has two crowns impaled on his sword. (Courtesy of the Rijksmuseum)

Left: King Edward III, wearing clothes decorated with the Order of the Garter, a richly jewelled crown and the arms of England and France over plate armour and spurs. (Courtesy of the British Library)

Right: The coat of arms of Edward III, who claimed the French throne in 1340. This coat of arms was calculated to enrage any French supporter with its presumption to the French throne. Yet it remained the royal coat of arms until the time of Napoleon.

Below: An older Edward III depicted in an illuminated manuscript. (Courtesy of the British Library)

Above: *The Battle of Crécy between the English and French in the Hundred Years' War*, from an illuminated manuscript of Jean Froissart's *Chronicles*. The victorious English are on the right.

Left: The capture of King Jean at Poitiers. The French king, dressed in a fleur-de-lys tunic, was taken alive and uninjured. The rules of chivalry meant his captor, the Prince of Wales, was to entertain him with a lavish banquet that very day. (Courtesy of the Bibliothèque Nationale de France)

No warrior king, the sickly King Charles the Wise nevertheless built a powerful French state that was able to take on the English menace before his early death. This painting is entitled *Charles V, known as The Wise, King of France (1337–1380)* and is by Gillot Saint-Eve. It belongs to *Portraits of Kings of France*, a series commissioned between 1837 and 1838 by Louis Philippe I and painted by various artists for the *Musée historique de Versailles*.

King Charles with his closest courtiers. Admiral Jean de Vienne is standing in the bottom right, with the eagle from his coat of arms on his breast. He was a rational and competent leader who ultimately failed in his lifetime of fighting the English, perhaps through bad luck.

Carisbrook Castle on the Isle of Wight was strengthened in the course of the fourteenth century, with crenelations, barbicans and bigger walls making it more secure, although the defenders surrendered when besieged in 1377. (Top: Author's collection; bottom: courtesy of Medwaymark)

Above: Mont Orgueil Castle on Jersey appears impregnable but did not protect the Channel Islands from invasion during the period. (Courtesy of Dan Marsh under Creative Commons)

Right: This manuscript illumination shows King Edward III granting the Black Prince the principality of Aquitaine. The two Edwards are dressed to lead armies into battle to reaffirm their ownership of the principality. (Courtesy of the British Library)

Cr parle dune grant feste que le kov richard denofleterie fift a londres

Above: The Dukes of York, Gloucester and Ireland dine with King Richard II. This scene illustrates the elaborate court style of the fourteenth century. The new high-status fashion of tights, pointed slippers and short tunics revealing buttocks was considered shocking by many, although even in battle such clothing was worn (*see cover*). (Courtesy of the British Library)

Left: Isabella of France landing near Orford with her son, the future Edward III, in 1326. (Courtesy of the Bibliothèque Nationale de France)

entrance to the Black Sea. It had been taken from Byzantine territory by Sultan Murat, and he had used it as an entrepôt for the spoils looted from the ancient cities of the Byzantine Empire, filled with centuries of riches. As the chronicler Rainaldi put it, Gallipoli was 'a very well-defended Greek port, to which the Turks were accustomed to carry the "sad" spoils taken from the European Christians, with whom they had fought'.

Count Amadeus led the landing, with the Turks ranged along the shore firing barbed and poisoned arrows at the crusaders. The crusaders were wearing full armour for the most part, which meant that they were able to continue their charge unabated. The Turks retreated to the fortress of Gallipoli but the crusaders were able to follow them in and, amazingly enough, the Turks fled, leaving Gallipoli to the Europeans. The huge store of valuables was taken away by the victors, which ensured that financially the expedition was going to be a success.

The Turkish system was to capture Christian children, and to train them to be high-class military slaves, adding professional ferocity to their military machine. In Gallipoli the Europeans were able to liberate many captive children and adolescents of Greek background, whom they took to Constantinople and delivered them into the arms of their Christian monarch. This act made the crusade doubly successful. By saving Christian souls from infidel captivity the true spiritual purpose of a crusade was being achieved, bringing benefits to men such as Jean de Vienne who was part of the expedition.

The highlight of the campaign however, came when the fleet entered the Black Sea and landed in Varna where the King of Bulgaria was holding Emperor John Palaeologus captive. Varna was an ancient Roman fortress, very well defended against attack. The season was passing, the weather was getting cold, and the crusaders were getting restless. It is an indication of how far Jean de Vienne had come in the knightly hierarchy that he was one of the two people appointed to talk sense to the Bulgarian king. The Bulgar was persuaded that it was better to stay on the side of the Christians rather than throwing in his lot with the Islamic hordes, and Emperor John returned to Constantinople in triumph, as did his new companions, including Jean de Vienne. When Jean do Vienne returned to his homeland he had gained in status and in experience. As a result of his abilities and achievements he was reaching the top of the tree.[19]

* * *

Later in 1366 the Danish King Waldemar's ships made a landing in East Anglia and commenced the usual round of looting and killing. It has been suggested that the fleet had been engaged on another mission and were blown to shore by a gale. Despite the fact that the men in the crew were professional fighters, it appears that the defensive systems set up in the 1330s and 1340s to guard against French attacks were still in full operation; the local levies formed up quickly and repelled the raiders, who made a hurried departure.

It is very unlikely that this raid was just a single isolated episode because the following year the Danish monarch entered into a treaty with Scotland and Norway against the English and 'agreed to ravage the English islanders and, what is more, to plunder England'.[20]

So it is probable that the East Anglia landing was part of a bigger series of hostilities that did not make it into the works of the chroniclers nor into later history books. The eyes of the English nation at the time were focussed upon the war with France, and a small Danish raid in an out-of-the-way part of East Anglia may have been overlooked in the build-up to the resumption of war on both sides of the English Channel.

In the years after the Peace of Brétigny there had never been peace. The extent of fortifications being built or improved tells us that the English did not see peace stretching ahead into the future. There was not a single year after Brétigny when there were no English forces in action somewhere in Europe, and Charles VI, while he was no warrior monarch, systematically and wisely spent the post-treaty years in readying France for war.

After Edward's defeat by the French weather nine years earlier, he did not take part in any more fighting. He was forty-eight years old, and he seems to have been suffering from medical disabilities. Whatever they were, he was no longer the audacious and headstrong warrior king of his early years, when his very presence on the battlefield would bring luck to an enterprise. It is possible that he had suffered from a stroke, or perhaps he had some form of progressive brain damage caused by repeated concussion in battle.

King Edward had plenty of children with Queen Philippa but rather like a rich and successful father whose 'trust fund' children underachieve despite their father's help, Edward's sons were not made of the same stuff as their sire.

John of Gaunt, despite being one of the wealthiest and best-connected men of his time, was unable to lead armies with any success and seemed to lack political judgement. The Black Prince was unable to follow up his triumph at Poitiers and while fighting the French in Gascony he became sick, possibly with dysentery, and had to be carried around on a litter until his premature death. Of the young aristocrats who had accompanied Edward more than thirty years before through the secret tunnel in Nottingham Castle and took part in the audacious coup against Isabella and Mortimer, Edward was the last survivor.

On resumption of war in 1369 Edward toyed with the idea of leading a daring raid across the English Channel to Picardy. Instead of entering a ship, disembarking, mounting his horse, and leading from the front, he abandoned the idea. From now on the king took little part in leading his country, and his ministers and family were no substitute.[21]

While England was in a state of decline, perhaps inevitable in an age when government in so many ways depended upon the character and energy of the king, France had been through its own 'year zero' after Poitiers and, under a leader who was diametrically the opposite of everything that Edward had been in his prime, it began a recovery – it began to shape itself into a fighting nation rather than an ineffectual giant. In these years France entered into a training regime with the intention of ensuring that when the time came, the realm's speed, punch and stamina would be as good as or even better than that of its smaller rival, England. In the early years of his reign, Charles had issued a series of *ordonnances* making it easier to recruit fighters. This included increasing the number and training of archers, a good idea considering how much the English archer had contributed to the catastrophic defeats of the French knighthood on the battlefield during the previous decades. A system was set up to provide training for military service which, in fact, was essentially what had existed in England from the very early years of the century.

It is impossible to wage war without having a healthy cash flow coming into government coffers, to spend on arms, armour, payments to warriors and, probably the biggest single item of expenditure, ships and shipping. New taxes were introduced, the *gabelle, aide* and *taille* for example, and by dint of skilful leadership from the king they were now paid in all parts of the kingdom, unlike the old-fashioned system in which each region had its own laws. The naval dockyard of Clos des Galées was where much of that taxpayers' money ended up, creating a French navy ready to resume the struggle with England.

The ancient forests of the Isle de France were a royal preserve and must have been largely untouched wilderness and home to a rich ecosystem of wildlife. (There are probably in the twenty-first century no such forests in the whole of Europe). The woodlands were used by royalty and the upper echelons of the aristocracy as a hunting preserve, in other words as a leisure resource. In post-Black Death France the wilderness would have become more impenetrable and its wildlife more abundant. We have to assume that the wolf, the bison, the wild cat would have been at peak numbers, and that great herds of deer would have roamed these oak woods. While the fourteenth century was a hostile era for human beings, we can assume that the natural environment would have greatly benefitted from the falling human activity in these years. The forests would have been massive and filed with ancient hardwood trees. For shipbuilding, the oaks were the most valuable resource and the centuries of undisturbed growth were a gift to the French state that planned to build as many ships as possible in as short a time as possible.

We can picture Rainier Grimaldi on horseback riding through this forest. The hardened warrior, well away from his natural environment, accompanied the King of France, Charles the Wise. Charles V was no sportsman and his idea of relaxation did not involve getting on a horse with a party of hunters and chasing the deer through the royal preserves. The party was riding in silence with none of the hunting cries and bugling typical of a royal hunt. On this day the King was en route to the forest of Roumare, accompanied by his top naval advisor, in order to inspect the logging arrangements. At first, from a distance, they would have heard the sounds of the work that was being undertaken. When they arrived at the logging camp, they would have seen workmen engaged in the slow and difficult job of chopping down huge oak trees. After the trunk was on the ground, the wood was processed into raw material for shipbuilding, either by sawing or by splitting. Whole straight tree trunks of suitable size would be being prepared for transportation to Rouen to be turned into masts and oars. We can guess that some at least of the logging crews' supervisors were of Monegasque or Genoese origin, selling their superior shipbuilding skills to the French state in a time of need.

Medieval kings did not usually display their royal personages to the lower classes of society – especially when actually carrying out physical labour. An indicator of how little these two orders of society mixed can be gleaned from manuscript illustrations of the time where it is almost unknown for the same scene to include both aristocratic knightly figures and those of the third estate, peasants and manual workers. The fact that Charles the Wise actually visited the source of the Clos des Galées raw materials indicates how committed he was to building an effective fighting machine in France, and that although he was no hands-on warrior, he immersed himself in the details of the rebuilding of the French war machine. He was more like a modern supreme commander than a medieval warrior monarch like Edward.[22] In order to keep close to the build-up of his navy, Charles took up residence in the Citadel of Rouen, to be close to the centre of the action. He was often to be seen in the Clos.

After the devastation in the years after Poitiers we can sense a revival taking place in this area of northern France. The newly healthy government cash flow was now being channelled into the ports around the Normandy coast, with shipbuilding, ironworking and sail- and ropemaking giving employment to craftsmen and administrators, all paid from tax revenues. The tentacles of wartime preparations went as far as Monaco and Genoa, and the superior expertise of the Mediterranean city states made them valuable employees – as well as mercenaries.

The alliance of France with Castile that had led to the great sea battle near Winchelsea had continued, and part of Charles' plans for standing up to the English was to use Castilian naval power and in particular the Castilian expertise in building and fighting from galleys. The Genoese and Monegasques were still part of the French alliance.

12

NEW FRENCH INVASION PLANS

From this time onwards France was engaged in what should have been a well-thought out strategy for taking care of the English menace. For thirty years the English war machine, much of the time led by Edward III, in later years by his sons, had been relentlessly struggling to undermine France – its territory and its leadership. If that meant destroying civilian lives and wrecking the infrastructure of entire regions, all well and good. But despite a string of brilliant military victories, the English forces were never large or strong enough to conquer all of France. Yet despite being a much bigger and wealthier country than England, France had – until the reign of Charles the Wise – never created a war economy, one that had the monetary resources to build a powerful army and navy and the manpower needed to act effectively. For the next twenty years, until the end of the 1380s, that is the path that Charles chose for his country, to become a military superpower.

By 1369 the post-Poitier year zero must have seemed a long time ago, and the Black Death was no longer part of the day-to-day condition of life. The destruction and chaos of the early years of Charles' years as Dauphin were in the past. The nitty-gritty financial and manpower changes that Charles had brought in were working, and much of the money was being spent in Rouen and Harfleur, and in the Channel ports such as Honfleur and Dieppe. They were enjoying royal favour and the dockyards were busy. Sailors were being recruited and paid a daily allowance while on service. Castilian, Genoese and Monegasques experts were getting paid for their services. By now they were engaged in practical details such as laying in supplies of food and drink.[1]

This was to be the French response to English aggression. It was to be a full-scale invasion force, like the types of invasion that Edward had carried out with such devastating success twenty years ago but in reverse. The French fleet was not yet fully operational, but with the help of the Castilians, the Genoese and the trusty Monegasques many of the deficiencies could be made up. Most of the French ships were merchantmen impressed into service and converted to military use with fore and aft castles and with arrangements to stable horses in stalls in the hold. Unfortunately, French recovery had only come so far and most of the vessels were a mere 50 tons or so. For the Castilians the timing of the request for assistance from King Charles was unfortunate as they were engaged in their own internal problems – they were in the midst of a civil war.

Now Charles was spending much of his time in residence in Rouen, and he often appeared with his guests and companions to watch men busily at work preparing to best the English. Ships and sailing were not normally seen as worthy of the attention of a king and the subject never gets a mention in the extensive literature of the time that is devoted to the theory and practice of warfare. King Charles was reported to be delighted with the build-up of his fleet in the River Seine, and loved seeing the fighting force camped out along the banks of the river in tents, and one assumes with the sailors sleeping in their vessels.[2]

In mid-July of 1369 during the midsummer fighting season, when Charles was in Rouen, the leaders of the naval force were in the great cathedral of Saint-Denis where they received the oriflamme with all due solemnity, the sign that war had been authorised and that if needed, unlimited violence was acceptable in the cause of destroying the enemies of France. While the oriflamme was carried off, the ships were being kitted out with pennants and flags, and their sails carried the usual heraldic devices to identify the occupiers. The higher-status men were dressed in their finery. This included for the greatest knights helmets and body armour worn with brightly coloured tights that emphasised the musculature of the leg and the broadness of shoulder. There was a total of perhaps 5,000 people, which was reasonable but not an overwhelming force. (The Black Prince when he captured King Jean at Poitiers had at his disposal something approaching 7,000 fighters.) The Genoese and Monegasques, as it turned out, had no ships waiting in the Seine but they had supplied crossbowmen, and many of the crews were manned by sailors ready to leap out onto dry land and fight ferociously, led by Rainier Grimaldi. All they were waiting for was the order to go, watched by a whole court eager to enjoy the spectacle of a French navy setting out to destroy their ancient enemy. The royal administration was not quite ready yet, however.

The French preparations were closely followed in England, and in July of 1369 a writ was sent round the whole country. Referring to the French, Edward's proclamation warns his subjects that they

> ... have made ready a great fleet of ships and galleys upon the sea coast in divers parts with a host of armed men, hastening as speedily as they may to invade the realm, to conquer and destroy the king and people and overthrow his dominion; and whereas the king would by the grace of God meet such hurt and peril, making provision by all means for the safety and defence of his realm and people so far as he may.[3]

King Edward's luck was still not all used up. By an unnerving coincidence Edward's son John of Gaunt was at the very same time planning a midsummer incursion from English-held Calais into French territory, although with a force of only 1,000 it is not easy to understand what the overall English strategy was – however, as a war leader, John of Gaunt was quite capable of launching a campaign without a strategy. And an episode of French incompetence helped. His army was able to slip into Calais without the French noticing what was going on. Even after John of Gaunt had led his army over the border into French territory the royal party did not learn what had happened. As luck would have it King Charles was in conference with French leaders in his citadel of Rouen, raising extra funds to pay for the expedition, when the news arrived. Now the French had to turn their attention to removing English forces from their territory. The 1369 invasion of England was abandoned. What was King Charles to do with a whole estuary-full of navy?

John of Gaunt had not inherited his father's military leadership skills but he had learnt how to devastate the lands of his enemies as a simple method of warfare. By the end of October he was forced out of France, leaving behind him a huge swathe of French territory once again burnt and destroyed.

The English campaign was militarily a disappointment. John of Gaunt had failed and had to return to England with nothing to show for his men's labours. This was a long way from England at the height of King Edward's powers. Although the French had a lot to learn still, they were indeed learning.[4]

In the late summer of 1369 raiding started up. In September Portsmouth was attacked by a small force of French and maybe Monegasques and Castilians in what was probably an opportunistic attack from a small group of the large invasion force who were perhaps blown off course and decided to seize the opportunity. This incursion into Portsmouth was the third such attack since the start of the war earlier in the century. The port had been burnt in the 1330s and although a certain amount of rebuilding would have been carried out, Portsmouth could not have recovered by the time this raid took place. Only a few years earlier the port had been threatened with invasion from a Franco-Monegasque flotilla, and it was largely the result of a strong showing by the local defenders that the fleet sailed on to make landfall farther west. It is likely that key trading ports such as Portsmouth were repeatedly targeted to ensure that they did not recover. In addition to these actual physical threats, the economic disruption caused by the years of warfare in the English Channel would have ensured that the Portsmouth of 1369 was a shadow of what it had been.⁵

* * *

In the second part of 1369 King Charles put his newly developing war machine behind a second invasion plan. It would not have been surprising if in the late summer when it was becoming clear that the John of Gaunt expedition was failing, Charles and his advisors had wondered whether there might be some immediate use for the naval force that they had assembled. The use became clear with the appearance of a professional soldier from Wales. Froissart says that he was the descendant of a prince from Wales who had been dispossessed of his inheritance at the end of the previous century during the Welsh wars of Edward III's grandfather, Edward I. Later Edward III created the title 'Prince of Wales' for his eldest son, as heir to the throne. This title has maintained its meaning ever since.

From his arrival in France during the reign of Philippe VI as an itinerant knight, Owen of Wales had been treated well and was what could be described as a hanger-on in the royal court, where he was given some sort of recognition as a dispossessed minor near-royal. In France his Welsh name Owen of Wales became Yvain de Galles and he fought under Jean II at Poitiers. As someone who claimed to be the genuine indigenous leader of the Welsh nation, Owen would clearly be of interest to any French monarch who planned to destroy the hated Edwardian dynasty, and he was able to catch the ear of King Charles after the abandonment of the early summer invasion.[6]

At some time during the frustrating summer of 1369, when it must have been starting to look as though France was going to regress to what it was immediately after Poitiers, that is, at the mercy of armed bands causing death and destruction over swathes of territory, Owen was able to persuade Charles that he was not just a descendant of a genuine Welsh prince but that he was in touch with leaders still living in Wales who were eager to rise up against English oppression. By the time that Owen persuaded Charles to support his expedition, the original 1369 invasion force had been dispersed and so from August onwards a new force was hurriedly assembled. This involved impressing merchant ships into service and preparing them for warfare, the same process that had so often held up Edward's expeditions to France. Even once the ship had been found, the usual modifications had to be carried out by skilled craftsmen. At the same time the fighters had to be recruited.

There were a number of Welsh expatriates in the force, including Owen's number two, Ieun Wen, a soldier of fortune who had been fighting on the English side until after Poitiers, when he joined the French. There were pardoned criminals in the company, and a few knightly retinues. As an example of a typical company, the retinue of a certain Mathieu de Pommolain consisted of a knight, eight esquires, and fifteen crossbowmen, for which he received 390 gold francs from the French crown.[7]

An expedition of this type, which was to a certain extent a leap into the unknown, was a speculative investment that would, if successful, repay its initial costs many times over. In the event of failure, there were usually debts to be repaid. The overall plan would have been to a certain extent a parallel to Isabella's strategy for invasion – put together a group of discontented exiles and persuade a supportive prince to back an invasion plan by donating ships, mariners, and fighting men; then hope that when the landing took place there was support on the ground to allow the invasion to consolidate. In Isabella's case, as the invasion force progressed through England it grew support and eventually the king and his supporters fled. Is it possible that Owen had persuaded Charles the Wise that the two conditions existed in Edward's kingdom?

Firstly, that Owen had powerful supporters lying low in Wales waiting for him to appear for them to throw in their lot with the invasion; and secondly, widespread discontent with the regime, so that the invading force would grow in strength as it progressed after its disembarkation. These propositions were not tested at the time as the French naval machine was not ready to set out to Wales and victory until December. And anyone who knows the usual weather conditions in the English Channel, around Land's End and around the Pembroke Peninsula would know that this would not be an easy sail. But the weather was worse than usual. The sea conditions made sailing a top-heavy, overloaded cog, crammed with fighting men camped out on deck and horses in stalls in the hold, even more perilous. Surely the mariners who were recruited to transport the army must have advised that the weather would be against them. As Sir Patrick Spens says when he is instructed to sail:

> Oh who is this has done this deed
> And told the King of me,
> To send me out this time of the year
> To sail upon the sea?

The fleet endured what must have been a nightmarish twelve days of Channel storms and contrary winds without even getting past Land's End. Although the fleet succeeded in getting back to Harfleur and safety, many fishermen and traders were lost at sea in what was just one more example of contrary weather in these years. The *Chronicon Angliae* says that both 1368 and 1369 were very wet years in which crops and animals were destroyed by the wild weather.[8]

Taken as a whole 1369 was not a good year for Charles the Wise's long-term plan of removing the English menace. The French war machine was not effective enough and needed to be improved. The Clos des Galées looked like an impressive industrial centre, but it was doing a poor job. There were only nine barges under construction, and the work was going slowly. The galleys under the command of Rainier Grimaldi had not been well maintained and in 1369 six were in the Clos des Galées for repairs. The king needed to appoint a really competent admiral, who could organise and lead his complex fleet and make it into a strong and reliable fighting force.

* * *

The response from the England of Edward III – even an elderly burnt-out Edward – was what you would have expected. The *custodies pacis* of each shire, and even the mayor, sheriffs and aldermen of London itself, were all recruiting yet again from all available men. Groups of tens, and hundreds, were formed, and they were instructed to hold themselves ready to 'march for the defence of the realm as often as danger shall threaten by the inroads of the king's enemies'.[9]

In a post-Black Death England short of suitable fighters, even the clergy were told that they had to prepare to take up arms alongside their fellow countrymen. The inhabitants of the coastal areas were starting to pack up their possessions and move away, and for the landowning class the temptation was to attend to urgent business in locations at a safe distance from the invasion front. Writs were issued by Parliament prohibiting this.[10]

No doubt while this was happening Edward would have been reminding his entourage of his foresight in ordering fortifications at the entrance to the River Thames after peace had been declared six years earlier. As 1369 progressed, strategically positioned castles became building sites. Oaks were delivered to Southampton for use in building a town barbican in wood, the gates to fortified gateways, and walling.[11] Carisbrook and Portchester underwent rebuilding.[12]

Frontline towns were getting nervous, especially the most threatened towns along the South Coast such as Rye and Winchelsea. Rainier de Grimaldi's raid in 1339 had been destructive and although the armed invaders were driven off, they had inflicted much damage on the town. Rye Bay had been overwhelmed by Edward's entire court, in readiness for the action between the Castilians and the English in the Battle of Winchelsea in 1350. And a decade later, during the winter of 1359/60, Jean de Neuville's descent on Winchelsea was one of the most brutal and destructive raids of the entire century. The trauma the town suffered must have been long-lasting. Now it was another decade and another crisis for the people of Rye and Winchelsea. Across the English Channel in 1369 yet another fleet was massing. The citizens of Rye asked permission from the king to levy murage, a local tax used for building fortifications around the town, possibly using crenellations.[13] In the words of the petition:

For lack of enclosure the town has been lately burnt in time of war … in view of the perils that may ensue if the town remains unenclosed the mayor and commonality has ordained that 1½d of every 20/- worth of goods and money weekly was to be applied to the enclosure of the town until it was complete.

The king granted this request. The locally financed works on walling and crenellating the town continued, on and off, well into the 1380s – a constant reminder of the crisis that loomed over everyone's life.

The Isle of Wight was another location in which the on-going French menace would have been a part of everyday life for years on end. While the defence of the Thames Estuary and the approaches to London was going on, works started on strengthening Carisbrook Castle, right in the middle of the Isle of Wight. By 1369 crenellations, barbicans, and bigger walls were appearing. The logistics of transporting the stone from the mainland and the lodging of the craftsmen working on the building must have been considerable. The impact of the costs of the works on the island economy must have been huge but not entirely negative, bringing with it a 'war dividend' in the form of services bought and workers paid.

In 1370 the English plans for another Continental invasion were again affecting life along the South Coast. Rye was the harbour of choice of yet another planned English attempt to wrest control of territory from the French. As a result, 2,000 fighters with supplies, horses and materiel descended upon Rye harbour in the early summer, only to leave in early August into the usual high winds, storms and heavy rain. The doubtful privilege of being chosen as a port of disembarkation caused the usual problems of economic and social disruption.

The whole of Rye harbour would have been full of merchant vessels modified to act as troop carriers, and local shipping must have been squeezed out by the military. The areas along the shorelines of the harbour were populated by military camps, and the streets of the town of Rye itself – the settlement was no more than 1 mile from end to end – would have at times been jammed full of troops, animals and supply trains. There would have been a high level of violence and lawlessness, quite possibly putting the day-to-day life of the town on hold. The relief in Rye when the last of the ships slipped past Camber Castle and into the waters of the English Channel must have been immense. We can imagine that the lookout points might have been nearly as full of people watching the fleet as they had been ten years earlier when Edward's ships fought the Spanish galleys.[14]

Not only in Rye or along the south coast were people fearful about the future. Despite the new fortifications at the entrance to the estuary, London itself was considered to be at risk from the reorganised and strengthened French navy and nightly watches were set up, following an edict of the king.[15]

> In order to resist the malicious designs of the same galleys ... every night in the future ... watch should be kept between the Tower of London and Billingsgate with 40 men-at-arms and 60 archers; which watch the men of the trades underwritten agreed to keep in succession each night ... as follows... On Tuesday – the Drapers and the Tailors. On Wednesday – the Mercers and the Apothecaries... etc.

On the French side of the Channel, 1370 saw a continuation in building up the capacity of the French fleet. The Clos des Galées was working at full capacity, and Rouen had become an industrial centre designed to serve the material needs of the French navy. The presence of Monegasque, Genoese and Castilian fighters, seamen, engineers and shipbuilders made the town international.

Apart from the specialist carpentry required for building fighting ships, the Clos was an ironworking centre where everything from iron nails to anchors would be fabricated, necessitating wood-fired furnaces for iron processing. It was also a centre for the manufacture of the ground-breaking technology related to gunpowder, which involved the use of the (at the time) rare and expensive raw material such as saltpetre. In an age when high-status fighters went into battle dressed up to the nines, the royal fighting machine paid skilled specialists to produce the ornamental items of identification without which no fighting force was complete. Much of the ship, including the masts, would be painted in heraldic colours to match the devices sewn into the sails, on the flags, and painted onto shields.

France was now a more militaristic country, and English-held fortifications in the north of France were being taken by French forces. In 1370 preparations were being made to take back control of Poitou in north-west France. From now onwards, the French started to win battles and English holdings began to shrink. So in the coming years there was plenty of action on the ground in France and Spain. And at the same time systematic work continued in the Clos des Galées to build up a truly effective invasion fleet.

The French also had plans to launch a series of raids along the south coast of England. The naval force that left the mouth of the River Seine in July of that year was an impressive array. There were 10 galleys, each rowed by as many as 60 marines. They were backed up by 13 sailing ships, each fitted out for war with high castles at front and rear. But despite the impressive turn-out, surprisingly little was achieved. The fact that the main raid was made on Gosport tells its own story. Although fourteenth-century Gosport was a small settlement, it was strategically important as it controlled the pinch point that ships would have to pass in order to enter Fareham Water, on which the major targets of Portsmouth and Portchester are located. And successful invaders, if they held the area, would have access to the key cities of Winchester and Salisbury. It is not impossible that during the years of defensive building along the English coast up to this year that the the entrance to Fareham Water had a chain ready and waiting that could be pulled across the narrow straits blocking the entrance. Alternatively, archers on each shore could make the passage of the strait very uncomfortable indeed.

What is more, by 1370 Portsmouth itself was armed to the teeth. In 1369 we know that under commander Warin de L'Isle there were 15 knights, 27 esquires, and 53 archers all ready to do their worst to any Frenchmen who showed themselves. With this number of armed forces waiting upon a landing, most fleets would have made the decision to sail elsewhere. It is likely that the Gosport raid was one carried out because nothing better was in the offing.[16] There is little left in modern Gosport to remind us of this period as whatever fortifications it acquired were of a later date than the fourteenth century, however, it cannot have been a very good raid, otherwise the writers of the time would have recorded it more thoroughly.

After Gosport it appears that the French ships moved along the coast attacking small, less important, undefended settlements. We have no names to put to these raids but we can suggest a number of locations along the invasion front that might have been targets and seem not to have been mentioned often. Seaford is one example. It was a member of the Cinque Port league and although it was in decline, its location between Rye and Winchelsea to the east, and the major ports further west, means that on a number of occasions in the previous decades flotillas must have sailed past this port looking for prey. Despite the port being in decline, at the end of the fourteenth century it was still a port with some moneyed inhabitants.

At this stage King Charles was acting cautiously, concentrating systematically upon preparing for the big push against England. His navy was not yet ready for a set-piece battle. A large fleet of galleys is a labour-intensive form of shipbuilding because galleys are lightweight and unlike the robust cog, for example, they need a lot of attention. Charles' navy possessed a reasonable fleet of specialist ships such as galleys and Norman barges, but not yet enough of them. Badly looked after while beached during the winter, an entire fleet of galleys could turn out to be unseaworthy by the beginning of the following year's sailing season.

In 1372 the balance of power shifted towards France. The 1340s, when Edward and his family seemed invincible, were long gone and Edward was no longer the impetuous and lucky leader he had been. There was plenty of English action on the Continent in 1372 but no successes.

Edward's second son, John of Gaunt, had married into the Castilian royal family. Through his wife Eleanor of Castile, he had taken a leaf out of his father's book and claimed the throne of Castile. He demanded to be addressed as 'Monsieur d'Espagne' and made a triumphal entry into London with his new wife as 'the King of Castile,' a title he took to applying to himself. This clumsy diplomatic move prompted an alliance between Castile and France against the English danger. In the coming years Castilian ships greatly strengthened the French naval forces. John of Gaunt now embarked on a series of fruitless wars in Europe, designed to seize the Castilian throne by force, conveniently taking the pressure off the French. From now until the death of the old king, the English were not winning battles and the French were recovering piecemeal territory that they had lost in Edward's years of triumph.

In the meantime there was a new invasion attempt involving Wales in the offing. Owen of Wales had spent the previous year with his company of Welsh warriors in action as mercenaries in an unrelated war in Germany, paid for by the city of Metz, thus keeping his Welsh anti-English force intact, and earning the wherewithal to keep armed and armoured fighting men equipped to go into battle. Before the start of the 1372 season, he was summoned to the court of King Charles and asked to put together another Welsh invasion, using his small force as the core of their battle strength. One can imagine that Owen would have used all his powers of persuasion to convince his patron that this plan was feasible. If this invasion had been a success it would have changed the course of British history. Owen issued a statement of intent:

> Whereas the Kings of England have in the past moved by intemperance and greed wrongly and without cause treacherously killed or put to death my forbears the Kings of Wales and expelled them by force from their kingdom... Lately I came before my most powerful and well-regarded lord Charles by the grace of God King of France ... he has supported me with his men-at-arms and ships to recover my kingdom.[17]

Charles the Wise was ready to support the project but expected to gain an economic return for his efforts. The total cost of the expedition was approximately 300,000 livres d'or, as a loan, to be paid back from the profits of a successful campaign. The soldiers were to be paid while on duty, and Owen himself received 1,500 livres when he was ready to sail. France had moved a long way from the dark days after Poitiers when Charles, as Dauphin while his father was in captivity, had had to refuse an invasion offer from King Waldemar that would have cost the same 300,000 écus because he had not have the money.

The Castilians, afraid of a forthcoming invasion by John of Gaunt in order to claim the throne of Castile, were prepared to supply ships, and the trusty Rainier de Grimaldi with his team of hardened warriors was on hand to launch the expedition from the Seine port of Harfleur. Although Owen's army was tiny by medieval standards, the Welsh fighting force was beefed up by the presence of French men-at-arms. However, the aim of this invasion was not to overwhelm the Welsh defenders with superior force. Owen had persuaded the French court that the anti-English feeling in Wales was strong, and that the people of Wales would rise up against their English oppressors as soon as they had the opportunity, and that the Welsh nation would respond as soon as he appeared on home soil. What was envisaged therefore was something like Isabella's invasion nearly half a century before, when the invaders were returning to claim their rightful inheritance from an unjust and oppressive monarch. As happened after Isabella landed in Orwell, it was expected that Owen's small invasion force would be welcomed and gather strength as the triumphal procession moved though his homeland, following his royal standard as the true Prince of Wales. This turned out to be true for Isabella and from day one Isabella and Mortimer formed friendly relations with the Earl of Norfolk. And as they processed through England they were spontaneously joined by supporters. Was Owen another Isabella?

When the under-strength invasion force was assembled in Harfleur harbour in May of that year, there were 10 Monegasque galleys, each with maybe 30 paired oars pulled by versatile fighting men, carrying a group of high-status leaders on the stern-castle, probably under canvas away from prying eyes. The bulk of the French men-at-arms would have been crammed away on the decks of the bigger, fatter and higher converted merchantmen, of which there were perhaps 10. The holds would have been full of horses, in addition to carrying supplies of water and food. The fleet would have been faultlessly turned out. The personal standards of Owen, as Prince of Wales, would have been flying proudly – four lions passant quartered in gold and red, left paw raised. (No Welsh dragons for Owen). Flying too would have been the blue-and-gold fleurs-de-lis of France, and the red-and-white banners of Monaco. As usual the chanting of slogans and signalling of trumpets would have accompanied the launch of the expedition.

The force may have been in the region of 700 fighters, although Froissart believed, almost certainly wrongly, that there were as many as 4,000 members of the force. But this was just the start. There were more to come.

The plan was complex. They did not sail straight to Wales and commence an invasion. Their Castilian allies were in port in Santander, hundreds of miles away, and Owen was to recruit once he arrived there. The invasion started by moving west along the English Channel. After crossing the Bay of Biscay, they were to meet up with the Castilian fleet, hopefully waiting on the north coast of Spain. This 700-mile journey involved the dangerous crossing of a possibly stormy Bay of Biscay. For the Monegasques in their open galleys with low freeboards it followed a route that all of them had used before, but it was fraught with risk and physical challenges.

On the way west shortly after the start of their journey, they descended on the island of Guernsey, not 20 miles beyond the Cotentin, situated nearer to France than to England. The Channel Islands had been fought over on several occasions in the course of the fourteenth century. Guernsey had been attacked thirty years earlier, as well as being occupied for a few months sixteen years previously, after the 1356 invasion. In the aftermath of the Battle of Poitiers, there was fighting in the Cotentin Peninsula, just a few miles away from Guernsey and a group of French fighters had descended upon Guernsey and captured Castle Cornet while it was relatively unguarded. It took several months for the Governor of Jersey to respond to the situation and it was not until the following year that the force, made up of the leaders from Jersey with their followers, landed in Guernsey. They managed to tempt the French out of Castle Cornet and into battle. Luckily the men from Jersey captured the captain of the fortress, and an attempt was made to ransom him for the huge sum of 80,000 florins. After some inconclusive negotiation, it was agreed to exchange the castle for the captain and the French sailed away back to France.[18]

There are two accounts of Owen's 1372 raid, which do not agree with each other. One version states that Yvain's fleet landed in Vazon Bay, on the north-east coast of Guernsey, in an area of sand dunes. The islanders in this account had been forewarned, and had brought in an English force from the English governor of the islands, ready for the invasion. According to one account, the attacking force was prepared for a party of fighting seamen, or pirates, and must have been taken aback to see a professional fighting force.

There was fierce fighting all day and, according to the local account, the Guernsey men were reinforced by English forces from the English-held fortress of Saint-Sauveur-le-Vicomte on the Cotentin Peninsula that same day. This is unlikely considering that Guernsey is more than 30 miles from the French coast. Did the fighting last more than one day?

It is said that the English defence force, after it landed in Guernsey, was joined by as many as 800 Guernsey islanders, who were no stranger to fierce fighting against unwanted visitors. A full-scale pitched battle was fought inland from St Peter Port, and the existing Battle Street is said to commemorate the action. For the French it resulted in total victory, with large numbers of the English and Channel Islanders warriors being killed. The remnants of the defending army fled into the ruined Castle Cornet. The mixed force of Welshmen, French and Monegasques dug in for a siege, but the English held out.

The local account of this invasion claims that there was a great slaughter, with as many as 500 casualties. Other non-Guernsey accounts do not agree. This incursion has left traces on local tradition with, for example, a popular poem, 'The Ballad of Evan of Wales and the Invasion of Guernsey in 1372', where Evan is, of course, Owen. The battle that took place in St Peter Port is described in this way,

Above Saint Peter Port 'tis said,
The conflict they renewed,
Of friends and foes five hundred dead

The grassy plain bestrewed:
Our ladies wept most bitterly,
Oh! 'twas a dismal sight to see
Their cheeks with tears bestrewed.

The invasion of Guernsey stands almost alone in the history of the period in that the event left traces in the collective memory of the location. In the history of the Channel Islands, the incursion is known as the 'Invasion of the Aragounais', and strangely enough Owen of Wales, or Yvain de Galles as he is known in the Channel Islands, is recorded as having been governor of Guernsey between 1372 and 1377, although there is no record of the island being occupied by the French during this period.[19]

The Welsh-led fleet sailed on and arrived in Santander in late June, after having completed its crossing of the Bay of Biscay without mishap. The timing could not have been worse for Owen. While his galleys were battling the elements out to sea, a major naval battle was being fought that further shifted the balance of power between France and England. An English army had been on its way to take the fight to Gascony, and to chase the French out of the province forever. It was not to be. In a naval engagement in the mouth of the River Garonne lasting over two whole days the French wiped out an entire fleet of 30 English impressed merchant vessels and took many prisoners. Most importantly, they captured an immense amount of money destined to pay allies and mercenaries in France, thus making it next to impossible for the English to recruit soldiers to fight.

France and its allies immediately moved on to the province of Gascony in what was to be a successful bid to terminate much of the English presence there. Not surprisingly when Owen and his ally Rainier Grimaldi arrived in Santander, rowed through the half-mile entrance to its fine natural harbour, and docked, they probably did not receive as enthusiastic a reception as they had expected. The action was taking place elsewhere.

There were no Castilian ships waiting for Owen, and shortly after his arrival in Santander he was visited by Henry of Trastámara, the King of Castile himself, to learn that the situation had changed. The promises that the King of Castile had made were no longer operable, and Owen's Welsh invasion had been cancelled. Owen was ordered to travel to Gascony and fight against the English there. No more Wales. Owen/Yvain spent that year fighting his hereditary foes the English in Gascony and he actually participated in the driving out of the English from much of south west France. He finished the year in glory, and he was still ready to lead an invasion into his homeland of Wales.[20]

Curiously, the Guernsey 'Ballad of Evan of Wales' mentions an episode that was said to have occurred when Owen was on his way back to northern France. Sailing eastwards along the English Channel his fleet was attacked by an English force. His French and Genoese galleys were boarded by English fighters, his crew was massacred, his new wife Eleanor, maybe from Gascony, was raped. Owen himself met a horrible end when his head was encased in a red-hot helmet:

> The south- wind rose, and on the coasts
> Of Brittany they passed,
> An English fleet to stop their boasts
> Appeared in sight at last:
> Full sixty men a footing found
> On board Sir Evan's bark, and bound
> His crew in fetters fast.
>
> Sir Evan to the mast they tied,
> And then before his face
> Insult his young and beauteous bride
> And load her with disgrace;
> They take him to Southampton town

And on his head, in guise of crown,
A red-hot morion* place.

They dragged his men out one by one
And hung them up in chains,
And now not one of all the crew
Save Eleanor remains.
A beggar's scrip her only store,
She roams about from door to door,
And scarce a living gains.

*Morion – a sort of tight fitting iron helmet.

The year 1372 was a fateful one. It had started well in England when the Great Council met in Westminster for an unprecedented two weeks. It voted funds for the English to raise an army of mercenaries in Gascony to launch a response to the French action of the previous year, simultaneously laying the ground for a John of Gaunt action across the Pyrenees to seize his 'rightful throne'. The Earl of Pembroke was to lead the small but valuable flotilla carrying 12,000 gold English pounds across a dangerous war zone to La Rochelle, which was to be the base for action against the French. Enough coin to recruit several thousand mercenaries to fight on the English side for several months was granted. This was the campaign that went so wrong and stopped Owen's invasion plans.

The campaign was audacious, if misjudged. The idea was to secure English trade routes to the south-west, and to consolidate English positions in France by extending English-held territory in France. And as far as John of Gaunt was concerned, who was not taking part in the campaign of that year but staying in England with his new bride, any improvement in the situation along the western seaboard between England, Gascony and northern Spain could only be to the good when he decided to take an army to Castile and claim what he believed to be his rightful inheritance. But this did not work out as planned. While Owen and Rainier's flotilla was waiting in Santander to put together their Welsh invasion force, Pembroke's small but well-heeled English fleet was on its way south through the Bay of Biscay, en route to La Rochelle, the key river port for the English Crown possession of Gascony. It was, by the standards of the time, a tiny flotilla with no more than twelve modest-sized cogs of up to 60 tons each, carrying a couple of hundred fighters.

The Castilian navy, like the one that Edward only just managed to overcome in Winchelsea twenty years before, towered over the English vessels and the Castilians were able to rain down a deluge of arrows onto the badly prepared English. By the end of the second day's fighting, the Castilians were able to set fire to many of the ships and, very importantly, were able to capture the whole of the Earl of Pembroke's treasury. The previous big battle between the English and the giant Castilian nefs had been led and inspired by Edward and, due to some audacious acts of leadership, had not been a defeat for the outgunned and outsized English. However, with that great wartime leadership now missing, they were reduced to nothing. It is said that when news of the La Rochelle catastrophe arrived in Edward's court, the old king became silent and thoughtful. After a time he told the court that he was going to take his forces to Brittany and lead them against the French. By coming out of his long retirement, maybe his presence on the battlefield would do what his sons and associates were not able to do – deliver a knockout punch to the French king.

The 6,000-man army mustered in Winchelsea. As was usual when Edward was involved, the process was long, slow and confused. The fleet was not ready to sail until late August, just in time for strong south-westerly winds to start blowing up the Channel, making headway with the large and unwieldy single sails all but impossible. The army was at sea for six weeks without having been able to leave the Channel itself, and eventually turned back, having been defeated by the weather. Much of the fleet dispersed, the soldiers went home, and the ships were returned to their owners who needed them for the annual wine fleet operation. It is said that Edward stayed on board his ship for several weeks more, convinced that the weather would change and he would be able to lead his army to victory. By late October even he admitted failure.[21]

Rainier Grimaldi did not follow Owen onto the battlefields of Gascony. Instead he reappeared in English waters later that summer of 1372, still in charge of the Monegasque fleet, now comprising nine galleys, and spent the rest of the summer sailing season cruising the English coast and raiding. There are few records of the location of the raids he carried out at that time, but we do know that his force had captured several English cogs. Presumably after having disposed of their crews, the ships were taken across the Channel to the Seine ports to be pressed into service on the French side. In the French chroniclers' record of this series of raids there is a rare glimpse of an interaction between defenders and attackers in galleys, and it shows us that despite the growing resentment of the endless war, the population of the seaside areas was still robustly patriotic.

In an unknown location Rainier's galley was rowing along the coast, very close to shore, and we can guess that he and his crew are scouting out the scene, selecting a suitable place to beach and mount a raid. A posse of English defenders unexpectedly appeared, and Rainier decided to move away. But he had taken his galley too close to shore and in the out-going tide, the keel was grounded. He was trapped.

The English force was bigger than the Monegasque one, and it must have been well armed. They prepared for battle. Fifty to sixty well-armed men on board a ship with a deck maybe 2 metres above the waterline against a force of well-trained militias wading through the water to attack the ship – and their loyalty as fighters is to the person of their king – Edward III.

'Surrender to the King of France!' they call out. 'Surrender to the King of France!'

Rainier is puzzled. He serves the King of France – King Charles. What do they mean?

'What do you call him?' asked Rainier.

'His name is Edward, and we tell you to surrender to him!' they called out.

'My king is called Charles and I can only surrender to him!'

By now the galley was surrounded by English fighters and Rainier and his crew desperately fought off the assailants, and the waters round the galley was filling with dead bodies. There appeared to be an unlimited supply of fighters ready to join in, the beach was filling up with more and more fighters and Rainier knew that he could not go on indefinitely. He considered having to surrender in the name of King Edward.

Luckily, the tide started coming in and the galley was lifted off the beach, and the rowers got to work. It was a close-run thing. It had been forty years since Edward III proclaimed himself king of France. The war machine that he built over the decades to back his claim had not succeeded, but some of the ordinary people of England appeared to believe that Edward was the King of France![22]

The following year Rainier Grimaldi was taken prisoner while raiding in England, although the circumstances of his capture are not recorded. King Edward himself bought Rainier from his captors for the huge sum of 12,000 gold French francs. Rainier stayed in captivity until 1375 and was treated according to the Franco-English custom – with honour and excellent living conditions.

Compared to the situation that confronted his father Carlos Grimaldi in the 1330s when he was covering the same piece of southern English territory, Rainier had been dealing with a coastal territory where many ports were poorer, such as Southampton, which had still not recovered from the damage that had been done several decades ago. The raids were not the only source of damage. The frequent use of civilian shipping to transport English armies to France and elsewhere had done immense damage to the commercial life of those ports which had the dubious honour of hosting an army of invasion. Add to this the disruption in trade caused by the fact that the English Channel had become a war zone. As a result of the war, the wine trade with Gascony had deteriorated, leading to fewer merchants, fewer ships, and quieter ports. Compared to their Continental opponents, English traders now had smaller and fewer ships. The Battle of Winchelsea more than twenty years earlier had highlighted the superior size of the Castilian nef, and the battle had been won partly by luck and partly due to the extra something that King Edward had brought to any battlefield, even a naval one. After that battle another leader might have decided to improve the English fleet, but not Edward. Now the 'Edward effect' had gone.

In the years since the first stage of the Hundred Years' War had petered out, after the catastrophic defeats of Crécy, Poitiers, Sluys, and Calais, King Charles had been systematically creating the conditions for a French recovery. The state's fiscal affairs had been reformed so that it now possessed an income that could be used on financing war. Alliances with states that could provide strategic support, such as Castile, were in operation. In fact in the post-wartime recovery it could be said that France was truly emerging as the leading power in Europe, while England was declining. By now the figure who dominated his era – Edward III – was no longer the leader he had been. He was not to be seen much in public and had not appeared on a battlefield for more than ten years.

It is not clear what was wrong with the old king – it could have been a stroke, or a form of dementia. It is possible that years of hand-to-hand combat had resulted in long-term brain damage. His beloved wife of fifty years had predeceased him. His eldest son had died prematurely, and his successor, Edward Prince of Wales, the Black Prince, was ill and slowly dying. His younger son, John of Gaunt, who had been a baby when the young Edward was bravely extricating himself from the mess he had created in his early Flanders campaign, was now an immensely wealthy royal who repeatedly demonstrated terrible political and military judgment, leading his followers to failure with bravery and panache. He looked, but did not act, the part of a great leader. Edward's heir, the future Richard II, was still a child.

In the 1370s there was plenty of action by English armies in France and other parts of the Continent. The difference now was that the English campaigns were failures and did not change the political status quo. After Crécy if the political process had turned out right for King Edward, which it did not, almost all of France's Atlantic seaboard would have been an English possession, France would have ceased to be the leading nation in Europe, as that title would have been taken over by Edward, King of France and England.

From this time until the end of the century the position of England against France reverted to what it had been – England no longer punched above her weight and the superior size of the French economy meant that France was able to finance armies in the field so that, piece by piece, one by one, English possessions in France fell to the French. But the kings of France, Charles the Wise and his successors, still held a dream scenario in their minds. That an alliance between Scotland and France would lead them to grasp the biggest prize of all – Edward III, his family, his administration. Now the French had another ally – Castile.

Since 1066 the French kingdom had grown in power, so why not repeat the trick? The English, a smaller and culturally inferior power, had captured the king of France himself. This was a humiliation to be revenged. Maybe Edward in captivity accompanied by some of his family would even the score. And the fact was that even now, despite the rise of jingoistic propaganda in England against the French, much of English culture owed much to France. In a way France was only planning to regain its own. From now onwards the French strategy was to plan a full-scale invasion of England, using Scotland as an ally. To achieve this the French admiral had to be not just a shipman, but also an experienced fighter.

13

ENTER JEAN DE VIENNE

It was at this stage that Charles the Wise lived up to his name. Wisely he did not plan to appoint one of his male relatives as admiral, regardless of their skills. No French-style John of Gaunt leading whole armies into destruction, no marrying into the Castilian royal family and embarking on ill-planned military adventures aimed at seizing a foreign throne for himself. Instead, Charles's plan was to appoint the best possible person to lead the French fight-back.

That person was Jean de Vienne. In choosing him, King Charles found someone from well outside royal circles, with experience, and someone who was total committed to taking part in a final showdown against the English.

We first heard the name of Jean de Vienne at the end of the Siege of Calais when six starving burghers handed the keys of their city to King Edward himself. Their leader begged Edward to grant them and their citizens their lives.

The leader of the six was Jean de Vienne Senior, the uncle of the Jean de Vienne we are about to discuss. Jean de Vienne Senior was taken into captivity in England, where he was ransomed. After years the money was raised through the Viennes and Jean Senior returned to France, with a place in history.

The fate of his famous uncle must have haunted the young Jean de Vienne. His lifetime of warfare, almost all in the service of the King of France against the English and their allies, was surely linked in some way with the humiliation of his namesake standing before the King of England, barefoot, with a noose around his neck, holding his sword by the blade, and begging for mercy. Young Jean de Vienne came from a respected but not wealthy family. Many of his brothers and cousins were active knights, and his brother Jehan de Vienne was a bishop. Jean himself started fighting when he was just eighteen years old and by the age of twenty-one he had been knighted and awarded by King Philippe the gift of a village and its royalties. He fought tirelessly in the terrible years after Calais and Poitiers, when France fell into anarchy.

The Battle of the River Ognon is an example of the small-scale, savage, low-grade type of engagement that Jean de Vienne fought again and again during those years. When the Dauphin, the future Charles the Wise, heard about the engagement and summoned Jean into his presence and knighted him, he was recognising his future potential. The gift that the young Dauphin gave him of the lordship of the Village of Villey, which generated an income of 140 gold florins per year, helped him to maintain himself in the manner that a knight fighting the English enemy should.

The next step up the ladder was when Jean took part in the Crusade of the Comte Vert, as a member of the international community of warriors. It was then he met and impressed such influential international naval commanders as the Grimaldi family. By the latter stages of the crusade, he was among the inner circle of knights who negotiated with the enemy. Is it possible that the Grimaldis recommended Jean de Vienne to King Charles when he was looking for a suitable admiral?

It was not surprising that by 1373 Charles V ceremonially gave Jean de Vienne the little gold mariner's whistle on a chain that betokened his role as *Amiral de France*, an exalted position. Alongside King Charles, Jean de Vienne had the right to half of the profits of any naval action.[1] In just eleven years Jean had risen from being an unknown poor knight from a good family, to holding one of the most important military positions in the kingdom. He was now charged with doing what it took in order to dispose of the English menace. Much of this strategy consisted of doing just what the English had not done in the past decades, building up a real navy and avoiding going into battle without a plan.

Jean's predecessors had already formed the naval dockyard near Paris, employing the best possible expert craftsmen and marines on a permanent basis. The new admiral was to build up this force so that the French fleet plus its allies would be overwhelmingly more powerful than the English musters. This meant coordinating a wide range of skills.

Shipbuilding did not just involve building with wood. It meant metal working so as to make nails, anchors, and cannons. It meant sail making. Very importantly, arms and armour were also made in Clos des Gallées in Rouen. The entire Seine Estuary from Harfleur at its mouth, which is where Jean de Vienne lived, down to Rouen became an industrial zone. Rouen was loud with the noise of sawing, and hammering. The air was thick with the smoke from wood and charcoal fires used in its foundries. Clos des Gallées was at the centre of the new gunpowder technology which was about to change warfare forever. It involved using the scarce and expensive mineral saltpetre.

A naval fleet designed to be used as a tool for the destruction of the hostile enemy kingdom on the north side of the English Channel needed allies and over the next fifteen years Jean de Vienne led the struggle to put together a force that would overthrow the English regime.

Our period started with the invasion of England by Isabella, the mother of Edward III. That invasion was a success for the simple reason that many leaders in England were delighted at the opportunity to abandon their obligations to the despised Edward II. The invading force had support on the ground. In striking contrast, although for more than twenty-five years Edward III and his armies had won battle after battle against the French, and were able again and again to detach parts of French territory from control by the French crown, Edward III never came near to achieving his real aim – to take up his 'rightful' title of king of France. Most of the territory taken in battle in France melted away in the decades that followed. The gain that lasted longest, for at least 200 years, was the capture of Calais, but significantly the first English action after the taking of the city was an act of ethnic cleansing – to remove the entire French population and replace it with English colonists. A result of the decades of warfare against the French was the rise of hard-line anti-French English nationalism.

Until the 1370s the French had concentrated on short-term raids, but as the decade developed Charles V and his admiral planned longer-term incursions on to the English mainland. In order to get the support that the French needed, the Welsh and Scottish opposition was key, and on five occasions from the late 1370s until the end of the 1380s invasion plans involving help from these two sources were launched.

***

The years after 1373 were relatively quiet in the English Channel, with few if any raids onto English territory, and no significant naval battles. One significant military engagement took place in 1374 when the single large English holding in Normandy, the Castle of St Sauveur le Vicomte, was recaptured by French forces.

St Sauveur was located in the heart of the Cotentin Peninsula, close to the eastern Normandy beaches, not far from the west coast and the Channel Islands. The English who held the fortress were a source of constant trouble, raiding surrounding territories and supporting banditry and casual violence against ordinary people in the area.

The admiral himself, Jean de Vienne, was given the task of reclaiming this powerfully defended fortress for the French crown. In 1375 the 2,000 soldiers under his command arrived outside the fortress, to find that the English were ready for the siege and had cleared away all buildings for several hundred metres in all directions, leaving a killing ground.

The siege was remarkable for relying, possibly for the first time in a major campaign, on the new-fangled technology of gunpowder and cannons developed in Rouen. The castle was subjected to months of close siege, assisted by relentless attacks by 50-pound cannon shot from just one giant cannon using stone cannonballs. The walls of the fortress were not of sufficient thickness to withstand continuous cannon fire and after nearly twelve months, with walls collapsing, supplies running short, and defenders worn down by the twenty-four hour mayhem, the castle surrendered. Admiral Jean de Vienne had won an important victory. An essential part of his siege strategy was to build a bastide – that is a temporary wooden portable fortress that was erected near to the action in order to give cover to the French attackers. It was a novel idea that worked, as it made its reappearance in following years.[2]

Jean de Vienne was versatile; he was at home in the thick of battle, engaging in strategic planning, or involving himself with naval affairs. The coming fifteen years of action against the English would test his abilities to the utmost.

* * *

The big campaign of 1377 had actually been launched the previous year and was the result of a long and careful planning process. It perhaps began long before that in the world of footloose mercenaries, spies, and traitors on the Continent, trying to extract some advantage from the shifting tides of war. In 1370 a complicated English invasion plan was launched led by Sir Robert Knolles, a knight of of humble origins who had attained status and wealth. English forces were supposed to link up with a Castilian army on French soil and then carry out joint actions. Overall the campaign failed, probably as a result of Knolles' poor leadership and strategy. It was during this campaign that a certain Sir John Minsterworth entered the picture. He was a poor English knight from the Welsh marches who went to France with 200 fighters and 300 archers ready to serve under Knolles. It is likely that Minsterworth's fighters were of the lowest status, made up of pardoned criminals and outlaws. Minsterworth would have been taking a big risk by borrowing the money needed to recruit and equip 500 men. Once in France he would have been desperate to find a way to recoup his money and make his fortune. As the campaign progressed it became evident that Knolles was neither an effective military strategist nor military leader. In a short time Knolles' army was broken, and the remnants of this force managed to get away and back to England, including Minsterworth.

A couple of years later Minsterworth was accused of treason, probably falsely, and not surprisingly, after having been arraigned he slipped away out of England and introduced himself to Charles V rather than stay and suffer a terrible execution as a traitor. Sir John must have been just the type of person that Charles V would have wanted to meet. A competent English commander with a track record of leading men into the battlefield, and desperate; as a traitor, he had lost everything in England – property, land, respect.

It appears that after meeting King Charles, Sir John made the acquaintance of Owen of Wales, who was still staying close to the French monarch. These two men were made for each other; between them, Owen and Sir John put together an invasion plan. Most importantly they must have persuaded King Charles that their plan would work.

There would be three parts to it. Once the Anglo-Welsh invasion force landed in Wales, the people of Wales would rise up against the English oppressors. Owen had been saying this for a long time. Secondly, once Minsterworth appeared in his home territory on the English side of the Welsh border, his people would join the rebellion. From then on the momentum would build and the simmering discontent would culminate in widespread support for the uprising. The plan was to be supported by the type of operation in which the French navy had gained plenty of experience off and on over the past forty years or so, that is, raiding along the south coast in order to inflict the maximum damage in advance of the raid proper, softening up the field in advance of the movement of the French-supported armies across southern England.[3]

Then the plan was slightly simplified. Owen and Minsterworth were to sail together with an invasion fleet, carrying fighters, horses, materiel, and food supplies to a landing place in the Sound of Milford Haven. Pembroke Castle was to be seized, and the invaders were to move through the rest of Wales, gathering support.

It is not clear what King Charles had been led to believe by Sir John Minsterworth, but it seems he had persuaded the French court that he had supporters in England. As a result, Minsterworth embarked early in 1377 on a mission to Castile, supported by documentation from the French king and with large amounts of finance available to obtain the transports and mercenaries needed to get the invasion underway – as had Owen on a similar mission five years earlier. Once the necessary support had been put together, ships loaded with men and materiel would make their way north through the Bay of Biscay, round the Breton peninsula and into the English Channel, after which the invasion fleet was to sail up to Land's End and South Wales.

It was not to be. On his way to Castile, Minsterworth was kidnapped. He was in Navarrese territory, and was delivered to the English rulers of Gascony. With his incriminating documentation, he was put on a ship to England, bound for the Tower of London. Under relentless torture he informed the English of the French plot. Minsterworth's broken body was then dealt with in the usual way. His torso was cut open while he was still alive and before the moment of death, he was hanged. Then his body was cut into four pieces, each of which was to be shown in a different part of England as a warning of the fate that awaited traitors to their liege lord.

Owen of Wales had failed to get his invasion.[4] However, if Wales had failed yet again, Scotland was still 'on the table' and there was everything to play for. In the run up to the 1377 campaign King Charles did what he could to revive the Auld Alliance and sent emissaries to Scotland to persuade Robert, the new monarch, to throw in his lot with the French. By 1377 with Edward no longer active on the battlefield, the Anglo-Scottish border had gone quiet, and no new schemes were being hatched for the crushing of Scottish independence. King Robert Stewart was no warrior king, and he was relatively uninterested in the badlands of the Anglo-Scottish border. Nevertheless, King Charles attempted to bring King Robert into his system of alliances and sent one of his private secretaries, Pierre Bournaseau, on a mission to the Scottish monarch, to persuade him into an alliance. In a rather comic turn of events, Bournaseau's regal lifestyle attracted attention to him when he was ready to sail out of the port of Damme, via the harbour of Sluys. The ruling pro-English Count of Flanders put two and two together. A regal personage on his way to Scotland? The Count refused to allow him to sail for Edinburgh, and the Franco-Scottish alliance was not relaunched until later in the year. This almost random event did have consequences later.[4]

The year 1377 should have been a fateful one for France and King Charles. The great invasion planned for Jean de Vienne's navy was just the marine arm of a bigger campaign. English holdings all over France were to be attacked during the forthcoming fighting season, while Jean de Vienne's naval attacks were to bring the war to English shores. The more fronts the English were engaged on the better the chances of success for the French once the big invasion started.

The people of England who lived along the invasion front were by now very accustomed to defending their coastline, and were familiar with the fact that since the early days of the war anyone who lived near the coast was forbidden to flee on rumours of enemy invasion. Often the writ was given teeth by the threat that the Crown would seize the property of any coastal inhabitants who did run away.[5] Local landowners were obliged to lead their defence forces into action when danger struck. Evidence of how serious the situation was is illustrated by a writ from King Edward to the Archbishop of Canterbury, instructing him to summons clergy in his diocese to do their duty by forming companies of fighting warrior priests and monks to take on the French when necessary. It suggests that entire companies were formed made up only of holy men.[6]

In consideration of imminent peril by attacks of the king's enemies of France and their adherents, to arm and array all abbots, priors and ecclesiastical persons of his diocese between the ages of 60 and 16, every man according to his estate, possessions and means, putting them in thousands, hundreds and twenties ready at the archbishop's command to march with other lieges against the enemy.

As before, local people with few skills but sharp eyes could stand watch along the cliffs, beaches and low-lying ground, staring out to sea or along the shore watching for lit beacons and ready to light their own. Beacons were supposed to be ready to light on the first hint of danger. Although there is plenty of evidence that during times of trouble beacons were ready and waiting, and lit, there are few if any references in contemporary accounts of a beacon message playing an effective part.

* * *

While the broad invasion strategy involving Wales and Scotland failed to come together, in 1377 Jean de Vienne as Admiral of France had brought the French offensive fleet into a state of readiness and the time was right for some action to start. He could call upon thirty-five large nefs, well-turned out and fully furnished with armaments and supported by a host of smaller supply ships. The fleet was manned by nearly 5,000 men – both fighters and mariners. The fleet was given teeth by the eight specialist attack vessels – galleys from Castile and Portugal. It was an imposing fighting force.

It is said that before Jean de Vienne led the fleet out of the harbour of Honfleur, near the mouth of the River Seine, he and Rainier de Grimaldi rode inland up the hill that dominates the port to the south. The two men had had a close relationship ever since Jean de Vienne had travelled to Constantinople on a ship captained by Rainier, where he learnt about ships and shipping for the first time. Both of them had served the French kings almost continually since then, and Rainier had been part of a number of assaults on English territory. Indeed – his great grandfather, also called Rainier, had himself been appointed to Jean de Vienne's job at the start of the fourteenth century.

As the two colleagues – one already old, the other nearing the peak of his career – looked out over the estuary it would have been full of ships of war, with flags flying and sails decorated with heraldic devices. Looking out to sea they could not of course see the English coastline, well over 100 miles away. Nevertheless, looking toward the blue horizon, Rainier Grimaldi is supposed to have pointed to where the town of Rye was located. According to the chronicler, Rainer advised Jean de Vienne to start on Rye. 'In front of us,' said Grimaldi, 'is the town of Rye, defended by its ramparts, and enriched by the depredations of its inhabitants, against our French neighbours. It is from there that the hardy seamen come, who have outraged our coasts on so many occasions. The people of that town do not believe that we could descend on them. It is against them, believe me, that we should aim our first blows.' Rainier's view of warfare, as we see it here, seems more like the world of feud and vendetta than part of a strategy aimed at removing the English military threat to France.[7]

Anyway, in late June 1377, the fleet sailed in good weather conditions. It took just a few days to reach the English coast and Rye was the starting point for the campaign. The fleet would have been led into the harbour by the eight Monegasque war galleys, and although the chronicler does not say so, it is likely the Rainier Grimaldi was one of the leaders, and as a hardened veteran of English raiding his advice would have been followed. The estuary of the Rother would have reverberated with the sounds of drums and trumpets signalling between ships. It is possible that Rainier's galley would have moved between the front line of galleys and the warship manned by Jean de Vienne as they decided how to proceed.

Rye shared the wide shallow estuary of the River Rother with Winchelsea, and Rainier would have noticed that Winchelsea on the western banks of the estuary had not been rebuilt since the Neuville raid of 1360, when the failed attempt to rescue the captive French king ended in a routine and quite successful raid. So when the inhabitants of Rye, 2 miles further inland from the deserted remains of Winchelsea, saw the French fleet they would remember having heard from their elders of nearly a generation ago what to expect. And ten years before that, the major naval Battle of Winchelsea had taken place outside the harbour entrance, and no doubt members of the older generation would have described the unforgettable scenes when the huge Castilian ships had been sent on their way by the smaller English ships under the inspired leadership of Edward III himself, even though Edward's own ship was nearly sunk.

When Rainier Grimaldi's ships approached Rye Harbour he must have been thinking of the raid that his great-uncle Carlos Grimaldi had taken part in back in 1339. On that occasion the Monegasques were just getting started on an easy and potentially profitable raid, involving some civilian slaughter, when a large English fleet threatened to trap the raiders in the enclosed waters of the estuary, and the raiders turned tail and fled, and while Carlos escaped with his life, it was a moment of real danger for a semi-mercenary fighter.

Some years earlier the citizens of Rye had followed Edward III's urgings and constructed fortifications around the entrance to the town, but the walls may not have been completed by the time the ships appeared because they did not stop the invasion and the inhabitants fled inland. The Franco-Castilian-Monegasque forces were soon in the town itself. The usual combination of looting and killing of the old and immobile had started. It was reported that 42 tuns of wine were loaded onto the French ships and, what was an especial humiliation, the bronze church bells of Rye Church were taken down and carried off to France. When the people of Rye first saw that an invasion force was approaching it is possible that they started to ring the church bells in the continuous peal that was the fourteenth-century equivalent of an air raid siren. If that was the case it can be guessed that the invasion forces took pleasure in silencing them for ever![8]

While the moveable valuables were being taken to the ships the Castilian leader the Sire de Torcy and the French Admiral himself had a policy disagreement. They seemed to be in control of a key coastal settlement in a strategic location, and they would be able to use the site of Winchelsea itself as a type of fortress. The Castilian thought it would be possible for the French to try to create a sort of 'mini-Calais' on the English mainland. If they held onto this piece of English territory would it be defensible, and would it strengthen the French war effort against the English? Suppose the invasion fleet had turned into a force of occupation, and suppose that they had successfully held onto this back door to southern England; just 40 miles across the Channel from English Calais and 35 miles from the entrance to the River Thames it would have been a valuable asset. What is more, located just a few miles from the scene of the great French victory over the Saxons in 1066 it would have had a powerful symbolic value.

Many of the great victories of the English armies in the past forty years had been won as a result of flexible improvisation by a great leader. Was this an occasion when brilliant improvisation by Jean de Vienne might have supercharged the French war effort? It was possible, but instead Jean de Vienne took the systems-led position that they should follow the plan that had been laid down for the campaign by King Charles and his advisors and not be diverted.[9]

The pattern of the raid followed one that we have seen on many occasions in the past. The landing itself seemed to be unopposed, followed by the flight of terrified men, women and children. The attackers got started on their usual destruction and plunder. Word of the incursion carried by people in flight, the reports of the coast watchers and, in one case, by a member of the invasion force who had been captured and carried off, finally reached the local commissioner of array.

This was Hamo of Offyngton, the Abbot of Battle, whose seat was only 8 miles away from Rye. In his case the instructions to the clergy to serve in the defence of England by the Crown had hit the bullseye. Hamo was a formidable leader who had dominated his abbey for many years. A scion of a wealthy landowning family from West Sussex, Hamo probably had more in common with the director of a twenty-first century corporate landholding organisation than a modern churchman. As an administrator he had proved to be a true custodian of his holdings, and he had cut the incomes of beneficiaries of his estates in a truly twenty-first-century corporate manner. The chronicler says of Hamo that when he was called upon to defend his coasts against the invader, 'underneath his monkish habit was a soldier of mark and a stout defender of home, neighbours and coast'. Was Hamo's company made up of members of the local clergy, following Edward's instructions?[10] We do not know.

As soon as he was aware of the situation, and after extracting insider information by the use of torture, Hamo would have led his force through the forested Weald via Roman trackways to the open views across the estuary. Once he arrived after a 12-mile march, he avoided direct contact with the looting Frenchmen and wisely took up a position in the ruins of Winchelsea. The cautious Jean de Vienne, seeing a threat to the security of his campaign, started by trying to negotiate with Hamo's forces. When this failed the French made a direct assault on the English defence position in Winchelsea. This was a difficult manoeuvre as the fortified town, similar in design to a bastide from English Gascony, was as much as 35 metres above the level of the surrounding marsh and water. After several hours of inconclusive fighting Jean de Vienne made the risk-averse decision that he did not possess sufficient fighting power to continue with his assault at the same time as destroying the town of Rye. And, as it happened, by now a portion of the French navy had sailed a few more miles south-west along the coastline to Hastings. Hastings had been raided by Carlos Grimaldi back in the 1330s and the invaders would have known that it was not a great prize. It was decayed at the time of the first French invasion, and there had been no economic reasons for the town to have improved since then, so the invaders simply burnt the town after the inhabitants had fled inland and took off out to sea again.

In the meantime Jean de Vienne decided that he did not possess the forces required to fight off Hamo's posse while protecting the beached galleys and other ships and standing guard on the harbour entrance in case of attack by English shipping. He was afraid of a powerful English fight-back, with the risk of leaders of the fleet being held hostage, of major losses to ships, and the deaths of too many fighters.

While Jean de Vienne and his fleet were cautiously weighing up their options the course of English history was changing. King Edward's regime had been drawing to a close for many months. Unable to talk in his last weeks, the great leader would sit blankly on his throne, unaware of what was going on during court proceedings. Possibly the last time that the old king was seen in public, he was being taken on a barge along the Thames to Parliament, lying motionless in the boat, partially hidden from public view by a canopy.

He had outlived many of his children so the throne passed down to his grandson, who became Richard II. Like his grandfather Richard came to the throne young, but unlike his grandfather he possessed no precocious leadership qualities. As can happen with great leaders, Edward III's immediate entourage slipped away before he died, in order to ensure survival in the coming changeover. At the end only his mistress Alice Perrers was left, but at the moment of death she took the valuable rings off his fingers and fled the palace.[11]

For the present England was drifting, and it was to be many years before a new pilot emerged. While Hamo and Jean de Vienne were facing each other in Rye, everyone who mattered in the royal court was taken up with Edward's death, Richard's coronation, and possibly most important of all, who would be up and who would be down under the new regime. For a time England was defenceless. If the French and Castilians had reacted fast, Jean de Vienne and his advisors and allies would have found no one to stop them and they could have seized English territory. *L'Angleterre Française*! As it was, the entire might of French naval power had been turned aside by an impromptu raid of locals and clergymen led by an elderly Abbot.

Meanwhile, the Franco-Castilian fleet continued on its way west, past Hastings again. It is possible that the next raid had been identified in advance. The focus of attention was Lewes with its wealthy priory, not a coastal location. The journey west took the fleet past the desolate Pevensey Levels and the ancient and decayed Pevensey Castle dating from Roman times. John of Gaunt owned it and when it had been suggested that he should man the fortress in order to deal with invading French forces he refused, arrogantly saying that he was so wealthy that even if it was destroyed he would not suffer! This remark from a contemporary chronicler indicates that without the leadership of an Edward III, the powers at that time relapsed into the type of careless solipsism that had accompanied the collapse of the reign of Edward II.[12]

The fleet rounded the chalk cliffs of Beachy Head and continued west. The cliffs where the South Downs meet the sea would have been manned all the way by the well-trained local levies, and the flames of the beacons that must have tracked their coastwise movements would have told Jean de Vienne that his fleet was being tracked. The choice of Rottingdean seems to show local knowledge, as the stretch of coast from Beachy Head onwards is cliff-bound, and a Rottingdean landing opens up the way to the river port of Lewis with its rich abbey. The approach to Lewis, however, via the estuary of the River Ouse, would have been considered risky by Jean de Vienne as it involved a 6-mile inland journey along a narrow valley, no more than a mile wide, flanked by low hills, so there was a real risk that his forces would be trapped while carrying out their raid on Lewis, the same risk as the one that had led him to withdraw from Rye.

The decision to target Lewis was a good one as its defence had been neglected in another example of the decline in the will of England's leaders to wage war on the French. The Earl of Arundel, a member of the royal family and the leading landowner in Sussex, was the local commissioner of array, and owned Lewis Castle itself. It should have been a secure location. Yet the castle was in ruinous condition, and largely unmanned. Like John of Gaunt and his castle of Pevensey, Richard Fitzalan had more pressing personal political concerns at this moment of national danger associated with the death of the old king. The result was that when Jean de Vienne's fleet was approaching Rottingdean, Fitzalan was in London, and despite the fact that it was well-known in England that a big French push was to be expected that summer, nothing had been done.

In the fourteenth century the chalk cliffs extended maybe half-a-mile farther out to sea than in the twenty-first century. Although Rottingdean must have been a tiny settlement, much reduced in population after the Black Death, it had a church and maybe just one large house. The slopes of the South Downs would not have been covered in short turf but very likely in scrub.

After the French had landed their ships there was an attempt by the local residents to fight back. But the resistance by the locals against trained professionals failed and although we have no record of the details many local militia members would have died in battle, and any taken captives would have been killed, once the French leaders had decided that they had no value for ransoming. It is likely that at this stage that the remainder of the population of Rottingdean took refuge in the church. All able-bodied men between sixteen and sixty years of age would have been out in the field, armed and ready for the fight, or already dead in battle, so the population in the church would have been mostly women, children, men over the age of sixty and disabled men. The French-led forces set fire to the church and by blocking the exit, ensured that the entire remaining population of Rottingdean was burnt alive. The reddish-coloured burn marks that survive on the limestone chancel arch stonework are a very rare piece of physical evidence from these events.[13]

To burn all of those people alive while stopping them from escaping the flames and being indifferent to the screams of terror and agony would be considered a terrible atrocity today, but it was not unusual or necessarily against the chivalric code of honour. The counter-attack came down out of the hills of the South Downs in the form of a cavalry charge of maybe 300 soldiers, led by a figure in full armour covered in a red surplice, another of the clerical homeland defenders that answered Edward's call to arms. This red knight was Jean de Cherlieu, also known as Jehan Caroloco, the sixty-year-old Abbot of Lewes Priory. It is surprising that the defence of Lewes fell upon a Frenchman, as during the same period a stream of anti-foreigner edicts were flowing out of the Chancery of King Edward in his name, eventually leading to actual removal of French-born members of foreign religious institutions. Lewes Priory, as a French-owned Cluniac monastery with co-establishments all over Europe, should have been targeted but on a number of occasions King Edward had stated his love and support for Lewes Priory, which was a huge landowner all over the south of England.[14]

Jean de Cherlieu was not to repeat the success of Hamo in Rye. As an amateur, Cherlieu led his fighting force of 200 men straight into a trap. Jean de Vienne retained a significant fighting force at the seaward end of the valley, but only to draw the fighting abbot and his seconds-in-command into an exposed location. Once they were in position the French and Monegasque fighters hidden in the undergrowth in the valley sides above the village houses poured out of their hiding places and fell upon the defenders. Froissart gives us a vivid picture of the ensuing melee in which English longbowmen were able to inflict much damage on the French attackers, and of the ghastly treatment of the dead:

> A squire born in France being in the service of the said prior fought manfully against men of France, in so much that his belly [was] cut, he fought sore, his bowels remaining behind him a great space, and followed his enemies. In which conflict a hundred Englishmen were slain, and many more of the Frenchmen; which took the dead men away with them, others else they burnt their faces with iron that they should not be known, and that Englishmen should not take solace of their death.[15]

During this engagement Jean de Cherlieu himself was captured by Jean de Vienne, alongside his seconds-in-command. Following the code of chivalric honour, Jean de Cherlieu would have been treated with great honour, and treated in just the same way that a member of the French Admiral's society would expect to be treated. He was later taken to France and ransomed for 7,000 marks – a huge amount of money, equivalent to a whole year's rent from the whole of the giant Lewes landholdings. Jean de Cherlieu spent two years in gilded captivity in France as a guests of Jean de Vienne before his priory was able to raise this amount of money.[16]

Jean de Vienne's withdrawal in Rye had been driven by fear of being cut off from his fleet by an attack on his flanks, and by charging down the valley of Rottingdean the English defenders had put themselves in a similarly vulnerable position and paid the price.

The Rottingdean raid was a profitable one in itself. It opened up the way to the town of Lewes, its rich priory and the wealthy hinterland. In the course of the fighting Jean de Vienne learnt of the death of the old king from captives who were tortured for their information. He must have realised that this was the end of an era. Undoubtedly Jean de Vienne must have understood that his job as Admiral of France had become easier and that an England ruled by a twelve-year-old made a successful invasion of the historic enemy far more likely to succeed. A Norman barge was immediately sent across the English Channel to take the news to King Charles.

The invasion force was undoubtedly encouraged by this news and the realisation that for now at least the surrounding territory would be relatively undefended. It is difficult to put the information of the post-Cherlieu actions into a straightforward chronological order. We can guess however that the French forces might well have advanced up the dry valley of Rottingdean and over the hilltops of about 500 feet, then down into the low-lying valley of the River Ouse, upon which Lewes Abbey and the town of Lewes itself was located. It would be a journey of maybe 7 miles and it is possible that that captives from among the failed defence force would have, under torture, told the invaders of the best approach to the prize of Lewes and its Abbey.

Before battle commenced, fugitives from Rottingdean would have brought the terrible news of death, slaughter, burning and hostage-taking. The remaining forces would have frantically prepared themselves. Before the arrival of the land forces the drums, cornets and battle cries of the Monegasque galleys rowing up the Ouse Valley may have been audible. At nearly the same time the sound of an army would have come to them from the hills overlooking the Abbey and then all of a sudden the hilltop would have been full of knights in glittering armour, with pennants and banners. They would have been accompanied by men in full armour on foot, yelling their battle cries, and running down the hill to the battleground.

The English were capable of defending themselves. Each archer would have his sheaf of arrows, and the arrows would have started their deathly work even before each side could physically engage with the other. Froissart tells us that Jean de Vienne's forces fought another force of defenders in an open space outside the Abbey itself:

> As they entered Lewes there was a deal of fighting, and many French were wounded by arrows; but they were so numerous that they drove back their enemies, who gathered in a convenient square in front of the monastery to await the foe approaching in close order for a hand-to-hand fight. Many noble feats of arms were performed on both sides, and the English defended themselves very well considering their numbers, for they were few in comparison with the French. For this reason they exerted themselves all the more, while the French were all the more eager to inflict losses on them. Finally the French conquered the town and dislodged the English; two hundred of them were killed and a large number of the more important men taken prisoner, rich men from the surrounding parts who had come there to win honour; the prior and the two knights were also taken. The whole town of Lewes was ransacked and burnt or destroyed, together with some small villages round about. By high tide the French were already back in their ships, and they set sail with their booty and their prisoners...

We are able to name some of the 'small villages' in the area. Ovingdean Church has signs of burning and there is a tradition that it was attacked and burnt at this time.

The French forces at the Battle of Lewes would have been supported by some at least of the Franco-Castilian navy, who would have sailed up the Ouse Valley to Lewes. It is known that Exceat was burnt at this time, and Seaford was attacked when the house of John of Newburgh was destroyed and looted by the Franco-Castilian Monegasque forces. Although it is not mentioned by any chronicler it is highly unlikely that the invaders stopped with John of Newburgh's house, even though Seaford was a port in terminal decline and it is likely that the invaders found little of value, which led to the raid leaving fewer traces on the record.[17]

The early summer expedition ended with a series of quick incursions into a number of other locations along the south coast. Many were return visits to ports that had been trashed by the French in previous decades. Portsmouth was raided. It had been attacked by a Franco-Scottish force in 1335, when many of its inhabitants were killed, and again in 1339, when an elite force armed with new-fangled gunpowder technology had wrecked much of the remainder of the town. Again in 1369 Portsmouth was burnt. The French were following a policy of destroying leading coastal locations as often as possible in order to hamper the recovery process. In late June Folkestone was put to the torch, and then the French turned on Portsmouth again. Terrier puts it very well:

> Although Portsmouth was not a base for attacks upon the French coasts, it was nevertheless a breeding ground for tough sailors, and from this time, its dockyards produced many ships. But it was however badly defended. By destroying the town and all its storehouses, Jean de Vienne did huge damage to England's naval power that was hard to repair.

Plymouth was the leading port in the south-western approaches, and it was a key target that was attacked again and again; in the early years of the war it had been attacked and burnt on three occasions between 1338 and 1360. There were many small raids, we do not know all the locations but apart from Portsmouth, Dartmouth and possibly Fowey are likely, with other smaller coastwise settlements such as Weymouth, Lyme and Exmouth in Devon also possible targets.

In late June Jean de Vienne and his Franco-Genoese-Castilian fleet returned in triumph to Honfleur. He was received by King Charles with honour. As the chronicler of the time says: 'Never before in living memory had the French inflicted such damage on the English.'[18]

While all this action was going on in the south of England, a small-scale Scottish event in the Borders gave a hint of what maybe was to come. George Dunbar, Earl of March, a leading Scottish magnate on the Border, started in July to attack English strongholds in Scotland in reprisal for small-scale fighting that had taken place between English and Scottish forces. The action escalated when Dunbar and his forces entered the fortress town of Roxbrough. In a striking parallel to the type of action that was happening in the south of England George Dunbar's men broke into the town, massacred the inhabitants, and burnt the town to the ground. It is strange that this was possible, as Roxburgh was at this time one of the main English bastions in the lawless Borders, and the fortress had been extensively restored just a few years before the raid. Is it possible that it had been left unmanned? Or had the defenders been bribed to absent themselves on the fateful day?[19] There are hints that French agents were still active in Scotland, ready to push the Scottish king in the direction of war against the English. This is a small episode but it was to become in later years part of a bigger story.

To return to the French royal court and the triumphal return of Jean de Vienne, Sanchez de Tamar, Rainier Grimaldi and the fleet. It was decided that the campaign must not stop at this point. There was plenty of summer sailing remaining and the fleet had to get back out to sea as soon as possible. The crew was paid, and re-engaged for the next expedition. They should exploit their winning streak by going for the biggest prize of all, Calais.

The Duke of Burgundy was put in charge, and the fleet was quickly loaded with the sort of equipment that a besieging army might require – plenty of artillery, a large quantity of scaling ladders, wooden defence walls and axes. Jean de Vienne was by nature a cautious commander who believed in planning and although we do not know what his opinion was of the Calais plan he might have had his doubts. In the end the Duke was of superior status to Jean de Vienne, so Jean may well have had to follow instructions.[20] However, after leaving port towards the end of August Jean de Vienne hatched a plan. Maybe the English had got wind that he was planning to take part in an invasion of their city of Calais? If the fleet sailed straight there might not the English fleet be waiting, ready to ambush them? Maybe the best way would be to sail away from Calais, in a westerly direction, making the English think that Jean de Vienne was going back to England for more of the same. At the same time Jean de Vienne secretly planned a quick but destructive raid on Southampton, one of England's leading ports, which may still have been in recovery from the terrible attacks of the 1330s. The plan was, after a successful incursion, to sail back across the English Channel for the Duke of Burgundy's operations outside Calais.

At this stage weather in the English Channel turned against the French, as had happened many times before. The unwieldy nature of the ships meant that the fleet ended up somewhere it did not want to be. Before they could make it to the entrance to the Solent, Jean de Vienne's vessels were blown onto the shores of the Isle of Wight, and they made landfall somewhere on the east coast, although the exact location is not recorded.

It is easy to picture the fleet sailing through the Channel in a late summer storm, trying to stop the easterly winds from blowing the fleet onto the shore, being watched by lines of islanders, ready with their longbows, pikes, and daggers. Out of the mist and sea spray, the ships appear, in obvious difficulty, making headway very slowly against the strong winds. A war fleet freshly out of port would have been a sight that few of the islanders had had seen before with its usual paraphernalia of flags, pennants, painted decorations and embroidered coats of arms and motifs on sails. Once the decision was taken that there was no option but to land on the Isle of Wight the leaders would have looked for a suitable landing place, almost certainly to the east of Sandown where for about 700 yards there is a flat area. As the fleet approached the shore, galleys, possibly led by Rainier Grimaldi, would have been in the lead while the landward defence forces were assembling ready for action. The French were ready to fight their way out of their ships and across the beach but to their surprise the islanders waited and no order was given for attack. The inexperienced islanders were not aware that an attacking force is most vulnerable when landing in rough waters. The defending forces had in mind something like a pitched battle where two armies range up on a piece of open ground and then start fighting after an agreed signal. Documents of the time do not say where this order came from but it could well have been from the leading military man on the Isle of Wight, Sir Hugh Tyrrell. As the Commander of Carisbrook Castle, he would have been consulted, and it appears he made a faulty decision. Needless to say the hardened warriors easily overwhelmed the islanders and the entire island was open to the invading force. It was said in government papers that every settlement on the east and south of the island was 'utterly burnt and destroyed'.[21]

Two of Jean de Vienne's raids of 1377 were defended by elderly leaders who until then had also been clerics. Sir High Tyrrell was another elderly defender, and he may have been in his late seventies when this responsibility fell upon him. In this case it would appear that he did not mount an adequate defence of his island, and wasted the military advantage that Carisbrook Castle could have given him.

The onus passed onto the castle itself and its commander. Carisbrook Castle was a powerful fortress located just where a fortress should be – on the highest ground, about 60 metres above the surrounding area, including the village of Carisbrook itself. It had been well maintained all the way through the fourteenth century and possessed every feature that a proper castle should possess. It had a fine fortified gatehouse, a portcullis, a drawbridge. It was right in the middle of the island so the defenders of the castle could see exactly what was happening through 360°. The commander of the castle made another faulty decision – he did not plan to fight the invaders but rather to retreat into his fortress and wait. As a result, the French forces were able to ravage the island almost unopposed, although the well-trained English archers in the castle were able to dispose of some of the attacking force. Eventually Sir Hugh surrendered to the invaders, and a ransom of 1,000 marks was negotiated in return for the French forces' withdrawal.[22] A good ransom payment made this expedition worthwhile.

In the meantime the fleet continued on its way, with better weather conditions. Needless to say, England's biggest and most important ports were by now well defended. Southampton, Portsea, Poole – all along the coasts forces were waiting for the French, in each case led by a royal earl or duke. The expedition ended in anti-climax. After a cruise along a well defended south coast, apart from the successful sack and burning of Folkestone, when the fleet returned home to Harfleur the plan to invade Calais had been abandoned.

The English planned to retaliate with a new expedition to Brittany. A huge invasion fleet was put together, yet again with the intention of attacking French territory and seizing key locations. After a series of disasters, a part of the fleet sailed in December of 1377 for Brest, led by the late King Edward's youngest son Thomas. It was successful, Brest was occupied and the royal Earl returned in triumph.

Not surprisingly, early in 1378 it had been decided in the English Great Council that there was to be a new series of attacks on French territory to follow up the Brest success, but by now times had changed. Decades of warfare had led to a feeling of war weariness in England. It was getting harder to recruit troops. Merchants in ports such as Sandwich did what they could to avoid allowing their ships to be used on expeditions. Press gangs made their appearance for the first time.

Over the next three years Edward's war leaders continued to do what they had done before, launch attacks on France. An entire generation of aristocrats lived almost entirely for the ideal of chivalry, a philosophy that set the highest possible value upon warfare as a noble thing that brings glory upon a victorious nation:

The noble chivalry of the realm was long well nourished, cherished, honoured and nobly rewarded for their great deeds ... through which the realm was greatly enriched and filled with all good things, and its inhabitants feared by their enemies.

The raids and incursions on the English coastline saw trained warriors often led by fighters who, although they lived within the chivalric ideal, were confronting non-chivalric inhabitants of the coastal settlements. Certainly few of the recipients of French aggression would have felt 'greatly enriched' by their experiences! In fact over the coming years English leaders such as John of Gaunt continued to fight on the Continent, but there were to be no more victories. The absence of the English fighting machine for long periods on the Continent had the result of opening the English coastline to the French. So when in August of 1378 John of Gaunt was looking for a suitable location to land in France, Jean de Vienne and his Castilian allies were planning a new series of raids on the English coastline. The Franco-Castilian fleet targeted the western approaches to the Channel, thus avoiding the usual south coast target, which we can guess would be in a state of alert against the French.[25]

Rather as happened in 1339 when the Franco-Monegasque fleet unexpectedly descended on Plymouth after cruising along the well-defended coastline further to the east, in 1378 the Franco-Castilian fleet descended on Cornwall and maybe other areas of the West Country. It is known that they attacked Fowey, but there is not much more information available. It is known that the fleet on returning to France had plenty of valuable booty and had not suffered any serious losses, and that they were able to inflict plenty of damage on the coastal areas of Cornwall. Thomas of Walsingham expresses the English mood:

> We are ashamed to pass on such unhappy events and we would rather pass over them in silence lest they become occasion for triumph for our enemies.[23]

The people of Cornwall send a petition to Parliament complaining about the fact that the English crown was unable to protect them from enemy attacks:[24]

> The people of the Duchy of Cornwall entreat as they are so badly wounded and put to such great mischief by the war of our enemies year after year ... and this year the Spanish galleys have come and burnt all the nefs, ships and towns which are in the ports and on the seacoasts – and these enemies have put a great part of this duchy to grievous harm because of our power and force to fight against them.

It appears that Jean de Vienne's fleet was operating on English territory between June and December 1378. In 1379 and 1380 the raiding continued, with attacks recorded in a widely dispersed range of places. Although no raid on Scarborough has been recorded by any chronicler, according to Parliamentary writs one was very destructive, and much of the population of the town had left and gone elsewhere.

In 1380 another set of invasions was launched all over southern England; Jersey and Guernsey were occupied by Jean de Vienne's forces and a new raid was carried out on Winchelsea. This time Abbot Hamo returned but was not able to stop the invaders, and the raid was a real success for the French. They burnt Winchelsea, by which it would appear that a start had been made on repopulating the town. The raid continued up the Rother Valley, possibly as far as Bodiam Castle, a few hours ride away. Later in the year they were back, and this time they dared to do what no fleet had tried in the forty-odd years since the outbreak of hostilities, when they sailed up the Thames. This time the fleet penetrated as far as Gravesend, sailing past Queenborough and Hadley Castles without being challenged.

In an example of closing the stable door after the horse has bolted, fortifications were built to protect London from future raids. A letter-book from Richard II indicates how serious was the threat of French invasion into the heart of the English nation. The proposal was as follows:

> For the building of a stone tower that was to be made on one side of the water of Thames opposite to another like stone tower, which John Philpott ... had promised and granted that he himself would build on the other side of the Thames; 60 kin's feet in height and 20 feet wide within the walls of the tower; and that on his own costs and charges.

Philpott seems to be a fourteenth-century version of the 'great and the good' who gain plaudits by carrying out services to their community.

14

FRANCO-SCOTTISH INVASION OF ENGLAND: 1385–6

The 1380 raid on Gravesend had been audacious. More than 30 miles up the River Thames, past the two castles guarding the entrance to the river, it would have been an impossible manoeuvre if there had been any systematic defence forces in operation. The fact that Admiral de Vienne's fleet dared to make this raid indicates just how far England's defences had deteriorated under their teenage King Richard II and his close advisors, such as John of Gaunt. It also suggests that the French had good spies on English territory.

The following year the whole of England was in chaos with what is often called the 'Peasants Revolt', although many classes of society took part in the mass demonstrations against the regime that broke out all over the kingdom. King Richard himself was trapped inside the Tower of London, helplessly watching the crowds roaming the streets. It is telling that John of Gaunt's Savoy Palace, by far the finest house in London, was targeted by the rebels and systematically trashed by furious but well-disciplined mobs who did not steal anything but concentrated upon destroying the luxurious building and its priceless treasures, brought back from the Continent as loot or bought with the proceeds of expeditions to France. The Savoy Palace was a symbol of what the ordinary people of England had grown to hate about the regime. Other attacks were carried out by citizens against symbols of the status quo. For instance, lawyers were targeted, their offices were attacked and legal papers were burnt. The universities in Oxford and Cambridge were attacked, prisons were invaded and prisoners were released *en masse.*

The 'Peasants' Revolt' was not specifically a rural movement and many people on the middle rungs of society were supporters. It was not just an expression of anger at decades of high wartime taxation, although that played a part. The decades of chaos and disruption caused by cycle after cycle of invasion fears, followed by real destructive incursions, the economic decline of coastal settlements as a result of French pressure, and the compulsory membership of all fencible men to take part in defence with no obvious benefit were important contributions. By 1380 England's defences were so badly organised that the French had sailed up the Thames without being challenged. The fact that even after the capital was threatened the state was unable to provide defences, leaving it up to wealthy benefactors such as Philpott to fill the gaps, told its own tale.[1]

The events of 1381 had profound effects on English society and government. The rules of engagement between France and England seem to change after that year. Most importantly, forty-five years of raids stopped. From now onwards the focus of the *Admiral de France* Jean de Vienne was a single large-scale land invasion of England, leading to regime change.

The concept of an invasion of England in which Scotland acted as an ally had been a scenario since even before King Philippe issued his *arrière-ban.* The expression 'Auld Alliance' always suggested two nations coming together in order to manage the risks and dangers posed by their unruly and aggressive neighbour, seemingly addicted to endless warfare. It also suggests war on two fronts. A plan of this size was a massive logistical challenge. French shipping had to be able to sail at will in the English Channel and the North Sea. There had to be sufficient shipping available to carry two armies across the seas at about the same time. The armies had to possess sufficient supplies of military equipment and also of food in order to stay active in the field for as long as necessary. Jean de Vienne was not willing to embark on the type of expeditions favoured by John of Gaunt, hoping that valour would make up for the deficiencies in organising supplies.

Just one ship of fully armed and equipped fighters, supported by cargo vessels carrying materiel and food supplies, represented a huge financial investment. Now the Admiral had to organise hundreds. Such a vast undertaking was only possible for a country which had the reserves that had been built up systematically since the dark days after Poitiers, under the judicious financial management of King Charles. The French crown had a formidable war chest and Jean de Vienne had access to it, so, to an extent, the naval plans in the coming years went ahead independently of the problems that developed after the death of Charles the Wise. France's diplomats had been busy all over Europe during the past years, under the direction of King Charles, forming alliances. England had none, apart from Flanders. However, Flanders was the best ally that England could have. Flanders bordered on the English-held territory of Calais, close to the narrowest point of the Straits of Dover. Flemish territory was uncomfortably close to the huge French-held port of Sluys as forthcoming events will demonstrate.

* * *

A first step was to renew the Franco-Scottish alliance. Robert II of Scotland was cautious and uninterested in waging war against the

English. His son John, Earl of Carrick, however, wanted war with England and he wanted to renew the Auld Alliance. An exploratory raid took place in 1383 in the traditional manner, led by the Earl. A small lightly armed Scottish force crossed the Border hills and raided the fortress of Wark, situated on the River Tweed. Even today the area is bleak and sparsely inhabited and although the castle has long been demolished, its mound still looms over the river bank. A properly defended castle in such a location should have been impregnable.[2] Probably because the Border country had been relatively peaceful for quite a number of years the Earl and his small mobile band of fighters quickly took the fortress, killed the garrison and did as much damage as possible before moving on. Just a day's gallop along the banks of the Tweed would have taken the Earl and his men to Berwick-on-Tweed, a frontier town of great symbolic value. But the Scottish force did not follow up their small victory. Many decades of attacks from King Edward's English forces had taught the Scots to keep a low profile and avoid direct action against battle-ready English forces. This was just a limited border raid, not unusual, but was one small part of a bigger picture that was developing.[3]

At the same time that the Earl's men were trashing this obscure border fortress, Scotland's leading cleric, William Wardlaw, who happened to be familiar with the inner workings of the English court, was in Orléans, talking to his French counterparts. It was agreed: when the current temporary truce ran out the following year, France and Scotland would become allies. France would contribute a subsidy of 40,000 gold francs, 1,000 French knights, and equipment for 1,000 Scottish knights to dress in the same way as the French. From now onwards the security situation on the Border deteriorated and in the councils of France, under the nominal leadership of the young and inexperienced Charles VI, a full-scale invasion plan was being put together.[4] This plan would be launched in the early summer of 1385. Jean de Vienne was to take a force all the way up the North Sea from Sluys to Scotland, carrying all the men, resources, ships and gold that had been agreed to the previous year by Wardlaw and his interlocutors in Orléans. Over the following months Jean de Vienne and the Scottish King Robert were to pool their resources and launch a full-scale invasion of the north of England over the Border hills, the scene of many a bloody minor battle in the past decades.

The Scottish campaign was merely the opening salvo. The main force would wait in port in France and, when the time was right, land an entire army somewhere in southern England. In an echo of the invasion of England by Edward III's mother, when the nominal leader of the invasion force had been the teenage Prince Edward, this great force was to be symbolically led by thirteen-year-old Charles, the son of Charles the Wise. In a strange parallel, both foes were led by teenagers – the English King Richard was only eighteen at this time.

When rumours of the impending French attack filtered through to the English court a generational split in the royal family emerged. The warmongering older generation led by the by now elderly John of Gaunt raged at his nephew King Richard, and insisted that England should behave as his father or grandfather would have done – fight back fast, ferociously, and maintain pressure on enemy territory, that is, on French soil.

The new generation, of which Richard was part, were for peace and if war was necessary, no more than self-defence. The passive argument won the day. The older generation were infuriated by the new approach. Gone were the days of Edward III, always dominant, able to command respect, lead and win on the battlefield. From now on the English court would be riven with dissension, plots and in-fighting. In the run-up to the big invasion there was much Anglo-French diplomatic activity aimed at ending the war.

In spring 1385 the Royal Council of France started to make its plans. Although King Charles was nominally the leader, his

uncle the Duke of Burgundy, who the previous year had planned
to invade Calais itself, was the effective head of the operation.[5]
This invasion plan was the biggest and most ambitious since the
days of the Crusades. The operation needed so many ships that the
authorities had to find suitable vessels from all over Europe. There
was only one port in all of the English Channel that was suitable.
Sluys was huge, with its 8 miles of sheltered waters in and among
a number of low-lying islands. For a pan-European fleet, it had
an essential central location just a few miles from the entrance to
the River Rhine and within a reasonable sailing distance from the
French naval bases in the River Seine. For a fleet that was able
to control the approaches, the narrow entrance to the harbour
provided real security. But nothing is secure in warfare, especially
in medieval warfare.

In the spring the English showed a great deal of efficiency in
putting together a defence force which would, if not take on
the French forces in their operations, at least harass them while
they made preparations. A defence force was put together with
impressed shipping, and the ships were mustered in the East
Anglian ports of Harwich and Orwell, about 90 miles across the
North Sea from Sluys. Amazingly enough, when in May this fleet
arrived at the entrance to Sluys harbour, they were able fight their
way in, capture some shipping and burn some in a lightning raid.
With their overwhelming numbers the French ships drove the
English vessels out, and they took off back to England.

After the Sluys raid a group of West Country independents went
into operation as an independent force. The sailors from these
West Country ports of Dartmouth, Fowey and Plymouth had all
suffered from the French raids of 1377 and were eager for revenge
and the restoration of honour. They were successful in the waters
near and around Sluys. They burnt ships and were able to capture
one very high-status vessel, which might have been the flagship of
a Constable. These episodes demonstrate the success of the English

quick and deadly style against the French approach of being slow and thorough.[6]

The French invasion of England was intended to be supported by land operations in France itself. There were to be attacks on English strongholds such as Calais, and in Gascony. Remembering the disaster of 1369 when the invasion of England had to be called off when the Flemings attacked Damme on the approaches to Sluys harbour, there were to be French forces in Flanders to ensure Sluys would remain a secure base. Even as the expedition was being planned Flemish Ghent was being besieged in order to expel all traces of the English alliance from the territory. In addition, there were to be plenty of extra French fighters. They were to stay in place, ready to move into action at the slightest hint that the John of Gaunt's philosophy of warfare at short notice with a minimum of planning got the upper hand in the councils of Richard II. If any reports had come back to the French court from their spies concerning English warships mustering in English ports, the spare French defenders would immediately have been in action.

It looked like a faultless plan. Financially, France was able to underwrite this hugely expensive project, and in case the war chest bequeathed by Charles the Wise to his descendants was not enough, the French Treasury had resorted to currency devaluation by printing money, recalling its silver currency, melting it down, adulterating it with tin and reissuing it at the same face value. The project had been years in the making – too long maybe. The years between the death of Edward III and the Peasants Revolt would have been the best time for a large-scale invasion. But after 1382 the English state was reorganising itself. By 1385 the English were far more ready to respond to a French attack than they had been, for example, in 1381. Slow and steady does not always win the race.

Finally in early May 1385 Jean de Vienne arrived at the port of Sluys ready to start. There were hundreds of ships in the harbour. The waterways that snaked past the low-lying islands were crammed with ships of all types. As many as 180 cogs had been fitted out to carry the large number of promised horses. There were hundreds of other support vessels. Fitting out such a huge fleet involved an enormous supply and manufacturing operation, so the low islands by the sides of the channels would have been covered with temporary accommodation for craftsmen, builders, woodworkers, painters, sailmakers, and metalworkers. There would have been many horses and men. As was usual the painters and decorators had been hard at work. Many of the ships were decked out in the blue and gold of France or the colours of their owners. All roads to the port had been crammed with traffic for weeks and it had even been necessary to resurface some of the roads in order to take the traffic.[7]

Almost inevitably, at the very moment when the fleet was ready to sail, the the winds changed direction. Westerly gales trapped the French in harbour and favoured the English ships to the west that were waiting to pounce. The French were able to fight off attacks from the English but marooned in port, the entire expedition was now at the mercy of the weather.

Finally after some weeks, the winds switched direction and the fleet slipped out of its moorings into the North Sea. The English were still waiting out to sea and when the wind was in the right direction they launched a fire ship at the French fleet. This was a dangerous moment. The burning ship was full of inflammable resin but also with gunpowder. If it had blown up at the wrong moment it could have torn the fleet apart.

Luckily the winds favoured the French again and the ship was blown away from the French fleet. Then the winds changed direction and the French fleet was unable to make headway northwards. There was nothing to do but return to port and disembark. At this point some of the members of the expedition panicked, and demanded to be allowed to abandon the expedition and go home. Jean de Vienne managed to persuade them to stay and on 20 May the fleet set sail.[8]

The news of the embarkation was passed all round France and prayers were offered up to Heaven to bless the French with favourable winds. Their prayers were answered and within ten days sailing, the fleet was in Scottish waters. Their passage along the east coast of England had been watched by English ships, but none dared to attack the French. The fleet entered the Firth of Forth under uncharacteristically cloudless skies and made for the port of Leith.

* * *

The French forces, coming from the richest and largest state in Europe, would have noticed immediately after their landing that Scotland was an entirely different world. The events that followed indicate that the French leaders had not been prepared for what late fourteenth-century Scotland was really like. A combination of terrible weather, the Black Death, and constant war with the English had resulted in a country stripped of its resources, where almost everyone lived in temporary shacks, even in the capital, Edinburgh. Jean de Vienne and his French knights would have been able to see this as soon as they arrived on dry land.

The French were a spectacle never before seen in Scotland. Froissart gives us a picture of the lengths that the French had gone to in order to make the appearance of their war machine overwhelmingly magnificent.[9]

They made pennons and flags of silk that were a marvel to behold. The masts were painted from top to bottom, and some, in a display of magnificence, were covered in gold leaf, the arms of the owner being fixed at the head. I was particularly informed that Sir Guy de la Trémouille had so richly ornamented the ship in which his men were to cross that the decorations and paintings had cost two thousand Francs.

Events were to show that it was perhaps a mistake to enter such an impoverished country as Scotland with such an overwhelming display of wealth. If the French wanted to make trusty battlefield allies of the Scots they maybe should have approached them in a different style. The French were surprised how cool their reception was. There were some pro-war noble families, and the king's son himself belonged to them, but not all the Scottish leaders were of the same mind.

Surely a glittering parade of French knights processing from their port, ready to wage war alongside their Scots allies would have been greeted rapturously?

Edinburgh itself was just a short gallop away. Everything would have been freshly painted, polished, where appropriate, gilded; brand new pennants and standards were fluttering everywhere; the horses were magnificent destriers – heavy war horses – in beautiful condition, doubtless brushed and groomed for the occasion. The craftsmanship of the full armour that the knights wore was the best in Europe. And their march was accompanied by trumpets and drums.

Upon arrival in Edinburgh the French must have been expecting something that looked like a European city such as Paris, Dordrecht, or Genoa. But to their surprise the settlement that straggled around Edinburgh Castle on its craggy rock (only recently built by the English) looked like a village of a few hundred poor houses and little else. Most to the point, King Robert was not there to greet them.

At this point Jean de Vienne may have begun to wonder if the diplomatic process that the Scottish churchman had carried out the previous year was a faulty one. King Robert's warlike son Count John had got his French alliance, but the King's absence indicated that something was not right. There was no evidence that anything was prepared.

The contrast between the flower of French aristocracy, newly arrayed in their best battle gear, with the shacks and hovels of Scotland's capital must have been stark, even shaming. The French had treasure and beautiful equipment stored in the ships, ready to share out. They had treasure chests filled with coinage. They had fine thoroughbred horses from France, ready to be given away to their Scottish allies, so different from the poor half-starved nags they saw around them on the road from Leith to Edinburgh. Did the French think that once arrayed in French gear a Scottish knight would look like a French one? If so, they were wrong. If you put a Scottish soldier in a suit of French armour and give him a French war horse you will not make him act like a French knight!

Edinburgh was certainly not Paris. Their lodgings were impoverished and not at all what they had expected. Worse, the poverty of the country led to a dearth of provisions. Even worse still, what supplies were on offer were sold at ridiculously high prices. Did the Scots see the French as a 'money machine'? The ultimate shock was when foraging parties were sent out in order to take supplies from local people by force they were attacked and driven away by enraged peasants accustomed to taking the law into their own hands – this is not what they were used to in France.

The visual magnificence of the best display that French chivalry could put on had badly misfired. By displaying their wealth so tactlessly in a ruined, impoverished country they were telling the Scots that they understood nothing of the real world of warfare that the Scots lived in. It also at this early stage of the campaign possibly told the Scots that the French had more money than sense, and maybe too the idea was forming that the Scots would not let Frenchman tell them how they should run their affairs just because they were poor. Indeed, Froissart expresses very clearly the opinion that the French nobility had of the Scots:

> In Scotland you shall find no man of honour of gentleness; they are like wild and savage people ... and are greatly envious of the honour or profit of any other man.

Froissart explains from his chivalric point of view why the Scots did not give the French army a warm welcome.

> Anon tidings sprang about in Scotland, that a great number of men-at-arms of France were come into their country; some thereat did murmur and grudge and said 'Who the devil hath sent for them? What do they here? Cannot we maintain our war with England well enough without their help? We shall do no good as long as they are with us. They understand not us nor we them.'

During the voyage a number of horses had died. When the French tried to buy new ones they were not only shocked at how poor the condition of the Scottish horse was, but also at the absurdly high prices that they were being charged.

When King Robert appeared, fresh from his 'urgent business' in the north of Scotland, said by Froissart to be 'vulgar of appearance and bleary eyed', he did not show much martial spirit.[10] Robert had not readied his army and he made it clear that the starting point of their relationship was French money. The French had to pass over to the Scots all of the money and materiel that had been negotiated the previous year, that is, 6,000 gold francs to be paid directly to King Robert. Now that the payments were starting, the Scots began to organise. June was spent recruiting and by July there were 1,000 armoured soldiers and 30,000 foot soldiers ready, many arrayed in French gear. On 8 July the force moved off in the direction of the Scottish Border, following the road to the key fortress of Roxburgh, a waypoint on the road to Newcastle upon Tyne situated on the upper Tweed valley. Once Jean de Vienne took the strategically important Roxburgh Castle they would have a power base in the region.

In late July the Franco-Scots force, having spent days marching through the desolate, depopulated Border hills, arrived in the Tweed Valley, bypassed the Border fortress of Roxburgh and marched over the high ground along the Border through country devastated by war. Encountering a few impoverished inhabitants, the Scots and the French took everyone they could and killed them by cutting their throats.[10]

When the Franco-Scots army reached Wark in England, which is where the Scots were the year before, they found it to be properly manned, no doubt in response to the disaster of the previous year. Naturally the French were ready to besiege the fortress of Wark, which is where the Scottish incursion started the previous year. But their Scots allies refused to take an active part in the attack. Once taken, the two armies moved forward – taking the fortress of Alnwick, then moving south to the Morpeth. This was a key location on the way to Newcastle, now just 15 miles march away. Once an army takes Morpeth it should easily take Newcastle. A powerful French army in Newcastle ready to link up with an even bigger invasion in the south of England would be a force to be reckoned with. Who knows how far they could have gone? In Newcastle they were ready to make further moves in response the second French force in the south.[11]

The French and the English had been at war for more than forty years, off and on. This was the first time since the Isabella-led invasion of 1326 that a large-scale army was on English territory equipped and able to overthrow the current weakened English regime led by King Richard. Jean de Vienne was moving through an English territory that was accustomed to being raided but according to the French chronicler the savagery of the invading French army was worse than anything seen before. The army fell upon everyone, slitting throats or disembowelling everyone regardless of age or sex. This type of brutality was not compatible with the conventions of chivalric warfare, although similar brutalities had been carried out in France after the collapse of government following the Battle of Poitiers, and there can be no doubt that many of the French would have wished to wreak their revenge. Edward III had learnt the technique of the chevauchée in his Border wars as a young king, but the French had suffered from countless terrible chevauchées since those early days. Who can say how many of Jean de Vienne's army – high- and low-born alike – had personal memories of English strategic brutality?

When his army was in Morpeth a provisional victory was in his grasp. Then he received some unexpected news. While camped outside Morpeth Jean de Vienne was approached by a messenger from King Richard, carrying a missive. It was an angry reproach for daring to invade his kingdom, vowing destruction of the entire French army. In the process it was revealed that the English had raised an army in response to the invasion, and that they were now within shouting distance of the French.

As a true knight Jean de Vienne treated the messenger with great respect, invited him to dine with him, and sent him back to his king with a proposal that the issue between the two armies be solved by means of a pitched battle between, for example, ten Frenchmen against thirty Englishmen – the proportion by which the Franco-Scottish forces were outnumbered. It was ignored.[12]

How did the English get an army to the Scottish Border so quickly? Compared to the elaborate and slow-moving preparations that the French had gone through, the English response had been extraordinarily speedy. The English, following the wishes of John of Gaunt, had been planning an expedition to the European Continent. This project was abandoned once it was understood what the French were planning. The question was how to raise an army big enough to scare the French back home in just a very few weeks, with a government in the midst of a financial crisis, with no funds available.

Armies were manned by professional paid soldiers, remunerated at a fixed daily rate according to their status. Since the early days of Edward III and his near bankruptcy, it had been the custom for armies to be paid in advance. In a society that ran on hard cash it meant that the Exchequer had to hold stores of coinage ready to pay out to long lines of waiting men-at-arms, for example. The England of 1385 did not have strong boxes full of silver coinage in this volume, although the French did. It was quickly proposed to revive the feudal levy upon non-combatants known as scutage. The entire male population would be summoned to carry out their duty to their feudal lord, and those who chose to fight presented themselves ready to do battle, for free. Those who did not wish to fight paid a tax to the Exchequer which was used to raise funds for the forthcoming battle. Later forces were recruited without any payment from the Crown. English magnates, faced with the prospect of a full-scale invasion on English territory, donated funds to the Exchequer. The immediacy of the crisis acted as a recruiting sergeant, and as the army marched north it grew. With King Richard at its head, and accompanied by his uncle John of Gaunt, the army had reached Newcastle on the fringes of the action and by then had swollen to 14,000 men, with archers in the majority. The entire aristocracy had contributed supporters. The army marched in battle order, in companies each led by a royal earl. The Bishop of Durham lent the authority of the Church to the expedition, and he walked among the fighters holding his crozier and accompanied by the banner of St Cuthbert.[13]

Once Jean de Vienne had dealt with the English herald, he proposed to his Scottish colleagues that they should try to draw the English into a pitched battle. The Scots had many years experience of fighting their English foes. They understood how to deal with an enemy bigger and better armed than they were, and pitched battles were not the way. The Scots knew very well how to wear down a better equipped enemy without putting their limited forces at risk. The Scottish leaders wanted to persuade Jean de Vienne that a set-piece battle was neither possible nor desirable.[14]

The Scottish leader took Jean de Vienne to a vantage point in the hills to see the army of 14,000 knights and archers moving through the countryside along a front several miles wide, burning, pillaging and destroying. It must have been a daunting sight as Jean de Vienne then agreed that they should not do battle. It was hopeless to resist them and that night, following the advice of the Scots, the French army slipped away silently and secretly. The English did not even see them go. The Scottish guided the French army through the wasted and barren Border country towards the English territory of Cumbria, which had not been wasted by war since the 1330s. According to the 'Life of Richard II' the response to the arrival of the English was dramatic. Many soldiers

> ... ran away from their place of encampment and scattered into many companies, it is not known where. Some of them hid in woods and marches... The rest of the population, except a few women and children, fled to the mountains and beyond the Scottish sea.[15]

Now the Scots were engaged in the sort of fighting that they liked best. The French and the Scots found a huge amount of booty in Cumbria, much to the delight of the Scottish army. But when they came to the fortified town of Carlisle in the flat and fertile area bordering on the Solway Firth, the combined Scottish army was unwilling to take what would have been a valuable prize. The fortress was neglected, the walls were unmaintained, and the citizens of Carlisle were unaccustomed to fighting. Given the right support the French army would have stayed on and besieged the town and taken it. This was the type of warfare that the French liked. But their Scots allies had a different idea of war. They had taken plenty of booty in Cumbria, they were living to fight another day. They were not prepared to risk any more.[16]

When the Scottish army returned home laden with booty it was unfazed by the fact that the English army had burnt and destroyed the lands between the Border and Edinburgh. Scotland was so poor that more burning would little more damage. When the English army arrived in Edinburgh there was nothing left to take – just abandoned dwellings that could be rebuilt in no time.

Once Jean de Vienne saw the English army marching north towards Edinburgh he did not necessarily see his plans failing. If the English army was busy in the north then now was the time for the big French invasion force to sail out of Sluys and do their worst in the south. The de Vienne army would be ready for them once word came through that they were going to land.

Jean de Vienne was supposed to be leading an invasion of England. But now in August he found himself taking part in raiding and pillaging in rural Cumbria, which pleased his Scottish allies, for by their standards the Cumbrian booty was valuable. But from the French point of view the operation was trivial. The Kingdom of France had not send months mounting a huge invasion force led by the Admiral of France himself in order to strip Cumbria of its moveable assets. At the end of the campaign the victor of the Crusade of the Comte Vert who had been received with honour by the Emperor of Byzantium himself had been unable to take Carlisle, a third-rate target. What had happened to the big plans?

At this stage Jean de Vienne believed that the plans were still feasible. The English army had taken Edinburgh, but it was worthless, stripped of its possessions, with the Castle itself impregnable. The entire country to the south had been wasted and the English army was running out of supplies. There was no option but retreat back the way the English army had come. John of Gaunt had once again taken an army on a big operation to nowhere in particular, only to find that his forces were starting to starve.

Didn't the French simply have to bide their time until news of the second French invasion came through? Not really. The real centre where the important action was nearly ready to take place was the giant port of Sluys. On 10 July everything was ready for the big invasion. Charles VI took up the oriflamme, with all that it symbolised, from the Abbot of Saint Denis, and took it to where the French army was waiting to embark. From there he went to his court in Amiens in order to prepare for his forthcoming wedding to a German princess.[17]

The estuary of the Zwijn in which Sluys was located was now crammed with men, materiel and shipping – it was said of the view the masts reflected in the water seemed like a forest and the roads around the port were almost worn out with traffic. The spaces between the giant transport ships would have been taken up with small supply vessels, and the ships belonging to the highest noblemen would have stood out with their elaborate decorations and beautifully gilded masts. This had been planned for months, and everything had been taken into consideration. Except of course, that is impossible.

Five days later, on 15 July a group of Flemish anti-French and pro-English rebels moved unseen into the town of Damme, situated just a few miles from the western end of the port of Sluys. Today it is a picturesque village 6 miles from the sea, joined to Sluys by 6 miles of canal, but late in the fourteenth century Damme was still joined to the Zwijn estuary by a shallow inlet which made it part of the port of Sluys. It was a swampy, unhealthy place, and because of its strategic position it had acquired a set of fortifications. It was just another 5 miles from the important French-held town of Bruges. Despite being part of the estuary of the Zwijn, and thus part of the network of waterways that the French invasion fleet was using, Damme was not well guarded and a group of pro-English Flemish fighters from Ghent scaled the walls and overpowered the guards who were unprepared for anything like this.

A military response was needed and just a few days later the newly married eighteen-year-old King Charles had abandoned his honeymoon and was nominally leading a French force to Damme. The invasion had to be postponed. Conflict raged on for the coming weeks and by October of that year, it was decided that the whole invasion was to be postponed until the following year – 1386.[18]

By late August Richard's giant army abandoned a deserted Edinburgh and took off through the devastated country in a warm August. The army was running out of supplies and by the time it returned to Newcastle it was sick, starving, and happy to see the last of Scotland, even though the men had only spent two weeks north of the Border.

When Jean de Vienne and the Scottish army arrived back in Edinburgh they heard the news that the campaign had been postponed. Jean de Vienne's first reaction was to stick to the master plan and wait in Edinburgh through the whole long Scottish winter for the arrival of the French fleet the following summer. After all, his army was almost intact and it would be able to fight during the following year.

Despite the fact that the two armies had campaigned together, there was no trust between the French and the Scots. The Scots were mean! They would not supply the French with the necessities of life. Valuable thoroughbred French warhorses were dying for lack of feed. The knights themselves were attacked by enraged peasants when they tried to find supplies in the surroundings of Edinburgh. In a society where wine was an essential social lubricant and status marker, the French had to drink poor beer.

Froissart, who did not have a high opinion of Scotland, describes the French feelings thus:[19]

> We never knew what poverty meant till now; we find now the old saying of our fathers and mothers true when they would say ... the long tarrying here in Scotland is to us neither honourable nor profitable.

And again –

> They hated them in their courage and defamed them in their language as much as they might.

But simply deciding to go back to France did not placate the Scots. The Scots had been keeping a tally of all the damage the French army had inflicted on their country. For example, whenever a posse of horsemen rode through a field of crops, which was a common enough custom, the Scots had actually kept a tally of the damage. Any supplies that had been seized by force had now to be paid for. Trees cut for firewood, damage to property by careless soldiers, all had their value listed and calculated. The Scots claimed that the French had done more damage than the English, and the relationship was deteriorating fast. The Scottish men-at-arms who had served under the French demanded their wages. The coin that the French fleet had brought with them at the start of the campaign was distributed. It proved to be insufficient, so Jean de Vienne, virtually a hostage of the Scots, who were determined to get their money out of the French, had to send to France for more coin.[20] As the end of the year approached the army slipped away in groups as and when ships became available. Many would have been glad to return to 'civilization'. They were relieved to go – and the Scots were pleased to see the last of them. There was no talk of the Auld Alliance over the coming years.

Not all of the French army returned home. Many of the fighters were young apprentice knights whose families had put themselves in hock to provide suitable knightly accoutrements. They did not want to return home to France with no deeds of daring to recount. These young men would have signed up to other adventures – maybe a crusade against the pagan Lithuanians, or against the Muslim Saracens in North Africa, or a European war against Christian nations.

15

THE FINAL ATTEMPT

Once Jean de Vienne was back in France a debriefing must have taken place involving possibly the King and his closest advisors. His plans for Scotland had failed, but this did not mean that invasion plans were to be dropped.[1] If the French plans for a southern invasion had not been upset by the Flemish attack on Damme, the campaign might well have succeeded. The neglect of the Flemish frontier when the invasion fleet was mustering was not the Admiral's fault. The Scots proved to be terrible allies but if the southern invasion had taken place as planned, the lack of Scots in the northern army would have not mattered at all. What is more, the fighting season on the Continent had been a success and many English-held bastions had been taken by the French.

So despite the failure of the 1385 campaign Jean de Vienne persuaded the Crown advisors that the English could still be bested on their own territory. Indeed, if the French invasion force of 1385 had been bigger he could have won in a pitched battle against the English army when they showed up in Northumberland. King Richard was too young to act as a military leader, and his number two John of Gaunt had a terrible record of losing battles.

It was decided that size mattered, and so Jean de Vienne's plan for the following year was the same again, but much bigger, minus dubious allies such as the Welsh and Scots. Money mattered also. A committed invasion force was an immensely expensive operation – probably the most expensive and complex endeavour that a medieval government could take on. France in the post-Charles the Wise era was in part like England, suffering from the economic consequences of decades of war; but the canny Charles the Wise had left behind him a government without significant debt, and a huge war chest of accumulated money. King Charles Junior, and his aristocratic uncles and advisors, treated this treasure chest as a legacy to be spent as fast as possible carrying out pet projects. For the present there was money available for an ambitious project. Long gone were the days when King Charles' father Charles the Wise was unable to find the 600,000 écus that Valdemar of Denmark was asking in order to launch an invasion of England and depose the troublesome English royal family.

By the spring of 1386 the Admiral and his officers were travelling around the ports of the English Channel, money no object, looking for suitable ships to carry a huge force of fighters and their equipment. For this, the ultimate big push, there were to be 100,000 foot soldiers, including archers and men-at-arms, led by 10,000 mounted knights. With just 2,500 fighters Jean de Vienne had decided not to confront an English army of 14,000 the previous year, after watching the huge mass of men moving through Northumberland pillaging and burning. This next expedition was to have forty times more soldiers.

On many occasions during the past decades, war campaigns had failed because of bad logistics. John of Gaunt had on a number of occasions led a starving army through France, and in Scotland the French army had been dangerously short of supplies in 1385. As money was no object the 1386 expedition was to carry enough supplies for a whole season. So the amount of stores and equipment needed was immense and had to be transported on 1,500 ships. Every friendly port from Spain as far as the mouth of the Rhine was scoured by the agents of the King of France for men, ships and materiel. All summer long the roads to Sluys were jammed with transport bringing all kinds of goods to the invasion fleet. Ships, people and supplies flowed into Sluys. Froissart, perhaps overwhelmed by the scale of the enterprise, lists the range of goods that were appearing, unusual for Froissart who rarely showed much interest in the practicalities underlying chivalric warfare. Nothing like this had even been attempted before, not on this scale.[2]

> They were supplying shoes, boots, spurs, knives, axes, pikes, mattocks, racks, iron and nails to shoe horses ... tallow candles, wax candles, boxes of grease, tow, canvas, sleeping quilts, cups, bottles, wooden bowls, tin bowls, chandeliers and basins, pots, grills, kitchen utensils.

One fatal flaw with this plan was the perennial problem of raising an army, arraying a fleet, and equipping it before the end of the sailing season, in a cold century with short summers, uncertain cold north winds and periods of incessant rain and hail. Even though planning started early in the season of 1386, there was so much to do that the invasion could not take place before September. And by September the invasion-friendly summer breezes blowing up the English Channel from the south-west could overnight be replaced by 'pro-English' storms from the north-east, bringing wild weather and pinning whole fleets in port for week after frustrating week. By trying to eliminate all uncertainties Jean de Vienne had opened up a huge window of uncertainty.

Another big risk in such a huge invasion force against a competent and fully prepared enemy was how to effect a landing in a country where the entire southern coastline was prepared for action, and had decades of experience in dealing with invasions. It is hard to imagine how long it would take to unload so many men, so much materiel, so many horses, each to be led slowly out of a hold of a ship.

Jean de Vienne responded to this quandary by modifying a type of wooden barbican that he had used years earlier during the siege of St Sauveur le Vicomte as a temporary fortress.[3] As was to be expected, this was not just an ordinary temporary fortification. In order to deal with the huge volume of men, horses and supplies it had to be vast, possibly the biggest wooden structure ever built in the fourteenth century. It was 20 medieval feet high, about the height of a two-storey modern house. It was said to be 9,000 paces in length. Every 12 paces there was either a tower or a gatehouse – that is a total of 750 defensive structures built into the wall. The enclosed area of 400 hectares would have been larger than that of the City of London inside its Roman walls. The post-Black Death population of London was maybe no more than 40,000 people, so if the great wall had been constructed on English territory and if the entire invasion force had landed inside it, the resulting conglomeration of people and equipment would have been many times bigger than the biggest urban centre in England![4] Just to guard this structure alone would have required 4,000 men-at-arms, each separated by only a couple of yards, backed up by a line of crossbowmen. The ancient forests of the Isle de France was stripped of its mature growth for this immense structure, and just to transport it across the Channel would have required 69 ships.[5]

So this time the invasion was really going to succeed. And among all the other skilled craftsmen employed by the French crown the painters and gilders were much in evidence. This time more than ever before the ships were done up in their Sunday best for the expedition, and some of the wealthiest of the aristocratic leaders went to great lengths to make their own ships stand out.

The Sire de Trémouille, for example, had spent 2,000 francs just in order to decorate his ship.

The weaponry was not neglected either and Froissart gives us a list including 'harnoys, darts, traits, canons, bombs, iron and steel bars, lead mallets, lances, aches, insarmes, daggers, spears, pikes, and many other things needful for fighting at sea'. [6]

As the huge preparations progressed the English became alarmed. It was obvious that something big was going to happen. Information from spies came back to the English court that the landing place was to be north of the Thames – possibly Orwell, on a sandy beach. This would be a sensible location, just 100 miles across the North Sea from Sluys, avoiding the risky waters of the eastern Channel and the English base at Calais. At the news England switched into invasion fear mode again. In East Anglia fortifications were built at the entrances to harbours. It is an indication of the strategic weakness of the English Crown that at midsummer John of Gaunt launched yet another Continental campaign aimed at seizing what he thought of as his rightful kingdom of Castile, thus denuding England of many of its ships. [7]

As had happened many times before during the century, the commissioners of array went into action all over the kingdom's coasts, but unlike past invasion scares the commissioners were required to supply fighting men for action in London, in order to protect the capital, or areas nearby. In October a navy made up of chartered foreign ships was put together on the Thames itself in order to protect the capital against the forthcoming French attack. Thousands of soldiers arrived from all over England to defend the capital. But there was no money to pay them. From a fiscal point of view Edward III had not left his heirs any legacy, just debts. [8]

The summer months slipped by. The English defensive preparations were on hold. The French were not ready to act as they were still getting together the huge volume of supplies needed to ensure that the invasion force would not suffer privations after landing in England. As summer ended the towns of Flanders and north-east France were being stripped of their supplies. Again Froissart puts aside his usual areas of interest and tells us just what was being loaded in order to ensure that the French army would not have to suffer the privations of the previous year:

> Flours, salt meat, tons of salt, onions, garlic, sour grape juice, fat, egg yolks, oats, hay in bales; then peas, broad beans, and olives. And also lots of useful implements, such as footwear, boots, spurs, knives, axes, picks.[9]

But the weather changed suddenly and a season of winds from the north east started.[10] The stormy season began with a bang, and a tempest of historic size hit France and Flanders. Trees were uprooted, houses blown down, with loss of life. The stormy weather continued. In just one day in September a fleet of sixty-nine French ships on their way to Sluys along the English Channel were lost at sea. The entire invasion fleet waited in port, including King Charles. One day the winds abated and the King, maybe throwing an adolescent tantrum, insisted on leaving port fully prepared for war, accompanied by his royal uncles, and started to sail for England. The winds returned and just a few miles out at sea the ship had to turn round and take refuge in port.[11]

It was not until the middle of October that Charles VI's army started to march north towards Sluys, which was a hint that the action was due to start shortly and Richard II's court in London received intelligence that the great invasion would not take place until November. When this information became public the English coastal defenders in some areas rebelled and slipped away and went home. The patriotic mood of earlier in the century had gone.

The French fleet was ready to sail. The wooden barbican preceded the departure of the troops. The transportation operation was made more difficult by the contrary winds, but a start on this operation was made. When the winds were more favourable, two or three ships took off northwards in the direction of the East Anglian coast. By an almost unbelievable stroke of luck for the English, the winds changed just when the ship was sailing past the Thames, blowing it into the estuary. The ship was boarded and taken to London with its crew. The French chief carpenter was forced to erect the sections of wall in London itself, while the rest of the structure stayed in harbour in France.

But the invasion was still meant to go ahead. The men and materiel had taken a week to load, and in late October Charles VI reviewed the invasion force ready for departure. Froissart himself was there and he note that the French were full of hatred for the English and were eager to get their own back.[12] 'Smash these English swine ... now is the time to avenge our fathers and mothers and our dead friends.'

The winds continued until the end of October, sometimes it was so windy that ships in harbour were damaged. At the end of October an attempt was made to leave port again, but no sooner were the ships at sea than a violent storm blew them back onto the coast of Flanders. By now the huge volume of campaign supplies were coming to an end. Gradually the owners of the individual ships were taking the law into their own hands and slipping away for the winter. The expedition was called off and King Charles sadly went back to Paris.

Jean de Vienne attempted to lead one more English invasion. In the following year of 1387, he decided that the 1386 plan had been too big, unwieldy and complex. He and his invasion forces had been let down by the Scots, and by anti-French fighting in Flanders. This time the invasion force was smaller, just 6,000 fighting men, with provisions for five or six months, and it was to be launched from Breton and Norman territory, including Honfleur at the mouth of the Seine. The invasion was to take place early in the year, and by May they were almost ready. The landing was to take place in Dover, after which the army would move on to London, a few days' march away, and maybe simultaneously into the interior of the kingdom.[13]

The auguries were good, and the fleet was in harbour in Harfleur ready for the signal to sail. Then totally unexpected political developments threw the whole plan into disarray. Extraordinary news came through from Brittany concerning the Duke, who had turned on certain members of the French royal family, making it impossible to go ahead with an invasion that would have involved Brittany. At the same time, one of Jean de Vienne's commanders, Olivier de Clisson, was captured by the English. In the political vacuum that followed, the invasion was forgotten and the 6,000 participants drifted away.

After 1397 the war between England and France was to continue for several decades. There were during the course of the coming century other invasions and after Richard III was deposed, his successor Henry IV was to continue fighting the French. But the chain of events that linked Queen Isabella's securing the throne of England for Edward her son, to Admiral Jean de Vienne's very nearly successful invasions plans was broken.

Appendix 1

SHIPS, SHIPPING AND THE SEA

The entire fourteenth-century Anglo-French conflict was defined by ships and shipping and the technologies needed to build, use and maintain them. Each country had its own individual personality and the position that ships played within each national narrative was unique to itself. Ships were probably the most costly items of moveable equipment that there was, and they required an elaborate infrastructure to produce them and maintain them in usable condition. This involved not just the services of a large number of skilled people, it also supported, especially in England, a merchant class of people living in ports who could have access to as much wealth as many of the traditional aristocracy.

The north and south coasts of the fourteenth-century English Channel would have had much in common. The inhabited Channel coastline of England and France would have been crowded with ships and boats of every size and type. The majority would have been small coastal boats, just big enough for one or two passengers, some using sail, others oars, many with a combination of the two. Some were designed for carrying cargos, some just for transporting people. Any inlet or river mouth would have taken traffic far inland and would have had its quota of boats. Rivers were medieval highways into the interior and shallow draft vessels allowed towns and villages far inland effectively to be ports. Fish was a vital source of protein in a world recovering from famine, and fleets of fishing vessels would have been seen all around the coastal waters in season.

It is, however, very difficult to reconstruct this inhabited seascape, as most of the information we possess is only concerned with higher-status larger ships. The chroniclers who describe the events of the conflict rarely care to mention the many ordinary boat- and ship-users who were caught up in the action. Ordinary people rarely appear in illustrations from the period. Even in pictures of naval battles, each ship is filled with fighting soldiers with not a single sailor to be seen anywhere, begging the question of how the ships were manned and managed for battle in the first place.

The key to medieval trading life in northern waters was the cog, the workhorse of the economy in the English Channel and east as far as the Baltic Sea. The cog was a fat, flat-bottomed, wide-beamed and sturdy boat with a deck high above the waterline, and a lot of cargo space in its hold.

A cog had just one big square sail, attached to a single thick and tall mast, often made of a number of tree trunks fastened together, and it was steered by a stern rudder. Its hull, curved at each end, made it a great cargo carrier and typically the hold of a cog on a trading journey would be filled with cargo such as tuns of wine, salt and minerals, while the crew would camp out on deck, living communally in the open air.

The sturdy flat bottom allowed the cog to come close inshore if, for example, there were no harbour facilities, to unload and sail away at the next tide. The combination of single square sail and small stern rudder gave the cog a certain limited manoeuvrability and with the wind behind it, a cog could move fast. But if the wind veered too far in the wrong direction, the rudder would not be able to maintain the ship's direction. Whole harbours full of trading vessels could be trapped by unfriendly winds for long periods, and it is a classic scenario of the period that huge and elaborate invasion preparations were stopped by a sudden shift in weather patterns.

The fact that England was an island with close commercial connections with Gascony and Flanders has a bearing upon how the English method of waging warfare differed from that of the French. The kings of England held Gascony in south west France as a personal possession – and the sweet strong wines from the region around Bordeaux were just what the English upper classes liked to drink. As the century progressed the farmers of the Bordeaux region abandoned general farming and specialised in wine production. The wine was stored in barrels and loaded onto ships bound for England. There was a heavy export tax, payable to the English Crown at this stage. The wine ships were unloaded in such ports as Southampton or Plymouth, where another duty was payable – again this payment went to the English Crown. The merchants operating out of English ports made huge profits on the trade between England and Gascony, with a single season's operations, for example, yielding 100 per cent profit or more. English merchants by their business activities related to shipping supported the English state. Fourteenth-century England was well endowed with tax-raising opportunities and could be describes as a wool and wine superpower. The English climate encouraged high-quality fleeces, and vast flocks of sheep roamed East Anglia and much of southern England. A close financial and trading relationship had developed by the early fourteenth century between England and Flanders, with England exporting wool to Flanders, and Flanders spinning it into cloth. Later in the century England started to produce cloth from English wool. As with wine, wool was taxed by the Crown at various stages of its journey between sheep and garment – and in the middle of this process was the merchant. As a result channel ports such as Portsmouth, Southampton and Plymouth were important wine and wool ports, helping to create a class of merchants who had money and who wielded economic power, although they enjoyed a relatively low position in the aristocratic hierarchy. A wealthy merchant with warehouses full of wine and wool could well be richer than many an impecunious aristocrat, who might be hard put to collect together the money for his warhorse, his armour, standards, and weaponry. The taxable profits from a merchant's trading were used to support a lavish court and, more and more the case as the reign of Edward III progressed, to pay for the huge cost of warfare.

Edward III's administration did not possess a wartime navy, and to a certain extent there was little need for one when the Crown could make use of the merchants' property as and when necessary. Ships were needed during English campaigns on the European mainland to transport fighters, equipment and supplies across the English Channel. For this job of transportation what could be better than the trading cog? With its wide deck space, capacious hold and shallow draft it was perfect for carrying troops and their equipment to landing places in France. Before the ships were ready for military use, however, there were modifications to be carried out. The most distinctive sign of a cog modified for military service were the castles fore and aft and a topcastle on the mast, looking a little like terrestrial castles. The castles gave to the already high cog even more height, which made it a great vessel for raining down arrows on enemies from on high. The wide and clear deck was perfect for battles at sea, which were often fought hand-to-hand on deck, as on a claustrophobic battlefield. When a fleet met with the enemy, cogs would be pulled alongside with grappling irons, bringing the two decks together, and a battle could ensue upon the limited space of the decks.

The process of modifying cargo ships for military use took time and needed armies of carpenters, not to mention supplies of wood and iron, so it is not surprising that months could go by before a fleet was ready for action. Stalls were constructed in the hold to take horses, and hurdles were designed to stop the horses getting injured in stormy weather. Huge quantities of animal feed had to be loaded. Getting the horses on board ship required major reconstructions – often a door was constructed in the side of the ship that opened up and allowed each horse directly into the hold, as in representations of Noah's Ark. Once closed the door had to seal perfectly and it required skilled craftsmen to do the job.

The cog's limited ability to tack when the wind was not behind it was on a number of occasions a huge problem. Invasion fleets would kick their heels in frustration whenever the weather gods decided to support the other side in the conflict, moving winds in the wrong direction, so that the sailing ships were unable to leave port. In the English Channel winds can be strong and changeable. On many occasions a fleet spent months on end preparing for a major expedition only to find that when they were ready to go, the winds had turned, blowing into harbour, thus making it impossible to set off. Or the gods could show favour because by following the wind, an attacking fleet could pin the opponents inshore, unable to go into attack. In later generations, sea battles where both sides ranged up opposite to one another ready to do battle were common and important. But these had to wait until sailing technology had advanced, leading to more certain navigation and the ability to tack effectively. Battles between fleets at sea were rare in the fourteenth century – although on the few occasions that this happened, the results could be spectacular, as happened at Winchelsea in 1350.

With so much shipping at his disposal Edward III did not bother to build himself a navy, but rather relied upon his merchants to supply England with the ships needed to carry his armies and patrol English coastal waters. This led to immense disruption to lives in England's coastal towns. If Edward III decided to launch an invasion from a certain port – Sandwich for example – the entire process could take months. The period could even extend from one sailing season to the one following. The consequences of this for England were huge. Entire ports declined economically as a result of having to host an English fleet for a season. Towards the end of Edward III's regime the merchant class were exhausted economically by the costs of the disruption, and high taxation. This contributed to the decline of the dynasty.

The French approach to running a navy was quite the opposite. One could describe the English approach as one that used private enterprise to provide services with which the state was not willing to get involved. The French, on the other hand, built up their navy under the auspices of the state. In the late thirteenth century a naval dockyard belonging to the French Crown had been built in Clos des Galées, in Rouen. Unlike England, France was a Mediterranean power as well as an Atlantic one. So the king in Paris had access to the more sophisticated world of the Mediterranean, North Africa, the Byzantine Empire and Italian states such as Venice and Genoa, whereas the English had limited or no contact with them. So at the start of hostilities in the 1320s the French naval dockyard of Clos des Galées was an exotic workshop manned by Mediterranean naval experts and builders, where conversations were carried out in scarcely comprehensible dialects. Two micro naval states especially were present in Clos des Galées for decades and the names of individuals such as Doria of Genoa and Grimaldi of Monaco were known and feared by the English when their galleys attacked the English coasts.

The Mediterranean galley was a descendant of the Greco-Roman warship. It was everything the cog was not. While the cog was fat, the galley was slender. The cog had a huge hold but the galley had limited space on board. A large cog towered above smaller craft. A Genoese galley of the 1330s could be 40 metres long, and only 5 metres wide, with a limited depth of 2 metres and maybe 100 rowers. On the stern of the galley there was an above-water-level battering ram, a change from the below-water rams of the Roman galleys. The Romans used the ram to hole their opponents below the waterline, while the Mediterranean galley's beak was designed as a landing device. The Genoese galley in use in the English Channel was not meant for battling at sea around the English coasts but rather as a landing craft. A galley could have more than 100 men rowing, which gave them an impressive turn of speed for short distances, although the heavy physical work of rowing limited the range of a galley that was not under sail. The sail was an essential item of equipment as it allowed the galley, if wind conditions were right, to sail close to its target then row into its landing place, with the crew ready to switch roles to fighters the moment the ship was inshore. The galley was not suited to long-distance operations; it was most effective carrying out localised strikes – getting in and out quickly. A typical French fleet making for English shores would consist of both cogs and galleys. The galleys would spearhead the landings. In the English Channel a galley fleet could cruise out of port in France under sail, follow the winds across the Channel to the English coastline and, then, under human power, search out just the right landing place and attack. The rowers switched roles immediately and become a band of maybe 200 fighters. While the raid progressed the galley would be ready to turn and flee whenever danger threatened. The cogs could wait still out to sea, and one of their vital roles was to take on board the plunder. A member of a galley crew was a highly skilled marine, capable of feats of endurance, and ready to carry out acts of terrifying brutality and violence if circumstances required them.

Astonishingly enough, on the occasions when the French called upon the services of the Mediterraneans as paid allies, the Genoese and the Monegasques travelled with their galleys through the Straits of Gibraltar, up through the Bay of Biscay, and round the western approaches of the English Channel. It was a harrowing journey.

A fleet of galleys from Monaco glimpsed from the southern English coastline was a frightening sight. In the fourteenth century England was not using galleys and the mere sight of the hundred-odd rowers powering the warship along a coastline meant imminent danger – enough to set in motion the defence routine, to start the church bells ringing in the continuous pealing that signified the risk of a raid.

For most of the fourteenth century, England, led by King Edward III was the aggressive power in Europe, attempting to impose military force, with an insatiable need for fighting ships and militarised troop carriers. The French situation was quite different as not until the late 1370s did the French Crown plan to land an entire army on English soil. The strategy that the French followed in these earlier years was rather to maintain economic pressure upon England, with the intention of degrading the English infrastructure and cutting down the English ability to pose a threat to France.

Appendix 2

ENGLAND AND FRANCE – THE FORM OF THE STATE

When Edward III decided to mount a challenge to the King of France by disputing his right to wear the crown, it must have come as a shock to many in the orbit of French culture. By the 1320s France had become a European superpower, while England was far lower down in the European pecking order.

The population of France in 1328 after a Royal census was between 15 and 18 million people. The disasters of the fourteenth century were to diminish that figure, but during the years when Edward and Philippe were squaring up for the forthcoming struggle, the Kingdom of France under Philippe Valois was the leading nation state in Europe, in territory, in population, and in national wealth. Its central position on the European map gave France a presence in Mediterranean affairs, in the Atlantic world, and via its feudal ownership of Flanders, of the North Sea. In an age when much wealth derived from agriculture, France owned the largest allotment in Europe – from the wine and olive lands of the Mediterranean to the wheat-growing country along the English Channel. The city of Paris was Europe's biggest city, and a whole slew of regional centres such as Avignon, Bordeaux, Rouen, were important economic centres, with, by the standards of the time, significant populations.

France's dominance was not limited to mere numbers. The French language and aristocratic culture led Europe. The University of Paris was a centre of European learning, and French Gothic architecture had for 200 years been one of the standards by which other countries' architecture was judged. In relation to the aristocratic ideal of the fighting man, the French system of chivalry was the standard against which would-be 'perfect' knights judged themselves. The Capetian kings of France were fortunate in that their years of dominance, the latter part of the thirteenth century and at the start of the fourteenth, had largely been a period of peace and prosperity; in retrospect the term 'High Middle Ages' seems an appropriate term.

When we turn our attention to the Kingdom of England the picture is very different. England was a much smaller country of a mere 6 million people, maybe fewer than half the number of France. Paris at 300,000 inhabitants was far bigger than London with its 40,000 people. No other English city came near to any of the French regional centres such as Bordeaux and Marseilles in terms of economic or political importance. France's agricultural productivity made it a superpower against England's modest and declining potential. The north and west of England had large areas of relatively barren upland with poor soils and marginal climates – far more so than France with its much friendlier climate and fertile soils. The Great European Famine during the first decade of the fourteenth century had hit England very badly so that whole areas of northern England, Wales and the south west had abandoned high-value agriculture almost entirely, resulting in simultaneous mass starvation of the peasantry. What is more, England, the island nation, a day's journey by ship from northern France, her nearest neighbour, was isolated from European affairs, while France was at the very heart of Europe, having frontiers with Castile, Genoa, Burgundy and the Holy Roman Empire. The Mediterranean coast of France gave access to the sophisticated world of Byzantium.

On the face of it, therefore, England should have been no more than a second-rate challenger. This was not the case. Again and again, Edward's David overcame France's Goliath. England turned out to be a dangerous enemy. Under Edward III's tutelage, it developed a highly efficient fighting machine, making the English army a quick-moving and agile adversary. The French state in complete contrast was slow-moving, inefficient, unfocussed. The reason for this contrast lies in the history of each state.

The Kingdom of England was largely what might be tentatively called an artificial – rather than organic – creation, set up, ironically enough, by the French-speaking William of Normandy in the aftermath of his successful invasion in 1066. The Normans cleared out almost the entire Anglo-Saxon ruling class and replaced it with their own people, and in the process created a centralised state, broken up into counties, many of which survive today, often with identical boundaries. The king's representative in each country was the Sheriff, carrying out the instructions coming from the Crown. There were few exceptions to this simple system whereby a royal edict was instantly passed on to where it belonged, and was immediately acted upon.

How different were the government arrangements in France. The territory that Philip VI ruled at the start of his reign had been acquired piecemeal over the previous 200 years, and the French state possessed no single unified structure. Some parts of French territory were ruled directly by the Crown, such as areas central to Paris where the king usually resided, including the Isle de France, Normandy, Picardy and parts of the Loire Valley. Many parts were not. The Fief of Flanders, which extended as far along the coasts of the North Sea as Bruges and Ghent, was virtually an autonomous polity. It was French in that its Duke owed feudal fealty to the King of France, but in other ways it was very much in the English orbit by virtue of England's exports of raw wool that was woven in Flanders. Brittany was an independent Dukedom, still very Celtic with its Breton language, which was closer to the Cornish, Welsh and Cumbric languages of the British Isles than to French. The most difficult anomaly in the make-up of the French state was Gascony, also a semi-autonomous unit, which happened to be ruled by the English Crown. Edward III had inherited the title of Duke of Gascony from his father Edward II. Although the Dukedom was Edward's personal asset, it was not a colony of England as its government and people were French. Edward owned feudal fealty to the King of France and he had, when he was young, carried out a ceremony of formal obeisance to King Philippe.

Superimposed upon this ramshackle structure was a two-part division of France. The two regions were the Languedoc in the south, looking to the Mediterranean, North Africa and the Middle East; and the Languedoil in the north, part of the North Sea and Atlantic worlds. Languedoc had its own language, still surviving today, and also its own courts and feudal obligations and systems of taxation. When King Charles took power he had to wield it via a whole raft of separate polities within the French state, which made France slow to respond events.

Before the outbreak of war, the French King had access to just enough revenue to pay for the upkeep of his household, and little more. Raising large amounts of money to pay for war expenses was very difficult in France, and in moments of crisis the French monarch had to resort on occasion to debasing the coinage (recalling all silver coinage, melting it down and adulterating it with tin, and reissueing it at the same face value). This was a process that infuriated French citizens.

By contrast, England, according to Froissart, was the 'best governed country in the world'. The king's writ applied in all parts of England, via the representatives of the Crown in each county. The English tax system was very simple; until the outbreak of total war in the 1330s, the export tax on unprocessed wool was the main source of the income for the Crown. In times of crisis the Crown imposed supplements, which could include a charge on all imports and all exports on any goods that were traded, such as lead, tin, hides, and most importantly, wheat. In addition the English kings had access to the most sophisticated money markets of medieval Europe – the Italians. From the 1330s the Chancery and the Exchequer were based in Westminster, as was Parliament. A growing army of clerks and functionaries were able to quickly and efficiently issue writs, proclamations and royal ordinances, and get them delivered at a speed of about 30 miles a day to the appropriate Sheriffs and Bailiffs for action.

Edward III inherited a lean and efficient taxation system from his father, but he very wisely improved the system by asking the Parliament, which included both Lords and Commons, to approve expenditure, so that wartime levies and extra taxation would come to the counties from Parliament. For example, on 3 March 1337 Edward opened his Parliament in the Westminster Hall. The purpose of the parliamentary session was to confirm the Lords' and Commons' support for Edward's war plans, to confirm arrangements for a big tax increase, and to create a circle of personal supporters for the hyper-active and ambitious king. In 1336, the wool merchants had agreed to an increase in taxation on each sack of wool. Export taxation was increased, and the tax on moveable assets held by each country was levied at a rate of one-tenth or one-fifteenth by the 1337 March Parliament. The clergy were subject to a levy of one-tenth or one-fifteenth of their assets, which they agreed to in the current climate. It was a very wise political move on Edward's part that both Lords and Commons voted on this extras taxation, as this made Edward's forthcoming struggle against France into a national struggle – which in a way it was not. The efficient tax-raising powers gave the English a great advantage in the forthcoming struggle with France as they could respond quickly and effectively to circumstances, while the French could not.

However, England was a fractious and aggressive country, clashing with Scotland, Wales and Ireland. Since the start of the thirteenth century, English armies had been engaged in constant land wars with its weaker and poorer insular neighbours. Here is a list of engagements carried out by the English against their neighbours in the earlier decades, mainly the Scots:

1282 – Battle of Moel-y-Don and Battle of Orewin Bridge.
1295 – Battle of Moydog.
1296 – Siege of Dunbar.
1297 – Battle of Stirling Bridge.
1298 – Battle of Falkirk.
1304 – Stirling Castle captured.
1306 – Battle of Methven Park
1307 – Battle of Loudoun Hill.
1315 – Battle of Bannockburn.
1322 – Battle of Byland.
1333 – Battle of Halidon Hill.

Edward III and his knightly class were hardened warriors. For decades the English state had been through constant preparations for war. Its subjects, the knights, foot soldiers and archers alike, were used to war and many families would possess the memory of war from their ancestors. What is more, internally the English were fractious.

However as the century and the war progressed the picture changed. After the post-Poitiers breakdown of the French state and the captivity of King Jean the underachieving giant that was

France became a more dangerous foe. The English state began a slow process of decline, in parallel perhaps with the decline of Edward III's capacity to lead. When Charles the Wise died in 1380 he left behind a state which, although scarred by war, had a rational tax system and efficient army and navy, and as a result of years of prudent financial planning, a huge war chest. The England of Richard II by contrast, while also scarred by war, and suffering under heavy taxation, was labouring under a burden of huge debt.

NOTES

Preface

1. Thomson, E. M. – ed – Robert de Avebury *De gestis mirabilis Regis Edwardi terti* (Murimuth) – p 500
2. Murimuth op cit - 89-90; Thomson, E. M. – *Chronicon Galfrido le Baker of Swynbrook* – pp 63-64; Martin G H – ed – *Henry Knighton Chronicle* ii 8-9
3. Rymer, T ed – *Foedera, conventions, literae et acta publica* – 1338 - Page 7. Translation by the author.

Quia intelleximus a nonnullis quod alienigenae, hostes echniq, cum galeis, et navibus guerrinis in magni multitudine at partes Dorset divertere celeriter se proponent, ad easdem partes hostiliter invadend ...

Volentes hujusmodo periculis, cum Dei adjutorio, praecavere, vobis, in fide qua nobis tenemini, districtius injungerdo mandamus, quod statim, visis praesentibus, vos una cum familiaribus vestries, potentius quo poteritis ...personaliter vos trahatis; dictas partes, una cum aliis fidelibus nostris partoum illarum, contra hostiles incursus hujusmodi defensuri, et eosdem hostes viriliter expugnaturi, si invader praesumpserint partes illas.

Chapter 1

1. *Percy's Reliques of Ancient Poetry – Series 1, Book the First.* 'Sir Patrick Spens', page 11.
2. Lt Colonel Howard Greene, *Guide to the Battlefields of Britain and Ireland*
3. Wikipedia, History of Seaford

4. St Matthew 10–34

5. 1 Samuel 25–28

6. Rymer – Foed 1337 – p 958

7. *Political Poems and Songs Relating to English History* – ed Thomas Wright Vol 1 – p 26. Translation by the author: *Callida, syrena, crudelis, acerba, echni, … Sub duce Philippo Valeys, cognomina lippo.*

Chapter 2

1. Weir, Alison, *Isabella, She Wolf of France*, p 138

2. Weir op cit, p 194

3. Weir op cit, p 218

4. Weir op cit, p 224

5. Warner, Kathryn, *Edward II – The Unconventional King*, p 202

6. Froissart, *Chronicles*. Chapter 1, p 10, Berners translation modernised by author.

7. Froissart op cit, p 15

8. Mortimer, *The Greatest Traitor*, p 150 n 2

9. Warner, op cit, p 202

10. Mortimer, Ian op cit – p 151 – n 4

11. Weir op cit, p 225

12. *Chronicon Galfridi le Baker*, ed E. M. Thomson, p 24

13. Berners, *Froissart*, Chapter XIII, p 12

14. Le Baker de Swynebroke, p 33, author's translation.

15. Walsingham *Chronica Maiora*

Chapter 3

1. Mortimer, Ian, *The Perfect King*, p 63

2. Vegetius, III, 13

3. Mortimer, op cit, p 68

4. Mortimer, op cit, 108

5. Von Clausewitz, Carl, *On War*, Book 8 Ch. 6

6. Sumption, Jonathan, *Trial by Battle*, p 135

7. *Rotuli Scotiae*, 1334, p 299, 'De Scotia et eorum navibus ad litus Suffolkiae applicantibus'

8. McKisack, May, *The Fourteenth Century*, p 203

9. Foedera III 704, 770

10. Strachey, J., *Rotuli Parliamentorum II* 64, 165

11. Chaucer, Geoffrey, *The Canterbury Tales*, Prologue, lines 388–400

12. Given-Wilson, *Plea Memoranda Rolls* – Vol 1, membr 35, August 1335

13. *Rot Scot 1335, 363, Philippus de Clanenowe et alii assignantur ad custodiendum portus et echniqu Walliae, et ad arrestandum naves in*

portubis illis, et eligendum echniqu, ad capiendam naves Scotorum Angliam invadentium

14. *Rot Scot 1335, 363 – Rex Edwardus, metuens invasionem per Scotos et gentes externas in Kantia vel partibus vicinis faciendam, mandas constabulario Doverriae quod castrum illud muniat cum armaturis, victualibus, et hominibus, necessariis pro defensione,*

Chapter 4

1. Hay, D., *Europe in the Fifteenth Century,* p 78
2. Sumption, J., op cit, p 137
3. Sumption, op cit, p 156
4. Mortimer, op cit, p 129; Sumption, op cit, p 160
5. Alban, *National Defence of England,* p 4
6. Sumption, op cit, p 165
7. RS, I, 450–451, 453
8. Alban, op cit, 15; Foed II ii 996–4, Sept 1337
9. De Guerin, *The Early History and First Siege of Castle Cornet,* p 350

Chapter 5

1. Sumption, op cit, p 184
2. Sumption, op cit, p 214; *Chron Lanercost* p 291;
3. Sumption, op cit, p 196
4. *Chron Lanercost,* op cit, p 283, p 305–6
5. Sumption, op cit, p 226
6. Froissart, tr Berners, ed G. & W. Anderson, p 22
7. Sumption, op cit, p 232, Froissart *Chronicles I – 403*
8. Desjardins, Gustave Adolph, 1874, *Recherches sur les drapeaux francaises, oriflamme, banniere de France*
9. De Guerin, op cit, p 359
10. De Guerin, op cit, p 67–9
11. Stow, John, *A Summarie of the Chronicles of England,* p
12. Platt, Colin, *Archaeology in Medieval Southampton – Medieval Southampton,* p 107
13. Platt, Colin, *Medieval Southampton, The Port and Trading Community, A.D. 1000–1600,* p 114
14. Riley J., *Memorials of London and London Life,* p202
15. Rogers, N. A. M. – *The Safeguard of the Sea,* p 97
16. Nicolas, Sir Nicholas Harris, *A History of the Royal Navy from the Earliest Times to the Wars of the French Revolution, vol II* p 114
17. Sumption, op cit, p 264

Chapter 6

1. Sum, 261– 62; *Murimuth Chron* 257–61
2. Alban, op cit, p 14
3. Rogers, op cit, p 96
4. De Guerin, op cit, p 349
5. *Murimuth Chron,* p89–90
6. *Murimuth Chron,* p257–261
7. *Cal Doc Scot III no 1307; RS I* p557–60;

Chapter 7

1. Clowes, op cit, p 134
2. Rodger, op cit, p 96, notes 22, 23, 24
3. De Guerin, op cit, p 347
4. De Guerin, op cit, p 349
5. *Treaty Rolls,* op cit, v 2, p 617
6. Sumption, op cit, I, p 263; *Knighton Chron* II, 9
7. Sumption, op cit, I, p 265; *Knighton Chron* II, 9
8. De Guerin, op cit, p 350
9. Mortimer, op cit, p 161

Chapter 8

1. Mortimer, op cit, p 167
2. Sumption I, p 320, Murimuth, 103–4; *Baker Chron,* 67
3. Chazelas A, *Documents relatives au Clos des Galees,* xxvii 329–477
4. Mortimer, op cit, p 172
5. Froissart, op cit, p 64
6. Froissart, op cit, p 65
7. Stanton, Charles D., *Medieval Maritime Warfare,* p 250
8. Mortimer, op cit, p 177
9. Rogers, op cit, p 100; Alban, op cit, p 17
10. Sumption, op cit, I 347; *Baker Chron* 70; *Murimuth Chron* 109
11. McKisack, op cit, p 349
12. Mortimer, op cit, p 18; Murimuth, 116–17

Chapter 9

1. Sumption, op cit, I, p 399; Rymer, op cit, II, 1210
2. De Guerin, op cit, p 342
3. Terrier de Loray, *Henri-Jean de Vienne, Amiral de France 1341–1396,* p 11
4. Mortimer,op cit, p 258
5. Fagan, B., *The Little Ice Age,* p 47

6. Ziegler, P., *The Black Death,* p 117
7. Mortmer, op cit, p 278
8. Knighton, op cit, p 62, author's translation
9. Myers, A. R. vol IV, *English Historical Documents* pp 52–3 – nr 694, p 1182
10. Sumption II, op cit, p 67
11. Froissart, op cit, p 115
12. Froissant, op cit, p 116
13. Sumption II, op cit, p 67

Chapter 10
1. Barber, R, *The Black Prince,* p 152
2. Knighton, ii p 90
3. Mortimer, op cit, p 328

Chapter 11
1. Bordonove, Georges, *Les Valois – De Philip V a' Louis XII,* p 70
2. Bordonove, op cit, p 75
3. Mortimer, op cit, p 330
4. Sumption II, op cit, p 327
5. Rymer, op cit, III, 427–428
6. Germain, *Projet de descente en Angleterre,* p 24
7. Rot Scot, II, 50–77
8. Brittan, op cit, p 143
9. Sumption II, op cit, p 436
10. Luce, *Chronique des premiers Valois,* p 111
11. Sumption II op cit, p 437
12. Denifle, Henri, *La Guerre de Cent Ans,* Vol I, p 590
13. Terrier de Loray, op cit, p 43
14. Brown, R. A. H. M., Colvin A. J. Taylor, *History of the King's Works, the Middle Ages,* p 793
15. Foedera, Ill. ii. 704; Alban, op cit, p 36
16. Bordoneuve, op cit, p 75
17. Bordoneuve, op cit, p 77
18. Terrier de Loray, op cit, p 24
19. Terrier de Loray, op cit, p 49
20. Ibid – '*insulanos sibi in depopulationem Anglorum confoederabunt ... insuper Angliam spoliare*' p 181
21. Mortimer, op cit, p 369
22. Terrier de Loray, op cit, p 78

Chapter 12

1. Bordoneuve, op cit, p 65
2. Terrier de Loray, *Jean de Vienne*, p 46
3. *Cal Close Rolls, Vol 13*, pp 35–37
4. Sumption III, op cit, 37–41
5. Rymer, ll. i. 868, 925; W. L. Clowes, *The Royal Navy. A History from the earliest Times to the Present* i. 280
6. Carr, A.D., *Owen of Wales: The End of the House of Gwynedd*, p 19
7. Carr, op cit, p 22
8. *Chronicon Angliae ab Anno Domini 1328 usque ad annum 1388*; Carr, p 24
9. CCR 1360–74 p 18; CCR 1369–74 p 36-7
10. *Rotuli Parliamentorum II*, p 302
11. CCR 1369–74, pp 20, 29
12. CCR 1369–74, pp 26
13. Brown, Covin and Taylor, op cit, p 591
14. Sumption III, op cit, p 73
15. Riley, H. T., *Memorials of London and London Life*, p 345
16. Sumption III, op cit, p 126
17. Carr, op cit, pp 56, 57, 58
18. De Guerin, op cit, p 110
19. De Guerin, p 112
20. Sumption III, op cit, p 150
21. Mortimer, op cit, p 377

Chapter 13

1. Terrier de Loray, op cit, p 67
2. Terrier de Loray, p 101
3. Carr, op cit, Ch 25
4. Sumption III, op cit, p 277
5. *Cal. Close Rolls, Vol 1, 1339–41*, pp 101, 4114
6. *Cal. Close Rolls, Vol 1,* July 1377
7. Terrier de Loray, op cit, p 103
8. Alban, op cit, p 43
9. Terrier de Loray, op cit, p 106
10. *Vita Ricardi Secundi* ed G. B. Stow, (1977) p47; *Oxford Dictionary of National Biography* – Hamo Offynton; Chron premiers Valois 262–3; E. Searle, *Lordship and Community Battle Abbey and its Banlieu* 342
11. Walsingham, *Chron Maj I* 164–6
12. Sumption III, op cit, p 287
13. Rottingdean Church Guide

14. Smith D. M. and London, V. C. M., eds, *Heads of Religious Houses England and Wales* (2001), ii 222 235
15. Froissart, op cit, vol VIII, pp 234–6
16. Smith & London, op cit, ii p 222, 235; Saul, *Scenes from Provincial Lif,* 29–30, 35–6
17. Seaford Town Guide
18. Terrier de Loray, op cit, p 110
19. *Rot Scot I* 703; *Rot Scot I* 849; *Rot Scot I* 861
20. Terrier de Loray, op cit, p 112
21. Walsingham *Chron Maj I* 160–162; Rymer – III 1019, 1020;
22. Terrier de Loray, op cit, p 128
23. Walsingham, I, p 373
24. *Rot Parl 1378* no 18; 11

Chapter 14

1. Dobson, R. B., *The Peasants' Revolt of 1381,* p xxxvi
2. Laing D., *Wyntoun Oryg Cron iii* 9
3. Walsingham, *Chron Maj* I pp 706, 714
4. Sumption III, op cit, p 513
5. Terrier de Loray, op cit, p 188–91
6. Sumption III, op cit, p 543
7. Walsingham, *Chron Maj I,* 752–4
8. Sumption III, op cit, p 543
9. Froissart xi, 255–258
10. Terrier de Loray, p 191
11. Terrier de Loray, p 192
12. Terrier de Loray, p 196
13. Sumption III, op cit, p 548
14. Terrier de Loray, op cit, p 197
15. *Historia Vitae et Regni Ricardi Secundi,* pp 88– 90
16. Sumption III, op cit, p 350
17. Sumption III, op cit, p 552
18. Sumption III, op cit, p 556
19. Froissart, tr Berners, Chap III, author's modernisation
20. Sumption III, p 556

Chapter 15

1. Terrier do Loray, op cit, p 206
2. Froissart, Ch 3, p 35
3. Alban, op cit, 71; Walsingham, *Hist Ang* – ii 147; Knighton ii 212

4. M. Puseux, *Etude sur une ville de bois*

5. Terrier de Loray, p 210

6. Froissart III, 41 in Terrier de Loray p 215

7. Walsingham *Chron Maj i* 792; *Foed vii,* 545–6

8. Knighton, 354, 348–50; CCR 1385–9 187; Walsingham I, 796–8;

9. Froissart, 3–35

10. Terrier de Loray, op cit, p 216; *Chron Charles VI,* vii, 9

11. *Chron. Charles VI– VII,* 10

12. Froissart, XIII, 75

13. Rogers, op cit, p 113

BIBLIOGRAPHY

Alban, J., *National Defence in England, 1337–89.* (1976)

Anderson, R. C., *Oared Fighting Ships, from Classical Times until the Coming of Steam.* (1962)

Barber, Richard, *The Black Prince.* (1978)

Bordonove, Georges *Les Valois – De Philip V à Louis XII.* (2007)

Britton, Charles E., *A Metereological Chronology to AD 1450.* (1937)

Brown, R. A. H. M. Colvin A. J. Taylor – *History of the King's Works, the Middle Ages.* (1963)

Calendar of Close Rolls – 1892. (1954)

Carr, A. D., *Owen of Wales: The End of the House of Gwynedd.* (1991)

Casley, Nicholas, *The Medieval Incorporation of Plymouth and a Survey of the Borough's Bounds.* (1997)

Champenois, Jehan, *1893: Le Compte du Clos des Galees de Rouen as XIVe siecle, 1382–1384, publie et annote par C Breard*

Channel Islands Study Group – Le Patourel, John – *Earlier Invasions of the Channel Islands.* (1945)

Chaplais, Pierre ed – *Treaty Rolls.* (1955–72)

Chaucer, Geoffrey – *The Canterbury Tales*

Chazelas, A. ed, *Documents relatives au Clos des Galées de Rouen.* (1977–8)

Clowes, William Laird, *The Royal Navy: A History from the Earliest Times to the Present.* (1897–1903)

Coppack, Glyn, *Medieval Merchant's House,* Southampton English Heritage. (2003)

Curry, Anne & Michael Hughes, eds, *Arms, Armies and Fortifications in the Hundred Years' War.* (1994)

Daumet G. *Etude sur l'Alliance de la France et de la Castille aux XIV et XV Siecles.* (1898)

De Guerin T. W. M. *The Early History and First Siege of Castle Cornet* – Transactions of the Guernsey Society of Natural Science and Local Research. (1904)

De Guerin T. W. M. *Some Important Events in Guernsey History.* Transactions of the Guernsey Society of Natural Science and Local Research. (1913)

Decaux, Alain, *Monaco and its Princes.* (1997)

Denieul-Cormier, Anne, *Wise and Foolish Kings – The First House of Valois.* (1980)

Desjardins, Gustave Adolph, *Recherches sur les drapeaux francaises, oriflamme, banniere de France, etc.* (1874)

Dobson, R. B. *The Peasants Revolt of 1381.* (1970)

Eddison, Jill, *Medieval Pirates – 1204–1453.* (2013)

Fagan, Brian, *The Little Ice Age.* (2000)

Fowler, Kenneth, ed., *The Hundred Years War.* (1971)

Friel, Ian, *The Good Ship: Ships, Shipbuilding and Technology in England 1200–1520* (London 1995)

Friel, Ian, *The English and the War at Sea* in Hattendorf & Unger

Froissart *The Chronicles of Jean Froissart*, tr Lord Berners

Given-Wilson, C., *Parliament Rolls of Medieval England*

Godfray, H. M. *Documents relatifs aux attaques sur les iles de la Manche 1338–1345 – Bull. De la Soc Jersiaise iii* (1897) 11–53

Greene, Lt Colonel Howard, *Guide to the Battlefields of Britain and Ireland.* (1973).

Hattendorf John B. & Unger, Richard W., *War at Sea in the Middle Ages and the Renaissance.* (2003)

Hawkes, Ken, *Sark.* (1992)

Hay, Denys, *Europe in the Fourteenth and Fifteenth Centuries.* (2014)

Hernon, Ian, *Fortress Britain.* (2013)

Hewitt, H. J., *The Organisation of War under Edward III.* (1966)

James, Margery Kirkbride, *Studies in the Medieval Wine Trade.* (1971)

Jones, Robert W., *Bloodied Banners – Martial Display on the Medieval Battlefield.* (2015)

Jusselin, M., *Comment la France se pre'parait a la guerre de cent ans BAC lxxxiii 209–36 Bibliotecque de l'Ecole de Chartres.* (1913)

La Ronciere, Charles de, *Histoire de la Marine Francaise.* (1932)

Laing, D., *Andrew of Wyntoun – Original Chronicle of Scotland.* (1872)

Le Patourel, John, *Earlier Invasions of the Channel Islands* in Channel Islands Study Group. (1945)

Lempriere, Raoul, *History of the Channel Islands.* (1980)

Luce, S. ed, *Chronique des quarter premieres Valois*

Macpherson, D. ed, *Rotuli Scotiae* (1814)

Bibliography

Martin D. & Martin B., *New Winchelsea, Sussex – a Medieval Port Town*. Field Archaeology Unit (2004)

Martin G. H., ed, *Henry Knighton Chronicle*. (1995)

Maxwell, Sir Herbert *Lanercost Chronicle*. (1913)

McKisack, May, *The Fourteenth Century*. (1959)

McLaughlin, Roy, *The Sea was their Fortune, A Maritime History of the Channel Island*. (1997)

Mirot, Leon, *Une tentative d'invasion en Angleterre pendant la Guerre de Cent Ans – Revue des Etudes Historiques LXXXI*. (1915)

Mortimer, Ian, *The Greatest Traitor; the Life of Sir Roger Mortimer, 1st Earl of March, Ruler of England 1327–30*. (2003)

Myers, A. R. *English Historical Documents, vol iv*

Nicolas, Sir Nicholas Harris, *A History of the royal Navy from the earliest Times to the Wars of the French Revolution*. (1847)

Nicholson, R. *Edward III and the Scots – the Formative Years of a Military Career*. (1965)

Percy's Reliques of Ancient Poetry – Series 1.

Perroy E., tr W. B. Wells, *The Hundred Years' War*. (1945)

Phillips, Seymour, *Edward II*. (2011)

Platt, Colin, *Medieval Southampton, The Port and Trading Community, A.D. 1000–1600*. (1973)

Pusieux, M., *Etude sur une grande ville de bois construite en Normandie pour une expedition en Angleterre en 1386*. (1864)

Riley, H. T., *Memorials of London and London Life*. (1868)

Riley H. T. ed, *Thomas of Walsingham. Historia Anglicana*. (1863–4)

Rogers, Clifford J. ed., *The Oxford Encyclopedia of Medieval Warfare and Military Technology Vol. 1*. (2012)

Roger, N. A. M., *The Safeguard of the Sea*. (2004)

Ronciere, Charles de la, *Histoire de la Marine Francaise* (1900)

Ruddick, Andrea, *English Identity and Political Culture in the Fourteenth Century*. (2013)

Rymer, Ted, *Foedera, conventions, literae et acta publica*. 1816–69.

Saul N., *Scenes from Provincial Life Knightly Families in Sussex 1280–1400*. (1986)

Searle, E., *Lordship and Community, Battle Abbey and its Banlieu*. (1974)

Sherbourne, J. W., 'The Hundred Years' War. The English Navy: Shipping and Manpower 1369–1389' in *Past and Present 37* (1967)

Smith D. M. and London, V. C. M., eds, *Heads of Religious Houses in England and Wales II*. (2001)

Spinks, Stephen, *Edward II – A Doomed Inheritance*. (2017)

Stanton, Charles D., *Medieval Maritime Warfare*. (2015)

Stevenson, J. ed, *Chronicon de Lanercost.* (1839)

Stone, L., *Sculpture in Britain – the Middle Ages.* (1955)

Stowe, G. B. ed, *Historia Vitae et Regni Ricardi Secundi.* (1977)

Strachey, J., *Rotuli Parliamentorum 1767–832*

Sumption, Jonathan, *Trial by Battle – The Hundred Years War.* (1990)

Sylvester, David, 'The Development of Winchelsea and its Maritime Economy'

Tait J. ed, *Chronica Johannis de Reading 1346–67.* (1914)

Templeman, G., 'Two French Attempts to invade England during the Hundred Years' War', in *Studies in French Language Latderature and History* presented to R. L. Graeme Ritchie ed J. J. Milne (1949)

Terrier de Loray, *Henri Marquis, Jean de Vienne, Amiral de France 1341–1396.* (1877)

Thomson, E. M., ed, *Robert de Avebury De gestis mirabilis regis Edwardi terti.* (Murimuth) (1889)

Thomson, E. M. *Chronicon Galfrido le Baker of Swynbrook.* (1889)

Turner, H. L., *Town Defences in England and Wales.* (1971)

Vegetius, ed C Lang, *Epitoma Rei Militaris.* (1885)

Von Clausewitz, Carl, *On War.* (1832)

Williams, Trevor, 'The Importance of the Channel Islands in British relations with the Continent during the Thirteenth and Fourteenth Centuries' – Société Jersiaise. Bulletins Vol XI (1931)

Williamson, James A., *The English Channel: A History.* (1959)

Warner, Kathryn, *Edward II – The Unconventional King.* (2014)

Weir, Alison, *Isabella: The She-Wolf of France.* (2001)

Wright, Nicholas, *Knights and Peasants: the Hundred Years' War in the French Countryside.* (2000)

Wright, T., *Political Poems and Songs relating to British History.* (2012)

INDEX

Index

Also available from Amberley Publishing

STEPHEN SPINKS

ROBERT
THE BRUCE
CHAMPION OF A NATION

Available from all good bookshops or to order direct
Please call **01453–847–800**
www.amberley-books.com